MEMENTO MORI

Published by Avalonia

BM Avalonia
London
WC1N 3XX
England, UK

www.avaloniabooks.co.uk

Memento Mori
Copyright © 2012 Kim Huggens

ISBN (10)   1-905297-14-9
ISBN (13) 978-1-905297-14-6

First Edition, September 2012
Design by Satori
Cover Art *'Polyptych of Earthly vanities and Heavenly redemption' (c. 1485) by Hans Memling*

British Library Cataloguing in Publication Data. A catalogue record for this book is available from the British Library.

MEMENTO MORI

*A Collection of Magickal
and Mythological Perspectives
On Death, Dying, Mortality and Beyond*

Edited by Kim Huggens

With Contributions by:

*Peg Aloi, Chad Barber, Emily Carding, Sophia Fisher,
Kyle Fite, Tina Georgitsis, Kim Huggens, Michael Howard,
Ivy Kerrigan, Humberto Maggi, Dave Moore, Mogg Morgan,
Tylluan Penry, Karen F. Pierce, Caroline Tully
and Julian Vayne*

Published By Avalonia

www.avaloniabooks.co.uk

TABLE OF CONTENTS

Kim Huggens, Editor: Published Work

The Tarot Illuminati: companion book (forthcoming 2013), Lo Scarabeo, with Erik C. Dunne

Pistis Sophia: the Goddess Tarot (forthcoming 2012), Schiffer Books, with Nic Phillips

Tarot 101: Mastering the Art of Reading the Cards (2010), Llewellyn

Vs. (2010), Avalonia, editor & contributor

From a Drop of Water (2009), Avalonia, editor & contributor

Sol Invictus: the God Tarot (2007), Schiffer Books, with Nic Phillips

Kim Huggens' work has also been published in:

Both Sides of Heaven (2009), Avalonia

Horns of Power (2008), Avalonia

Priestesses, Pythonesses and Sibyls (2008), Avalonia

The Mithras Reader vol. 2 (2008), Web of Wyrd

Conjure Codex (2011), Hadean Press

The Contributors: Published Work

The Celluloid Bough: Cinema in the Wake of the Occult Revival (forthcoming 2013), I.B. Tauris, co-written with Hannah Johnston

Faery Craft (2012), Emily Carding, Llewellyn

The Transparent Tarot (2008), Emily Carding, Schiffer Books

The Transparent Oracle (2010), Emily Carding, Schiffer Books

The Tarot of the Sidhe (2011), Emily Carding, Schiffer Books

The Children of Cain; A Study of Modern Traditional Witches (2012), Michael Howard, Three Hands Press

Modern Wicca: A History from Gardner to the Present (2010), Michael Howard, Llewellyn

Tankhem: Meditations on Seth Magick (2004), Mogg Morgan, Mandrake of Oxford

Supernatural Assault in Ancient Egypt (2008), Mogg Morgan, Mandrake of Oxford

The Wheel of the Year in Ancient Egypt (2010), Mogg Morgan, Mandrake of Oxford

The Essential Guide to Psychic Self Defence (2010), Tylluan Penry, Capall Bann

Magic on the Breath (2011), Tylluan Penry, Wolfenhowle Press

The Book of Baphomet (2012), Julian Vayne & Nikki Wyrd, Mandrake of Oxford

Pharmakon: Drugs and the Imagination (2006), Julian Vayne, Mandrake of Oxford

Priestesses Pythonesses Sibyls (2008), Sorita d'Este (ed), Avalonia, contributions by Sophia Fisher, Caroline Tully

Both Sides of Heaven (2009), Sorita d'Este (ed), Avalonia, contributions by Emily Carding, Michael Howard

From a Drop of Water (2009), Kim Huggens (ed), Avalonia, contribution by Emily Carding

Hekate Her Sacred Fires (2010), Sorita d'Este (ed), Avalonia, contributions by Emily Carding, Tina Georgitsis

Vs. (2012), Kim Huggens (ed), Avalonia, contributions by Emily Carding, Sophia Fisher, Michael Howard, Karen F. Pierce

Diabolical (2009), Scarlet Imprint, contribution by Humberto Maggi

Conjure Codex (2011), Hadean Press, contribution by Humberto Maggi

NASCENTES MORIMUR:
TO BE BORN IS TO DIE

CONTRIBUTORS

Peg Aloi

Peg Aloi is a media studies scholar whose main research and publication areas include representations of the occult and paganism in cinema and television. Her book *The Celluloid Bough: Cinema in the Wake of the Occult Revival* (co-written with Hannah Johnston) is forthcoming from I.B. Tauris. She served as the Media Coordinator for *The Witches' Voice* website from 1997-2009, and maintains her own blog focused on pagan media, *The Witching Hour*.

Chad Barber

Chad Barber is a folk magician, card reader and *espiritista*. Born and raised in Southern Africa, he hails from a family line addled with mediums, dreamers and madmen. Chad is a Lucky Mojo certified practitioner (1479G) and in addition to working as a root-doctor he serves his local community as a spiritist medium at mesa blanca gatherings. As a Santeria initiate and practitioner of espiritismo - a form of Afro-Caribbean spiritism - he is especially interested in the important role that the Creole traditions are playing in an emerging new synthesis of western spirituality and magic. He currently lives in Amsterdam, Netherlands with his spouse where he reads cards, writes and conjures irrepressibly. www.balthazarconjure.com

Emily Carding

Emily Carding lives in Cornwall with her amazing husband, ethereal daughter, the glorious Albus Dumbledog, (who has created his own oracle deck, due out from Schiffer Books towards the end of 2012!) and the newest addition to the family, the three cats known as the Supurrrnal Triad; Kether Kitty, Chokmah Cat and Binah Puss.

Here she has created various offerings, such as *The Transparent Tarot*, the *Transparent Oracle*, and *The Tarot of the Sidhe* for Schiffer Books. She has also contributed book covers, articles and artwork for several works from Avalonia Books. To date these titles include *Towards the Wiccan Circle*, *Both Sides of Heaven*, *From a Drop of Water*, *Hekate Her Sacred Fires*, and *Vs..* Avalonia also recently published *Gods of the Vikings* which features cover art and numerous illustrations by Emily. She is a regular columnist for *Mermaids and Mythology* magazine and is currently putting the finishing touches to *Faery Craft*, a new faery lifestyle and magical practice book due out from Llewellyn in Autumn 2012.

Sophia Fisher

Sophia Fisher is a devotee of Papa Baron. After completing her law degree she pursued a diverse range of spiritual interests, but found her true home in the religion of Vodou. She is now an initiated spiritual worker with multiple websites, workshop and ceremony facilitator and second-time mum. This is her third contribution to the Avalonia anthologies. www.sirenabotanica.com

Kyle Fite

Kyle Fite is a social worker and artist residing in Wisconsin with his family and four-legged friends. He is a member of the Typhonian Order, Sovereign Grand Master of the OTOA-LCN and Founder of the Boullan Academy of Spiritual Service. His view of the Magical Universe is one which recognizes the Sacredness of Life, endeavouring to approach the Mysteries of Death as a critical and necessary element of the Cosmic Life in which all beings participate.

Tina Georgitsis

Tina has had a deep love and appreciation for the occult all her life and is deeply respectful of the Ancient Greek and Ancient Egyptian spiritual paths that she practices. She is a Priestess Hierophant within the FOI (running the Lyceum of Heka), Hereditary Folk/Hermetic Witch and an initiated Priestess of Wicca. She is a qualified reiki, seichim and sekhem master and a tarot councillor within the ATA. She has studied various modalities within natural/alternative medicine and operates a spiritually based business which includes readings, healings, magical items and workshops in various metaphysical and occult subjects whilst also working in the education sector.

Michael Howard

Michael Howard is a writer, researcher and editor. He is the author of over thirty books and numerous articles and since 1976 has been the editor of the witchcraft magazine *The Cauldron* www.the-cauldron.org.uk. His latest book is *The Children of Cain; A Study of Modern Traditional Witches*, published by Three Hands Press USA and available in the UK from Midian Books.

Kim Huggens

Kim is a freelance researcher, author, editor, proof-reader and public speaker in the fields of occultism, Paganism, mythology and Tarot. She has written papers for several journals and anthologies on her postgraduate research, specializing in ancient Graeco-Roman malefic-erotic magic, necromancy, slander spells and *'voodoo'* dolls. Previous work has appeared in *Both Sides of Heaven, Horns of Power, Priestesses, Pythonesses and Sibyls, The Mithras Reader vol. 2*, and the *Conjure Codex* (2011.) She is also editor and contributor for two anthologies, *From a Drop of Water* (2009) and *Vs.* (2010). Kim has been studying and reading Tarot since the age of 9, and is the co-author of *Sol Invictus: the God Tarot* (Schiffer Books, 2007) and the forthcoming *Pistis Sophia: the Goddess Tarot* with Nic Phillips. She is also the author of *Tarot 101: Mastering the Art of Reading the Cards* (Llewellyn, 2010.)

Kim enjoys travelling around the UK giving lectures and workshops at events such as the Mercian Gathering, Tarosophy Conference, Pagan Federation (Mid-West and Wales) Conference, Occult Conference (Glastonbury), etc. She is also an initiate of Ordo Templi Orientis (Tamion Encampment) and initiated as Hounsi Lave Tet in Sosyete Gade Nou Leve, a Haitian, Dominican and Sanse Vodou house.

In her spare time Kim works as a PDSA veterinary receptionist, makes jewellery and Vodou bottles, and does tabletop roleplaying. She has a passion for zombies, cats, pirates, antlers, electroswing, mermaids, sparkly things and cake. Mmmm, cake.

Ivy Kerrigan

Ivy Kerrigan has been practicing witchcraft and other magical traditions for over 10 years. Her main avenues of practice include shamanism, dream work and working with the Greek chthonic spirits. She also practices Haitian Vodou, is an initiate of the Hearth of the Sangreal (of the Clan Coranieid) and has a close relationship with several of the spirits of the *Grimorium Verum*. She lives in a seaside town in Southern England, with her husband Drac.

Humberto Maggi

Humberto Maggi was born in Rio de Janeiro in 1968. He is an ex-Probationer of the A.: A.: and a Knight of East and West from the true Ordo Templi Orientis. His approach to Magick is deeply connected to a scientific view of the Universe. He published articles in the anthologies *Diabolical* from Scarlet Imprint and *Conjure Codex* from Hadean Press.

Dave Moore

Dave Moore lives on the Dorset coast and has degrees in Computer Science and Astrophysics. He is a Thelemite and member of Ordo Templi Orientis. Like the Ancient Egyptians, he is extremely fond of cats, and is currently servant of and food provider to two such fine creatures.

Mogg Morgan

Mogg Morgan is a senior occultist, author, publisher, commentator, theologian, historian, lecturer, teacher and researcher. Following his earlier experiences with Kenneth Grant's Typhonian OTO he has continued his own journey into the Pagan/Kemetic tradition. He shares his vision through a series of books including *Tankhem: Meditations on Seth Magick*, *The Bull of Ombos*, *Supernatural Assault in Ancient Egypt* and *The Wheel of the Year in Ancient Egypt*.

Tylluan Penry

Tylluan Penry is a solitary pagan witch, and author of *Seeking the Green, The Magical Properties of Plants ...and how to find them*, *The Essential Guide to Psychic Self Defence*, and *Magic on the Breath*. She writes regularly for various pagan magazines, has made several appearances on the Avalon Whispering Show on One World Radio and is a regular speaker at various festivals including Witchfest International and the Artemis Gathering.

Her blog is at http://tylluanpenry.blog.co.uk, and you can also read more about her at www.thewolfenhowlepress.com

Karen F. Pierce

Karen Pierce has been a practising pagan for over 15 years. Whilst a student she took an active role in running two pagan societies (at Cardiff and Lampeter). In 2004 she completed a PhD on Helen of Troy, and now works as a librarian. She is passionate about stone circles and a couple of years ago embarked on a mission to visit 40 of them in Britain, writing up her experiences as she went along; this journey continues. She also has a deep interest in mythology, and mythical interactions with the landscape. She has previously contributed to *Vs. Duality and Conflict in Magick, Mythology and Paganism*, and has a piece in the forthcoming *Megaloi Theoi: A Devotional Anthology for The Dioskouroi and Their Families* (published by Bibliotheca Alexandrina).

Caroline Tully

Caroline Tully has many areas of interest including ancient Mediterranean religions, Reception Studies, the Hermetic Order of the Golden Dawn, historical Witchcraft and contemporary Paganisms, particularly Pagan Reconstructionism (the practice of historically-accurate ancient Pagan religions). She has been published in many international Pagan publications and has contributed to several Pagan anthologies. See her blog, *Necropolis Now*, at: http://necropolisnow.blogspot.com/

Julian Vayne

An explorer of the occult for over quarter of a century, Julian Vayne is the author of six books & numerous articles and papers covering many aspects of magickal practice. He is best known for his interest in chaos magick and the spiritual use of psychoactive substances. He is a devotee of Baphomet and really likes a nice cup of tea.

Der Apt.

The Abbot. Woodcut from the series known as
The Dance of Death, Holbein, 1538.

INTRODUCTION

By Kim Huggens

The nature and process of death has been for millennia one of the central concerns of most religious traditions, philosophical schools, and mythological tales. The condition of the soul or spirit after death, and the possibility of an afterlife, is a subject that has crossed everybody's minds, and the fact that one day each of us will go the way of our ancestors is a heavy truth. But here is glorious death, the great equaliser! The nature and process of death has been for millennia one of the central concerns of most religious traditions, philosophical schools, and mythological tales. The condition of the soul or spirit after death, and the possibility of an afterlife, is a subject that has crossed everybody's minds, and the fact that one day each of us will go the way of our ancestors is a heavy truth. But here is glorious death, the great equaliser! In death we recreate the passing of every other being on this planet, back to the dawn of time. In death we are reunited with our ancestors. In the face of death we live our lives all the more spectacularly – sometimes in an attempt to escape the inevitable, and sometimes to embrace it without fear.

Magical, occult and pagan traditions have a lot to say on the subject of mortality. The Underworld and all its associated beings and myths – such as Persephone's descent into Hades, Kwan Yin's redemption of hell, Inanna's death in the Heaven Below, and Orpheus' journey to Hades to bring back his beloved Eurydice – has gained a rich oral and written tradition in modern day occultism. Deities associated with death, either because they are death or because they look after the dead, are still worshipped and served by magical practitioners – Baron Samedi, Hekate, Erishkegal, Kali, Shiva... Festivals centred on the theme of death are celebrated yearly: Hungry Ghost festival, Samhain, El Dia De Los Muertos, Fet Ghede and more.

A number of modern pagans also seek ways of celebrating and mourning their loved ones that are fitting with their beliefs. They choose woodland burials, funerary rites from ancient times, and ancestor reverence. They also create theologies that celebrate death and life, remove fear in the face of death, and treat the dead with respect and dignity. Further, the initiation rites found in most pagan mystery religions, both ancient and modern, re-enact or are inspired by some mythology of descent into the Underworld, approaching death in a metaphorical and ritualistic fashion.

"Kali", by Emily Carding, 2010.

I hoped to show through the papers in the *Memento Mori* series of anthologies that modern Pagans, occultists and those of like mind are not prone to letting a fear of death or a belief in what comes afterwards control their lives; rather the fact that they will one day die like all those that have gone before them goads them to action, emboldens their strength and heightens their passion for what the world has to offer. The ways in which they come to terms with or explore their own mortality or the death of a loved one are explored thoroughly in this anthology: tantric practices in graveyards, reclaiming the bones of dead animals as ritual items, serving the spirits of ancestors, mediumship, making altars to deities that bring or represent death, undergoing initiations that mimic the moment of death, exploring past lives, and destroying the ego. From this study it becomes overwhelmingly clear that whilst many have asserted religion to be nothing more than an attempt to cheat death or make sense of life in the face of an inevitable end, magical thinkers around the world are not ruled by such fear of death; their reasons for choosing to walk their path are not based on a fear or belief in a hereafter, of divine punishment or reward after death, but instead based on a life well lived, people well loved, and opportunities grasped firmly. Although the title of these anthologies is *Memento Mori* (Remember, you shall die), more rightly it should be subtitled '*Carpe Diem*' (Seize the day), for this is the effect that the awareness and engagement with the process of death and dying elicits in our modern pagan and occult thinkers.

Through reading the offerings contained herein, a few things become abundantly clear:

Nascentes morimur – to be born is to die

Pulvis and umbra sumis – we are dust and shadow

Incerta moris hora – the hour of death is unknown

We enter into life under pain of death; our mothers, by giving birth to us, are also bringing about our end. The womb is also the tomb. And, just as we are made of 'stardust' ("*Every man and every woman is a star*",[1] or an unknown and impossibly large number of miniscule parts) and nothing is ever truly created or destroyed, so the stuff that our ancestors, other beings on the planet, the dinosaurs, everything that has ever gone before, fills us with every breath we take. And one day, when we return to the earth our 'stardust' will be reused and recycled, and future generations will be created and breathe us in. Death is the price we must pay for the privilege of life and everything it has to offer.

Because of our transient nature (though we do not like to view ourselves as such), in the grand scheme of things we are but dust and shadow, passing very briefly through this world and, in most cases, doing nothing to warrant remembrance except perhaps passing on our genes and creating further generations who can

---

1 The Book of the Law (Liber al Vel Legis) 1.3.

undergo the same process. Unfortunately, we cannot always rely on the future generations to remember us, and so our names stand a good chance of passing into oblivion mere decades after our deaths. This is not unfair, because concepts of fairness and equality cannot be applied to this, except insomuch as all are equal in the fact of our dying. As such, we must accept not only that we are passing shadows in the great history of our planet, and conversely that we must fight to make ourselves worthy of remembrance. Yet even here we must concede that since our race is also a passing shadow, remembrance of our ancestors is limited.

As finite human beings we are faced with the possibility that death could take us at any time. Many of the anthology pieces contained herein make us aware that sometimes those who are most undeserving of death are the ones taken soonest – younger brothers, children, little sisters, young men and women. History has given us a great number of artworks portraying this fact: from the grim dance of skeletons leading people of all ages and walks of life to the grave, to the pleading with death of the young lady in *Death and the Lady* (a 19th century broadside ballad reprinted herein). The hour of death is unknown and nobody is promised tomorrow. To some this might be a reason to stay indoors and insulate oneself from all potential harm; yet many people still take part in dangerous activities that pose some risk, such as sky-diving, parachuting, swimming with sharks, riding motorcycles, flying in an aeroplane... even crossing the road and driving a car in everyday life poses a risk. It is impossible to insulate oneself from harm and therefore from the ever-present possibility of death. In the face of this, the thought in this anthology positively encourages an attitude that seizes every opportunity, every day, living life to the full with passion, tenacity, courage and sense of adventure. Whilst we cannot cheat death, in some way we can live so that we can laugh in its face.

Not all the pieces in this series are about death, yet somehow they all manage to shed some light on death and the process of dying. Many of them explore the symbolism and traditions associated with death, so that in the more universal language of myth and symbol we can come to understand death through the experiences of those who came before us (*Don't Fear the Reaper*, by Emily Carding). Some essays approach death from an historical perspective, examining how ancient cultures have dealt with their dead and their ancestors, and what associated rituals they practiced (*Ars Moriendi*, by Humberto Maggi, *Tomb-cults, Caves, Stars and Blessed Isles*, by Karen Pierce, *Demeter's Wrath: How the Eleusinian Mysteries Attempted to Cheat Death*, by Caroline Tully, *Ascending to the Imperishable*, by Dave Moore, *The Setian Way of Death*, by Mogg Morgan, *The Truth About Zombies*, by Kim Huggens, *Dogs and Death*, by Ivy Kerrigan, and *Eating with the Dead* by Tylluan Penry.)

Often, through devotion to deities that rule or are associated with death and the dead, practitioners find a peace and acceptance of their own death and a preparedness for what it may bring (*Papa*

Ghede, Petit Ghede by Sophia Fisher). In pieces in which the dead themselves are worked with, the familiarity with the spirits of our ancestors and the dead forms an intimate working relationship in which both the living and dead partner benefit and grow (*Cultivating the Dead*, by Chad Barber, and *Communicating with the Blessed Dead*, by Tina Georgistis.) The true beauty of these pieces is in their ability to remind us that the dead in many cultures are not so separate from the living; that they walk around us and among us, maintain relationships with us, look after us, seek our help, love us and sometimes annoy us. The Western idea of the dead staying dead and being far removed from life may not be as certain as we think, since the traditions of Spiritualism a la Allan Kardec and the necromancy of the Western Mystery Tradition bring the dead very firmly into the realm of life.

It might not be far from the truth to say that many of the authors are devotees of death in some form, whether it manifests as a deity, as a concept or morality, as a seminal experience that changed them profoundly, or as a simple awareness and continual walking with the dead. Whilst the modern world, in particular Hollywood, would like to view death's children as morbid creatures of the night, in fact we find that they are in many cases practitioners of some form of solar-phallic or nature *'worship'*. They lead pretty normal lives, and their experiences of death in their lives are surprisingly similar to those found in non-magical folks. A great number of them see the inherent humour in death and in mankind's futile attempts to avoid it, and most, if not all of them, would prefer to stand brave in the face of death when it comes, and until then celebrate every day of life allotted to them. Sometimes this comes across as irreverent, particularly in the cases of speaking with the dead or digging up graves or meditating in graveyards, or making filthy jokes about death. However, throughout this series it soon becomes clear that this irreverence is not a cause of our devotion or awareness of death, but a symptom: for what better way to deal with death is there but to live and live well? As the saying goes, *"Don't take life so seriously. You'll never get out alive."*[2] The conclusion one can draw from this anthology is that to embrace death is also to embrace life.

It is interesting to note that perhaps the idea of death as a journey is only true in certain cultures. Essays that look at the ancient Egyptians (*Ascending to the Imperishable, The Setian Way of Death*) and the ancient Greek mysteries (*Becoming Persephone, Demeter's Wrath*) indeed show us that some cultures view the instance of death as another doorway to be travelled through in order to reach another stage in the soul's evolution. However, for the modern Western mind the idea of death as a journey does not find as much support. Instead, it is viewed very much as an instant, a one-time thing, a cataclysmic event. If there is something afterwards,

---

2 This quote is thought to be attributed to Elbert Hubbard, but it also quoted by Bugs Bunny.

then the process of death is a blockage that must be broken through for the soul or spirit to be freed. It is only in recent years, possibly with an exposure to the African Traditional Religions such as Vodou, Santeria and Candomble that death has started to become more integrated in our magical practices, and the dead given a firmer place in our everyday lives.

When I die (and may it be many, many decades in the future!) I hope to be able to do so without fear, knowing that I have lived life well; knowing that I have not lived in fear, that I have not squandered my days, that I have laughed frequently and loved deeply, that I have pushed my own limits and overcome my weaknesses. To me, a life lived walking with death as a constant companion is a life in which true freedom can be attained. And since a number of Ghede lwa (with a nod and a filthy grin at Brav Ghede and Baron Samedi, amongst others!) have been close companions these past few years, I felt it was only right to offer an anthology on a subject so close to my heart, and one that I know is, or one day will be, close to everybody else's heart also.

Remember: you will die. Seize the day, for nobody is promised tomorrow. What else can you do?

Kim Huggens

On a train between Cardiff and Shrewsbury, around the Winter Solstice, 2011.

Tina Georgitsis Akhu Shrine, July 2011

COMMUNICATING WITH THE BLESSED DEAD

BY TINA GEORGITSIS

Unknown to me at the time, I first started working with the blessed dead as a young child. I call them the blessed dead because they have provided me with messages to aid the living, insight or knowledge applicable in life and guided me on my magickal and spiritual path. The blessed dead is a term I use, as it's a name used for our ancestors and deceased loved ones in the Kemetic tradition I am a follower of.

It all started in the middle of one night when I was woken up by a loud voice talking to me. When I opened my eyes I was at first startled when I saw a tall middle aged man standing at the foot of my bed, but as I focused, I realised he was familiar to me and so I wasn't afraid. He was talking to me without moving his mouth, was slightly transparent and being so young I didn't question this. I just accepted that he was there and didn't want to hurt me as he just wanted me to pass on a message.

He was telling me that I needed to tell his brother that he was gone and that his brother needed to know he was ok and not to worry. I got up and ran into my parents bedroom to tell them what this man had told me, but my mother thinking I had a bad dream, put me back into bed after bestowing upon me a blessing and protection prayer. Some time later, I was woken again by this man who was adamant I pass on a message to his brother and that he wouldn't leave until I'd done so. Again I raced into my parent's bedroom and this time when my mother tried to explain it was just a nightmare and everything was ok I started to throw a tantrum because I wanted to be heard. Whilst my mother was trying to calm me down I practically screamed out the message I had received which was that 'John' was in my bedroom and wanted to tell his brother that he was dead but that he was ok and not to get sad. My mother's eyes widened in a quizzical expression and she then asked what he looked like so I carefully described him. When I was done my mother crossed herself and shot my father a worrying glance. I started to cry in panic and she soothed me and put me back to bed whilst telling me everything was ok and thanked me for passing on the message from John.

The next morning I found my father crying at the kitchen table and when I asked him why he was sad he told me that his brother John had died. Uncle John was my father's favourite brother and best friend who lived interstate and had suffered a stroke and died during the night. I hugged my father and told him not to cry as Uncle John had visited and told me that he was ok. My father, believing in life after death, this message gave him comfort and solace. In the following days when I attended the funeral with my parents I wasn't shocked to see Uncle John lying in an open casket and was actually wondering why people gathered were upset since he told me himself that he was ok. When I told this to my mother she explained to me that not everyone talked to people who had passed away and gently warned me not to repeat to anyone what had happened as they wouldn't understand. She also explained that some people in our family could talk to the dead in order to help those who were left behind with their grieving. Since I had this gift she would teach me how to work with the blessed dead in a safe and helpful way.

That was the beginning of when I started working with the blessed dead, and to this day I continue to work with them in one way or another. I predominately work with my own blessed dead as they have guided me on my magical and spiritual path. When I conduct healings and readings I receive messages for clients from their loved ones which I pass on. I find that these messages, along with descriptions of their loved ones, are appreciated by the living as it helps them to move on and accept their loved ones are no longer in physical form and we don't need to worry about them.

Having lost both my parents by my early 30's, working with the blessed dead has allowed me to accept and let go of them with love in my heart as I am completely confident they are in a happy peaceful place. I had been warned about both my parents passing before it occurred through dreams and other blessed dead who came to me to tell me, and in both my parents' cases it actually helped them move on.

Over the years I've delved deeper into Hellenic and Kemetic magickal and religious practices. I have found this has added value not only to my personal life but also when dealing with the blessed dead. My interest in Hellenic and Kemetic traditions stems from my ancestry and I was also drawn to it through the guidance of my spirit guide who happened to be an ancestor well versed in these traditions.

When I was introduced to the concept of ancestor veneration in the Kemetic tradition it felt very familiar. This practice was something which I had always done in some way or another and it was refreshing to see others actively participating in the same practice in this day and age. I came to learn that '*Akhu*' also known as the '*Shining Ones*' or '*Blessed Dead*' are the spirits of our ancestors who became a star in the heavens in the body of Nuit. Nuit is a sky goddess who is depicted as a naked woman covered in stars who arches over the earth. She is also a goddess of death and swallowed and rebirthed the stars and sun. As stars shine their light down upon us, they remind us that our ancestors and departed loved ones are always with us and watching over us. This brought me great comfort and resonated within me in a most profound way.

Venerating the Ancestors is a practice where you honour (instead of worship) your blessed dead so their *Ka* (soul) continues to be fed and therefore continuing to exist. Through remembering and speaking their name and by leaving them offerings such as incense, water or things they enjoyed in life, it allows them to have the ability to intercede on our behalf and assist us in our lives. Venerating the Ancestors shows how much you care for your blessed dead even though they are no longer in physical form in this earthly plain. It allows us to thank them for being, as our own existence is due to theirs. When venerating the Ancestors it allows them to bestow blessings and offer insight into our lives. This is because it is believed that our ancestors stand in the *Duat* or underworld/land of the dead and can communicate to us or be go betweens to the Gods themselves if necessary. All that is needed to venerate the Ancestors is to acknowledge them in the form of prayers or offerings; this includes asking them for assistance and in return thanking them for their assistance when given. Also it is worthy to note that you don't have to be blood tied to your blessed dead as they can be a person you cared deeply for in life and want to remember and honour them in death.

People in many cultures including Eastern, Native American, Greek and Egyptian have been known to venerate their Ancestors for many thousands of years. Originally it was part of everyday life for the common man to do this and in the modern day these practices have remained in one form or another. This shows us that many acknowledge that honouring and/or working with the blessed dead gives them comfort or blessings and has a positive impact on us physically and psychologically.

I have an ancestor shrine which I maintain regularly, and which sits in a part of the house I frequently use, to ensure my blessed dead are acknowledged as part of the family. My shrine is an old desk I have covered with a star studded shrine cloth and I have placed various items on it which represent my ancestors and which symbolically feed their soul. Some items on my ancestor shrine include personal possessions of my ancestors, photos of my ancestors, a book containing ancestor's names and their stories, flowers, a libation bowl, a food offering plate, incense holder with incense and candles which are lit during the reciting of prayers. It is important to note that food offerings are always disposed of in the garbage separately to the household trash and are not to be consumed. Libations are left to evaporate or poured onto the earth outside.

I find an effective way to communicate with my blessed dead other than simply talking to them in shrine is by writing them a letter and reading it to them or leaving it on their shrine. I have personally amended a Kemetic prayer (A Hotep Di Nisut Prayer) with my own words at the end which has been framed and placed amongst photos of my blessed dead on my shrine which is recited frequently:

"An offering which the King gives to Yinepu-Upon-His-Mountain and to Wesir, Lord of Abydos: a thousand of bread, a thousand of beer, a thousand of oil and alabaster and linen, a thousand of meat and fowl and all things good and pure that heaven gives, the earth produces and the inundation brings; for the ka of Tina Georgitsis, ma'a heru.

Your names will live on forever, for you are the stars who watch over me."

If it wasn't for my ancestors, my blessed dead, I wouldn't be here and for that I am indebted. I am a part of them and they will always be a part of me, as I remind myself how much I love them through devotional veneration where I bestow offerings and prayers as a symbol of this love and remembrance. In return they bless, assist me and remind me of where I came from. Until I see my blessed dead when it is my time to cross over, I will continue to show them respect and be their messenger when needed.

EATING WITH THE DEAD: FUNERAL MEAL PRACTICES

BY TYLLUAN PENRY

The practice of eating a special meal at a funeral is probably as old as humankind and, even more intriguingly, seems to persist in some shape or form right down to the present. Nor is it restricted to a single country or even continent, but is found right across the world, from Ceylon to Nigeria, Sweden to the US and from Rumania to the UK.[3] However, the evidence, such as it is, can be very ambiguous. It's one thing to find the remains of an ancient tortoise feast at a burial ground in, say, the Hilazon Tachtit cave in Israel, but quite another to place it in its proper context. Even the terms *'funeral meal'* or *'funeral feast'* are fraught with problems. What exactly constitutes a meal or feast? When should it be held? Who attends? Is there an accompanying ritual? And unfortunately, the answer to most of these questions is simply that we don't really know.

Part of the problem of course is that even if we find the remains of a funeral meal, it doesn't tell us very much about why or how it was celebrated. Or who was invited to eat it. For example, excavations in Egypt have revealed the existence of a workmen's site dating from the New Kingdom period at Deir el Medina, on the West Bank of modern-day Luxor. Numerous archaeological remains include many different types of food offering in graves, including various types of bread, amphorae of grain, wine, and preserved meats; bowls of vegetable paste; seasoned vegetables; fruit including dates and grapes; a box of salt; bunches of garlic; baskets of juniper and cumin; sacks of dom nuts.[4] What such remains cannot tell us however is whether similar food was also consumed at a funeral feast by the mourners. The remains of a basket of dung for the fire seems to suggest that everything was expected to experience some sort of afterlife and that the food must have been intended to be eaten and even cooked at a later date presumably by the deceased in the hereafter.

Normally the presence of food implies that someone – or something – is supposed to eat it. With funerals however, we have to be careful not to leap to conclusions and the archaeological evidence often suggests a range of different answers. The presence of charred

---

3 Yoder, L., The Funeral Meal: A Significant Funerary Ritual, 1986:146.

4 Smith, S.T., They Did Take It with Them: Require-ments for the Afterlife Evidenced from Intact New Kingdom Tombs at Thebes, 1991:67.

animal bones for example, could mean that somebody ate meat at a funeral feast and tossed the bones on the fire afterwards. Or that the dead animal was ritually slaughtered and burned either whole or jointed without ever being eaten by anyone.

The common modern perception of a funeral meal is a group of people sitting eating near a grave or cremation pyre back in the mists of time. However much depends upon where and when the funeral was held. Sometimes the funeral meal could be the conclusion of several days' fast following a death. It may have been accompanied by ritual or other ceremony. There are so many things we just have to guess at, such as whether food was ritually shared with the corpse or simply eaten in his honour or whether the meal was held just before, during or after the disposal of the body. It is even possible that the mourners did not eat anything and that the food was provided solely for the use of the deceased, to provide him or her with sustenance for the voyage to the afterlife, or to keep him fed in the grave. In normal everyday life of course, the presence of food almost always implies the intention to eat. Someone – or something – is intended to eat the fruit or meat at some particular point in time. But at a funeral – particularly an ancient one, whose customs are virtually unknown to us - the answers are not so clear cut.

Herodotus, in Book IV [73] of his *Histories* describes how when a king of the Scythians died, the body was taken to a banquet held by each of his friends, and the dead man was actually '*served with a portion of all that it set before the others.*' This took place over a period of forty days, and we have to hope that some sort of embalming or preservation must first have been employed otherwise the corpse's presence would have been intolerable.

Human beings, however, do not normally eat their meals in graveyards, at crematoria or beside a corpse so the funeral meal must have had some special purpose, presumably religious or magical. The most likely explanations are that either the dead personal magically assimilated some benefit from a final meal with the living, or vice versa. Another possibility is that the corpse's portion was treated in the same way as the body i.e. burned or buried, perhaps to provide sustenance on the way to an afterlife.

Modern funeral meals, especially in the UK, tend to be more pragmatic. Everyone traipses back to the family home after the funeral for a couple of ham sandwiches and a glass of sherry. It is basically a social rather than a religious or ritual occasion, and the deceased is not expected to be remotely interested. Yet it persists, and the only reason for this must be that it is felt to bestow some benefit somewhere, even if few people nowadays have much idea what it could be. The traditional Irish Wake is another example of a funeral feast that continued well into the mid twentieth century. Despite its geographical proximity to mainland UK, it is quite a different type of celebration, a mixture of religion, feast and party. Held before the funeral, the mourners ensured that the deceased was never left alone although the food was usually consumed in another room.

It is always important to resist the temptation to try and project our own values back into the past. Our attitude to food is quite different; nowadays most of us simply buy our food from the supermarket, whereas in the past it had to be caught, gathered or grown within the community. This process of acquisition and preparation meant there was greater involvement with the food one ate, and the preparation of any communal meal must therefore be viewed as significant. It was presumably meant to bring people together in some way in order to share a common purpose.

It seems more than likely that people mourned at funerals, because that is human nature. The extent of the mourning and how it was expressed however, almost certainly varied then just as it does nowadays. In some societies women wail, tearing their clothes and hair, in others even shedding a tear is seen as embarrassingly emotional. In northern Europe at least, excessive mourning was frowned upon because it was believed to disturb the rest of the dead. In the Icelandic Eddaic *Lay of Helgi* for example, Helgi appears to Sigrun drenched with blood, because her tears are heavy and cold on the dead man's breast. This is also a fairly common theme in folksongs such as the *Twa Brothers* where the distraught sweetheart weeps until

'She wept the stars adown from the lift

She wept the fish out of the sea.[5]

This song, and others like it, all suggest the dead were thought to not only dwell in the grave, but also be affected by the actions of the living. If so the dead would require at least some of the necessities of life, such as food and drink. However, providing food for the afterlife is not quite the same as having a final funeral meal unless of course the final funeral meal magically assuaged all future thirst and hunger for the deceased.

Another problem we have in assessing how funeral meals were held is the nature of archaeology itself. Modern archaeology bears little resemblance to its Georgian and Victorian counterparts which had more in common with a treasure hunt. Items that were thought to have little intrinsic value (and charred animal bones or grains would certainly fall into this category) were disregarded, unrecorded and occasionally thrown away or forgotten. Anything that seemed valuable usually disappeared into a private collection or occasionally was recycled and re-used until it was beyond repair. This was the fate of a whole cache of glass drinking vessels found c. 1793 near a conical hill at Woodnesborough in Kent.[6] They were kept at nearby farms to be brought out at harvest time until virtually all were smashed and broken. Over a century later, a large deposit of burned

---

5 Harvey, The Unquiet Grave, 1941:52.

6 James Douglas, Nenia Britannica, 1793:71.

bones were found five hundred yards away. Since cremation and drinking were both traditionally associated with the Anglo-Saxon cult of Woden, it seems likely that this was important evidence of funeral feasts being held at this time near the site of the cremations. The importance of such a site might even explain why the early Christian missionaries built a church in the same area. It's difficult to imagine what evidence the finds might have yielded in more sympathetic hands.

However, even when we are presented with archaeological evidence, it can be very difficult to interpret. For example, animal bones are often found in cremation burials from the Bronze Age right up into Anglo-Saxon times. Yet they cannot tell us the underlying belief or motive for their presence, although we can make a few educated guesses. For example, a dog may have belonged to the deceased and been killed in order to accompany him to the afterlife. However in times of famine it may have been eaten and knife marks on the bones are not conclusive either way. Chopping marks could either have been made while butchering the carcass to cook for the funeral feast, or to make it easier to drag a large animal such as a horse or cow to the funeral pyre to burn. Alternatively the marks may show that the animal was hacked to death.

An Irish Bronze age cremation burial dated between c.2000–1850 BCE, in south County Dublin (Carmanhall) revealed a number of animal bones belonging to a cow and a dog. [7] Allowing for the fact that nobody normally has a pet cow, this means that the cremation must have taken place at a time when food was plentiful and the meat may well have been eaten. Yet against this argument we know that sometimes religious and cultural beliefs encourage people to give up things they cannot really afford to lose, just in order to fulfil cultural and societal obligations. So even when animal bones are present, we cannot be sure that any funeral feast included meat, although it does seem likely.

It is also difficult to be sure *when* a funeral feast actually took place in relation to the cremation or burial. At Carmanhall, the condition of the animal bones suggests they were cremated along with the body, but these may just have been a portion that was included for the deceased, while the other mourners ate the remainder. Elsewhere it is possible that the meat was consumed first as part of the funeral meal and the bones thrown onto the pyre. Indeed some scholars have even suggested that animal carcasses were included not as part of a feast at all, but as an aid to combustion![8] Although bodies, both human and animal contain a high percentage of fat, they are extremely difficult to burn especially on an open fire. While adding *some* rendered down fat to the fire to help it burn could be a good idea, adding the carcass of a large animal would run the risk of extinguishing it altogether.

---

7 Reilly, Bronze Age Cemetery, 2005:32.
8 Bond, Animal Bone in Anglo-Saxon Cremations, 1996:82.

Just because animal bones are found with a cremation or burial does not mean they were necessarily eaten as part of a funeral feast. The Anglo Saxons for example, seem to have eaten some animals but not others. Often the cremated bones of sheep and pig bones often show chopping marks, but not those of horses.[9] One explanation is that people preferred eating lamb and pork to horse-flesh. It is often claimed that the Anglo-Saxons never ate horsemeat, unlike the earlier continental Germanic tribes mentioned by Tacitus, a Roman author of the first century CE. However, there is written evidence that papal legates were complaining as late as 786 CE that Christianised Anglo-Saxons were still eating horsemeat, *'a thing which no Christians do in the East'.*[10] The evidence from Anglo-Saxon cremations suggests that in some parts of England at least, people probably avoided eating horsemeat as part of a funeral feast and placed the complete dead animal onto the funeral pyre. This in turn implies that horses had a quite different status from other animals, and its inclusion in the funerary rite was magical or religious.

Although Tacitus is far too early to have described the Anglo-Saxons, at least some of the Germanic tribes whom he wrote about were their ancestors. So when Tacitus,[11] in his work *Germania* described something similar where the deceased's horse was *'cast into the flames'* of the funeral pyre we have to wonder whether this was a tradition that was later brought to England. It does seem strange though that the Anglo-Saxons seem to have continued the practice of sacrificing a horse on a funeral pyre, yet changed their minds about eating horsemeat.

Providing food at funerals was widely practised in many different cultures for thousands of years. For example, postholes have been found in many ancient burial mound sites in North America.[12] These are generally thought to have been used to support temporary shelters, and nearby evidence of hearths, pottery and animal bones, in particular of white-tailed deer bones, all suggest feasting took place in these areas. Of course it doesn't tell us whether this was part of the funerary rite or whether it was connected to rituals designed to honour the ancestors. However it is probably significant that Native Americans regarded white-tailed deer as spiritually important and ate their meat in rituals intended to protect and ensure healthy crop yields.[13] This suggests the people who celebrated at these burial mounds with a ritual meal of deer meat, were deliberately reinforcing a magical link between the deceased, the burial site, the mourners and the food itself.

Certain food, such as bread, regularly appears in ritual meals associated with the dead. For example, in ancient Egypt, bread and

---

9 Bond, Animal Bone in Anglo-Saxon Cremations, 1996:82.

10 Hunter-Blair, Northumbria in the days of Bede, 1976:211.

11 Tacitus, trans. Mattingly Germania 27, 1970:123.

12 Bower, Banquets in the Ruins, 1998:331.

13 Bower Banquets in the Ruins, 1998:331.

cakes were placed in the tomb as food for the deceased's *ka*. Likewise at the Chinese feast of Yü-Lan Hui, the Feast of the Hungry Spirits, people made small cakes for the dead. In England the preference was for oat cakes, while in Rome almond cakes were offered. A slight variation on this was found in parts of Germany, where bread crumbs were collected throughout the week then thrown onto the fire on Saturday *'for the dead'*. Cakes and breadcrumbs may not be most people's idea of a funeral feast, but the principle remains the same. The dead need food, just like the rest of us. Providing this was not only a way of remembering and keeping them close, but also ensured their help and support for the living. Again we cannot escape the conclusion that at some level the dead were believed to need physical sustenance, just like the living. Yet real food decays, meaning that it either had to be consumed magically at once, or that some sort of ritual was employed to magically preserve it. This would ensure that although bread might go mouldy in this life, in the afterlife it would be fresh and edible for eternity.

In ancient Egypt, the provision of food for the deceased seems to have been an extremely early practice that continued right up to the nineteenth (c. 1298 to 1187 BCE) and twentieth (c. 1187 to 1064 BCE) dynasties, especially at Thebes. Gradually however, real food was replaced by ceramic copies, suggesting a shift towards more magical thinking. Obviously it was known that real food would decay, but it seems that during this period the Egyptian priests believed they had found a way to imbue the ceramic fruits etc., with the magical properties of their real-life counterparts. This must have been intended to provide a constant supply of nourishment for the deceased's *ka*, at least until the afterlife was reached.

A particular type of cake – Soul Cake – was common to most of the Celtic and Germanic peoples. They were usually baked in early November and often placed on graves. Some Soul Cakes were marked with a cross, rather like a modern hot-cross-bun but probably originated as a round loaf bearing the four spokes of the sun-wheel sometimes referred to as a *'sun wreath'*. During Charlemagne's reign, laws were passed forbidding this and ordering that sun wreath bread could only be marked with a cross. Normally the bread or cake was left for the returning soul to eat, although in northern Europe it was sometimes said that the more people managed to eat at a funeral meal, the more souls would be saved and the better they would be fed in Purgatory.[14] In the Netherlands there was a taboo on eating *doodsbood* (the bread of death), although to avoid waste it was often given to the poor, sometimes with a coin hidden in it. Presumably the poor and hungry were thought willing to risk any ill effects of breaking the taboo just in order to eat!

There was no taboo however on eating Arval or Avril Bread at burials in mid nineteenth century Westmoreland. These were a type

---

14 De Cleene & Lejeune, Compendium of Ritual and Symbolic Plants in Europe, Vol I, 2003:108.

of unleavened bread or oatcake that was given out to the mourners at the funeral. Although we should not automatically assume an unbroken link between such practices and earlier, pagan ones, Arval Bread does seem to continue the longstanding tradition of offering food at funerals. Although they were traditionally baked at home by relatives, friends or neighbours of the deceased, by the mid nineteenth century the breads were being produced for sale in shops in Windermere or Kendall.[15] This may have been an early example of the commercialisation of death, or alternatively may simply have reflected the size of funerals at that time.

Traditionally, Arval Bread was given to everyone who attended the funeral or who would have attended if they could and every effort was made to ensure that everyone who was entitled to attend received their portion. Sometimes the bread was wrapped in a piece of paper along with a memorial notice or pious verse. This was probably a Victorian attempt to Christianise a very old tradition, although most people were unable to read and write well into the late nineteenth century. The bread was usually given out after the funeral meal and just before the guests left. Therefore it was not eaten in the home of the deceased or anywhere near the burial, but in the mourner's own home and preferably before the end of the day of the funeral.

Since there is no physical reason why the bread could not have been eaten as part of the main funeral meal at the home of the deceased's family there must have been some other factors at work. One possibility is that by taking away the bread, the mourners were removing something that might otherwise harm the deceased or his immediately family. That something – whatever it was – could magically pass into the Arval Bread and then be safely consumed by others. Presumably any ill effects were diluted by being spread between so many people. This might also explain why so much effort made to ensure it was even given to those who could not make it to the funeral. The timing also seems to have been important, since if anyone who was invited to the funeral was unable to attend, arrangements were made to take the bread to them that same day.

Of course, there were other occasions when bread had to be consumed at funerals for rather different reasons, particularly if vampirism was suspected. In many parts of Europe, the tradition was to take a drop of blood from the corpse of someone suspected of being likely to turn into a vampire, such as a murder victim or a suicide. This was then added to bread dough that was cooked and handed out to the mourners in the belief that they would either be protected against vampirism or that the deceased would be prevented from turning into a vampire in the first place. It is quite possible that there may have been similar motivation behind such traditions as Arval Bread. It would certainly go some way to

---

15 Thompson, Arval or Avril Bread, 1918:84.

explaining the urgency behind eating the bread on the same day as the burial.

Right across Europe and even Egypt, celebrations devoted to honouring and remembering the dead were popular in early November. This is quite distinct from commemorating an individual at the time of death or burial which after all, could happen at any time. The Anglo-Saxons celebrated Blotmonath or month of sacrifices in November, while on the west bank at Thebes in Ancient Egypt, the *ntryt* festival was celebrated at the end of October.[16] There, people made necklaces of onions as offerings not only to Sokar-Osiris but also to their deceased friends and relatives. The purpose of the onions was to illuminate the face of the dead, which appears to have occurred due to magical properties within the onions. This is curiously similar to the northern Halloween and Samhain celebrations which, incidentally, were held at almost exactly the same time of year as the *ntryt*. At Halloween however, vegetables normally growing underground - such as swedes and turnips - were hollowed out and illuminated with candles, which is curiously similar to the Egyptian idea of illuminating the faces of the dead. The fact that these vegetables grew underground may have been a magical link with corpses in the grave. In northern Europe however the faces were traditionally carved into the vegetables instead. Anything that is illuminated glows, and anything that glows – such as fire – appears to have a life of its own. Magically speaking therefore, these vegetables were probably intended to reanimate or bring new life to the dead.

In the ancient Graeco-Roman world parsley and celery were dedicated to Hades/Pluto, deities both associated with death and the underworld.[17] Both plants were eaten at funeral feasts and in ancient Egypt celery was included in funeral wreaths, most notably that of King Tutankhamun. Although modern day celery is far too thick and brittle to twine into a wreath, in ancient times it had much thinner stalks, not much thicker than parsley stems. In fact the Egyptian *'mountain parsley'* was an early term for celery.[18]

Part of the attraction of plants such as celery and parsley in funerary rituals and meals must have been linked with their ability to remain green long after being picked. In Egypt the colour green was associated with Osiris, and symbolised rebirth. Therefore the magical properties of any plant that remained green long after others withered and turned brown may have helped the deceased obtain an afterlife. Even nowadays, funeral wreaths still often contain evergreen plants, although rarely celery or parsley! Parsley was so closely associated with death in the ancient world that the Greeks

---

16 Graindorge, C. Les Oignons de Sokar originally published in Revue d'Égyptologie, 1992:43, an English summary available online by Th. Benderitter, http://www.osirisnet.net/docu/e_fete_sokar.htm accessed August 17th 2011.

17 Dierbach, Flora Mythologica, 1833:147-8

18 Wilson, Egyptian Food and Drink, 2001:52.

had a saying: *'deisthai selinon'*, meaning *'to need celery'* – another way of saying that someone was extremely ill and not expected to survive. The saying was also used whenever there had just been a death in the house.[19]

One intriguing aspect of many funeral foods is that they often have a dual purpose as aphrodisiacs and were used at wedding as well as funeral feasts.[20] For example, not only was parsley used at funerals but it was considered so powerful that it could make women pregnant just by sowing or picking it. Nuts are another example: their dead, dry-looking shell could symbolise death, while the inner kernel represented revival and rebirth; any sapling that grew from it could then represent eternal life. Nuts have been found in bone deposits at cremations sites such as Carmanhall in County Dublin (along with cleaver seed, carbonised grass seed, an indeterminate cereal grain, an indeterminate legume and a stalk fragment, any or all of which may have been part of the funeral feast).[21] However, nuts were also linked with sex and nowadays the term *'nuts'* is a popular euphemism for testicles. In the ancient Graeco-Roman world nuts were often thrown at weddings, hence the Roman author Virgil [22] wrote s*parge marite nuces,* meaning *'Strew nuts, bridegroom'*. Nuts may no longer be strewn on the floor at weddings nowadays, but they have almost certainly survived in the form of sugared almonds used as wedding favours.

At first sight, this pairing of sex and death may seem strange to us, but it is common in many traditions. The ancient Graeco-Roman world held that there were two opposing yet complementary forces, the Greek gods *Thanatos* (death) and *Eros* (Life/procreation). This interplay between opposites could easily be recognised in everyday life, in the constant struggle between life and death, growth and decay, fertility and sterility. Since these things can be found in just about any walk of life, it probably also explains why it became such a popular concept in psychology. Indeed, Freud was to describe *eros* as a *'self preservative instinct'* and *thanatos* as a desire to *'lead organic life back into the inanimate state'*.[23]

Magically speaking, plants that help to create or empower life by increasing fertility can also help to end it. By the same token, foods with this dual role would perform an important function especially in any society that believed in rebirth/reincarnation. In particular, the *eros/thanatos* properties would help ensure reincarnation by

---

19 Thiselton-Dyer, English Folklore, 1884:3–4; Baker, Discovering the folklore of Plants, 1996:118.

20 De Cleene & Lejeune, Compendium of Symbolic and Ritual Plants in Europe Vol II, 2003:446.

21 Reilly, Bronze Age Cemetery, 2005:33.

22 Virgil, Eighth Ecologue, 8.29-30,

http://classics.mit.edu/Virgil/eclogue.8.viii.html.

23 Freud, The Ego and the Id, 1962:30.

encouraging conception as soon after the funeral meal as possible.[24] This would be made more likely by holding a *'bean-feast'* at a funeral, due to the widely held belief that just the scent of broad bean flowers would make a woman consent to have sex. It is probably no coincidence that both funerals and weddings were (and to some extent still are) traditionally accompanied by feasts. Even the humble onion, which makes a very unlikely aphrodisiac, was once considered so potent that the priests and followers of Pythagoras were forbidden to eat them!

Looking again at the Bronze Age cemetery at Carmanhall in County Dublin, it is interesting that at this particular site the cremation urns were upturned, quite the opposite of what we might expect from a vessel that contained human remains (or anything else for that matter).[25] This inversion is curious, and the nearest comparison I can find is the old practice of turning a cauldron upside down over the ashes at the end of the day for baking. We know that cauldrons were used in many Bronze Age societies and although it is sometimes claimed that they did not eat bread, saddle querns have been recovered from the sites of some lake dwelling communities, such as those at Moynagh Lough and Knocknalappa in Ireland.[26] This suggests that grains were ground and made into flour so the technique of baking beneath an upturned cauldron may well have been possible. But why treat someone's charred bones in this way? One explanation could be that inverting the pot meant that the opening was at the base, like a womb. The body was therefore symbolically being returned to the womb to await its rebirth.

It is impossible to do justice to the wide-ranging practice of funeral meals in a short essay such as this. We cannot even be sure what people felt they achieved. Scholars have suggested a variety of explanations from van Gennep's[27] suggestion that funeral meals were intended to reunite the surviving members of the group with each other, to Rowell's[28] belief that feasting relieved the *'tedium of their existence in the tomb'*. Some claim that anything done at the funeral – including a funeral meal – could only ever be intended to meet the personal, social, emotional and religious needs of those who survive.[29] Others argue that everything was intended to benefit the deceased.[30] Unfortunately nothing is certain, even the best artefacts can only give us clues about what was done, and usually raise far more questions than they answer.

---

24 Teirlinck, Flora Diabolica, 1924:149.

25 Reilly, Bronze Age Cemetery, 2005:33.

26 O'Sullivan, Archaeology of Late Bronze Age Lake Settlements, 1997:118.

27 Van Gennep, The Rites of Passage, 1960:164.

28 Rowell, The Liturgy of Christian Burial, 1977:10.

29 Jackson, For the Living, 1963:19.

30 Abercromby, Funeral Masks in Europe, 1896:364.

In the modern world, death has become depersonalised and we have a tendency to leave everything to the professionals, employing undertakers and even religious representatives rather than actually speaking out for ourselves. Indeed, the religious groups often prefer it this way, and woe betide anyone who wants to personalise a funeral service.[31] In the ancient world the deceased's friends, family and maybe even the wider community may all have been expected to play a *'priestly'* role in looking after both the deceased and the mourners.

Although we can recover so little knowledge about the purpose and function of funeral meals, the fact that they were so widespread suggests a common need to mark the passing of a member of the tribe or family, by coming together and sharing something – in this case a meal. What the meal involved and what it was expected to achieve is difficult to assess, but its enduring popularity suggests that even if the tradition has evolved with the times, it still has something to offer modern society.

Bibliography

Abercromby, J. (1896) *Funeral Masks in Europe,* in *Folklore* Vol. 7.4:351-366

Baker, M . (1996) *Discovering the Folklore of Plants.* Princes Risborough: Shire Publications Ltd (third edition)

Bond, J.M. (1996) *Burnt Offerings: Animal Bone in Anglo-Saxon Cremations,* in *World Archaeology, Zooarchaeology: New Approaches and Theory* Vol. 28.1:76-88

Bower, B. (1998) *Banquets in the Ruins,* in *Science News* Vol. 153.21:331-333 (May 23, 1998.)

De Cleene, M. & Lejeune, M.C. (2003) *Compendium of Symbolic and Ritual Plants in Europe,* Volumes I and II. Ghent: Man and Culture Publishers

Dierbach, J. (1833) *Flora Mythologica.* Frankfurt am Main: Sauerländer J.D.

Douglas, James (1793) *Nenia Britannica.* London: John Nicols

Freud S. (1962) *The Ego and the Id.* London: The Hogarth Press

Graindorge, C. Summary by Th. Benderitter, *Les Oignons de Sokar.* Can be read online in English at

http://www.osirisnet.net/docu/e_fete_sokar.htm accessed August 17th 2011.

Harvey, R. (1941) *The Unquiet Grave,* in *Journal of the English Folk Dance and Song Society* Vol. 4.2:49-66

Herodotus, & Rawlinson, G. (trans.) (2010) *A history source of Persian Empire.* London: The British Library

Jackson, E.N. (1963) *For the Living.* Des Moines: Channel Press

Hunter-Blair, P. (1976) *Northumbria in the Days of Bede.* London: Gollancz

O'Sullivan, A. (1997) *Interpreting the Archaeology of Late Bronze Age Lake Settlements,* in *The Journal of Irish Archaeology* Vol. 8:115-121

Reilly, F. (2005) *Bronze Age Cemetery,* in *Archaeology Ireland* Vol. 19.2:32-35

Rowell, G. (1977) *The Liturgy of Christian Burial.* London: S.P.C.K.

Smith, S.T. (1991) *They Did Take It with Them: Requirements for the Afterlife Evidenced from Intact New Kingdom Tombs at Thebes,* in *KMT Magazine* Vol. 2:3

---

31 http://www.telegraph.co.uk/news/religion/7804570/Bishop-of-Chester-criticises-celebratory-modern-funerals.html.

Tacitus, & H. Mattingly & S.A. Handford (trans.) (1970) *The Agricola and the Germania.* Harmondsworth: Penguin

Teirlinck I. (1924) *Flora Diabolica, De plant in de demonologie.* Antwerp: De Sikkel

Thiselton-Dyer, T. (1884) *English Folklore.* London: W H Allen & Co.

Thompson, T.W. (1918) *Arval or Avril Bread,* in *Folklore* Vol. 29.1:84-86

Van Gennep, A. (1960) *The Rites of Passage.* Chicago: The University of Chicago Press

Virgil *Eighth Ecologue,* 8.29-30 Can be read online at: http://classics.mit.edu/Virgil/eclogue.8.viii.html Accessed 1st September 2011.

Wilson, H. (2001), *Egyptian Food and Drink.* Oxford: Shire Publications Ltd

Yoder, L. (1986) *The Funeral Meal: A Significant Funerary Ritual,* in *Journal of Religion and Health* Vol. 25.2:149-160

http://www.telegraph.co.uk/news/religion/7804570/Bishop-of-Chester-criticises-celebratory-modern-funerals.html Accessed 1st August 2011.

Cultivating the Dead: The Path of Lilies and Water

By Chad Barber

Tracing the influences that forged spiritism as it took shape in the religious crucible of the New World, spanning Caribbean locales ranging from Cuba and Puerto Rico to New Orleans and modern day Florida, can make decoding what is really a pan-Caribbean phenomenon as complex as it is contradictory. It's a task that becomes all the more complex as *espiritismo* emerges on the world stage and continues to change, along with a constellation of African-derived Creole religions and folk-traditions as a global religious phenomenon.

Point of fact: my own understanding of the tradition is primarily based on the training and experience gained working as an *espiritista* (spiritist medium) in a dynamic, and remarkably popular, *espiritismo centro* in Amsterdam, in the Netherlands. This is all the more remarkable considering that the Netherlands proudly boasts one the most secular atheistic societies in the European Union. Yet our *centro* fills fortnightly to capacity with a mix of people of various ethnicities and socio-economic classes all conspicuously dressed in pure white, ready to participate in what is otherwise denounced as an irrational, superstitious act: communicating with discarnate souls.

Participants come to receive messages from the spirits, to sing, to be spiritually cleansed, to be inspired and often enough to cathartically sob and shake as they enter into profound spiritual congress with the dead. Sometimes the dead will manifest through *espiritistas* who are '*working the table*' in full possession in order to cleanse bodies with specially prepared branches, to warn or even angrily reprimand. At other times they will conspiratorially whisper formulae for benign sorceries and charms, or healing remedies, to help improve the health and well being of a congregant. It's a process with alarmingly *magical* implications in the modern western context and therefore seems to hold a kind of transgressive potential as it undermines the materialistic preconceptions that pervade European society. More commonly the spirits are subtly incorporated in the continuum of an *espiritista's* consciousness, enabling them to deliver messages while being only partially overshadowed by the *muerto's* personality, thereby still retaining control of their normal faculties and body. These sorts of messages are given more gently by calling individual congregants up from the audience to receive messages from the *espiritistas* near the ritual foci of this gathering – the *mesa blanca*, or white table.

These spiritist gatherings, called *misas espirituales* (spiritual masses), seem to hold the capacity to blur religious, social and racial categories in the Old World, just as they have done historically in the New World. And while *espiritismo* is ostensibly based on French spiritualism as transmitted by Allan Kardec, in the Caribbean the system underwent a number of important changes - adapting to existing and emerging indigenous, folk Catholic and Afro-Cuban cosmological schemes. In Cuba and Puerto Rico, for instance, African-derived religious systems such as Santeria (a composite of traditions of West African origin) and Palo Monte (a Kongo derived tradition) *"drew on and modified the séance-based ritual technology of Kardecist Spiritism to communicate with the dead"* and as Raul Canizares astutely remarks: *"although spiritism serves a valuable function in Santeria, it has not been absorbed by it"*.[32]

At our *centro*, for example, one will find that some *espiritista's* simultaneously function as *santeros* (priests of the Afro-Cuban orisha tradition) outside the context of the *misa espiritual*. There is a saying in the Santeria community: *"not all espiritistas are santeros but all santeros should be espiritistas"*. However, within the context of the misa, their status as Santeria priests formally affords them no special status among other *espiritistas* where a more junior Santeria initiate may well be a more experienced *espiritista*. Today in Europe, as in the Caribbean, the boundary between the two systems, while sometimes overlapping, is continually being negotiated so as to ensure the coherence of each system remains intact.

It's a religious landscape characterized by subtle binary oppositions; spiritual and material, the living and the dead, magic and religion, good and evil. Revealed religions tend to proscribe clear systems of moral and philosophical doctrine that delineate these sorts of binaries for their adherents. Creole African-derived religion by contrast seems to create a vehicle through which these binary tensions can be interrogated, explored and performed - an ongoing lived phenomenon with *"dichotomous alternatives, naturally embedded within potentialities of these practices"*.[33]

That dynamic tension is nowhere more evident than within the practice of *espiritismo* where the binary of matter and spirit, which is to say, the living and the dead, their interrelatedness and their opposition, sit at the core of what motivates the work of the *espiritista*.

---

32 Canizares, Raul. Cuban Santeria: Walking with the Night. 1999.

33 Santo, Spiritist Boundary-Work and the Morality of Materiality in Afro-Cuban Religion. 2010:72.

French Spiritualism and the Rise of Espiritismo

Spiritism's core beliefs were originally transmitted in the book of orations, *Le livre des esprits* (The Book of Spirits), by Allan Kardec who was born Hypolyte Leon Denizard Rival (1804-1869). First published in 1857, *The Book of Spirits* was followed by six additional works related to the doctrine of spiritism (all published by 1868) and translated into Spanish from the original French almost instantly. By the 1860s these texts were widely available in Cuba and Puerto Rico where *espiritismo* quickly grew in importance as soon as it arrived. Initially Kardec's ideas drew intellectuals and well-to-do urban elites, but then quickly filtered into almost every other sector of society. In Cuba especially it greatly appealed to the largely Afro-Cuban working class as well as the unemployed.[34]

In these locales *espiritismo* provided an avenue for healing treatments attracting peoples already familiar with African-based healing methods. As George Brandon notes:

"Espiritismo also took on the colours of its Creole environment. Espiritismo grew by accumulating elements of Spanish and Cuban herbalism, Native American healing practices, and the scent of African magic."[35]

This coincided with decline of the highly skilled Yoruba *egungun* specialist in Cuba, whom once performed the vital function of working with the ancestral dead in Santeria and thus playing a key role in funerary rites. This role was perceived to be potentially perilous for the practitioner and therefore assumedly became an unpopular vocation. With the *egungun* priesthood in decline *santeros* would resourcefully appropriate the séance-based ritual technology that allowed the spiritist medium to act as a communicational device, thereby linking the formerly unavailable spirits of the deceased with the living. In this way African ancestors could reconnect with their descendants in a New World in a more accessible and pragmatic style based, in part, on French spiritualism.

It's not that hard to conceive how Kardecist concepts would come to take root so easily in populations already permeated by reverence for ancestral forces and the dead. Kardecist spirituality in its various mutations would become a convenient vehicle for expressing what was really a pre-existing religious sensibility in a new, more egalitarian, form – one that appealed to a body politic that had grown frustrated and suspicious of Catholic authoritarianism.

While *espiritismo* would incorporate the Kardecist liturgies and basic form of white table mediumship, Kardecist theological and moral tenets tend to be interpreted more loosely. Often the spiritualist doctrine would be reframed in Afro-Cuban, folk-Catholic

---

34 Bettelheim, Caribbean Espiritismo (Spiritist) Altars: The Indian and the Congo. 1985.

35 Brandon, Santeria from Africa to the New World: The Dead Sell Memories, 1993:87.

and indigenous cosmological terms to varying degrees depending on region and line of practice. The degree of syncretism versus adherence to the original Kardecist world-view would come to characterize the numerous different streams of *espiritismo* that would spring up in Cuba and Puerto Rico; a process still under way after Cuban and Puerto Rican forms met and amalgamated in U.S. locales such as New York and Miami.

In Cuba this process produced a more syncretic *'crossed'* form referred to as *espiritismo cruzado* and *'purist'* forms such as *espiritismo scientifico*. Considering itself a closer interpretation of Kardec's teaching, *espiritismo scientifico* emphasizes a more rational *'scientific'* method for mediumship, making use of the idiom of science and medicine to define and describe its mediumistic doctrines, and very importantly, to set itself apart from what it considers as *'primitive'* syncretic forms of spiritism that locate their practice in an African-derived religious milieu.

Espiritismo cruzado by contrast takes a more lively approach that makes heavier use of the materials and music that it has absorbed from its Creole environment. Techniques such as song and dance, herbalism deployed in spiritual washes and remedies, spirit-dolls and pots, cigars and ritual possession all play an important role in the religious performance of the *cruzados*. Similarly, spirit guides and cosmological preconceptions of distinctly afro-Cuban flavour and therefore not recognizable from Kardecist doctrine populate the *cruzado* style of *espiritismo*. We find entities that recall a distinctly African and Native American heritage such as the ubiquitous Madama spirit; the Congos; Indian spirits and spirits of deceased slaves, or ancestral guides who once were elders of Lukumi and Palo traditions.

Materialising the Dead

"In contemporary Afro-Cuban religion, icons, artefacts, spirit representations, sacrificial offerings and other ritual objects or consumables do not just embody or represent; rather, they engender a complex set of cosmological and social relations, expectations and effects that go well beyond their production and use at any one given moment. In Cuba, matter matters, not because it is symbolic or expressive of (and thus, subordinate to) a transcendent spiritual world, but because for many religious people it is vital for the achievement and manipulation of the spirit world's presence in the physical world: among other things, as a means of miming the otherworldly into being."[36]

Espirito Santo's observation that matter is not necessarily seen as hierarchically subordinate to a transcendent spiritual dimension but indeed as crucial for *"miming the otherworldly into being"*

---

36 Santo, Spiritist Boundary-Work and the Morality of Materiality in Afro-Cuban Religion. 2010:65.

elegantly articulates the dynamic tension found in the use of ritual objects and consumables (food, alcohol, herbs, spirit dolls and figures, cigars etc.) as deployed in the more creolized practice of the cruzados.

Firstly, the espiritista must seek to cultivate a sound relationship based in reciprocity with his or her muertos. One of the ways this is done is by feeding the spirits foodstuff that it is understood to have liked in life including substances such as alcohol or cigars – which it is interesting to note, are often addictive! This process, in part, can be seen as a technology for drawing a spirit closer into matter, and therefore materializing it. And as Diano Santo remarks, *"notions of spiritual potency and power, in relation to degrees of materiality, are critically important in understanding how espiritistas cruzados locate their practice in the Afro-Cuban religious spectrum."*[37]

The more *'materialized'* the *muerto* becomes through this process, the greater the access that *espiritista* has to its knowledge and power. Power that is crucial for affecting the pragmatic changes such as healing or improvement of economic and social conditions – the very needs that draw people to services of the *espiritista* in the first place.

However, from the perspective of the Kardecist doctrine of spiritual evolution, the work of the spiritist is primarily to elevate and bring clarity (*claridad*) to the dead; a process that by its very nature once again distances them from the material, sending them higher into the spiritual sphere. This clarification and elevation of the spirits is accomplished by offering them prayers and *misas* that produces a kind of nourishing spiritual light (*luz*), which is much needed by the dead for their growth. It is a process which, as Kardec describes in a popular spiritist oration, *"hopes to seek elevation for my assigned Spirit Guide in Your* [God's] *magnificent celestial territory"*.[38] Distressed spirits are also counselled and soothed in order to help them recover from traumas they may have experienced in life. The elevation of the spirits in turn helps them become wiser and *'cooler'* and, resultantly, easier to work with - yet paradoxically more detached from the worldly affairs of men.

It's a dilemma that is continually being negotiated by the *espiritista* as he or she seeks to balance the need for *'materializing'* their *muertos,* increasing their power to effect changes in the tangible world and thus drawing them further *'down into'* the material realm, versus the desire to help with their continued evolution in the spiritual world. In a distinct sense this process is generative because of the way in which the spirits are materialized; though what they are fed or the dolls and icons and other materials they are given to give them form indeed *'creates'* a sort of spirit. Considering the close partnership that the espiritista enters into with his *muertos* and the

---

37 Ibid., 2010:66.

38 Kardec (ed. Gual), Collection of Selected Prayers: Devotion manual and spiritualist prayer guide, 2004.

mutual obligations that this entails, care needs to be taken that the practitioner is not led astray.

The dilemma plays itself out further in the problem of defining the moral orientation of the medium in a religious environment where the transcendent spiritual values of good character, spirituality and evolution can be starkly contrasted against the need for a practice that also provides socio-economic benefits.

As Diano Santo's informant, an *espiritista* named Jesus, relates to her: "*I must be certain within myself of what I have lived. Just as you see these glasses of water* [referring to the bovéda], *transparent and clean, a spiritist should be exactly the same way*". Another of Santo's informants, a Cuban man who is both an *espiritista* and a *palero*, remarks that the way of the *'pure'* spiritist is "*a 'camino de azucena, de agua' – the path of lilies and water.*"[39]

The Boveda Espiritual

The ongoing process of "*miming the otherworld into being*" is nowhere more evident than in the construction of *espiritismo* altars and its mediumistic device par excellence: the *bovéda espiritual*.

The *bovéda*, which can be translated as the 'spiritual dome,' forms the centrepiece of every *espiritismo* altar arrangement and naturally forms an energetic focal point for the *mesa blanca* (white table) during a *misa*. This large glass bowl filled with cool, clear water becomes a conduit for the *muertos* to enter into the ritual context and as such has the capacity also to absorb unwanted spiritual influences through the potency of the *muertos*. It conducts in and out of this world. In a certain sense it becomes transformed into a microcosm representing the intersection of the realms of living and the dead.

Usually an unadorned wooden cross is placed in the bowl to sanctify the water so that it might be a suitable conductive medium for the dead. Along with the customary séance table covered in a white tablecloth, adorned with white flowers and white candles - the *bovéda* becomes the axis upon which the mediumistic praxis of the *espiritista* turns. Ritually saluted by each participant by respectfully tapping on its rim three times whenever the white table is approached, the *bovéda* is paid the same respect as the spirits themselves. With all the white clad *espiritistas,* flowers and white candles this preponderance of white quite naturally exerts a calming effect on the participants.

Yet, I would also like to suggest that the symbolism might well have some connection to Christian funerary custom. I recently found myself walking with my godfather (both *santero* and *espiritista*) past a beautiful graveyard, and he remarked how the crosses were unadorned by the Christ figure just like the plain wooden cross we

---

39 Santo, Spiritist Boundary-Work and the Morality of Materiality in Afro-Cuban Religion.2010:71.

put in the waters of the *bovéda espiritual.* The observation suddenly impressed upon me the funerary atmosphere that *mesa blanca* format attunes itself to – an entirely appropriate resonance for contacting the dead. As Marta Moreno Vega poetically remarks *"the cross, as used in spiritualism, acknowledges the supreme being as well as the continuity of life after death. It is the point of transition as the session invites the spirits to join the living and the living to enter the spirit world."*[40]

Vega also draws a comparison between the *bovéda* and the Kongo cosmogram, the Yowa, (a sacred Kongo image of a circle quartered by a cross) and points out that the horizontal line represents the primal cosmic waters with the area above the line indicating the divine realm and below the line the realm of the dead, *kalunga.* It's interesting to note the manner in which the circle and cross structure of the *bovéda espiritual* (also containing water) visually and mythically rhymes with that of the Kongo cosmogram. The Kongo conception of the dead residing *"beneath the water"* becomes an important idea to hold in mind when thinking about the ritual function of the *bovéda* – especially considering the role that Kongo peoples, taken as slaves to all areas of the Caribbean, played in forming the basis of Creole religious conceptions relating to the dead.

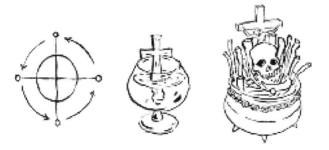

[Left to right] The Yowa, the *boveda espiritual,* and the *nganga.*

Similarly, if we draw a comparison to another important Kongo-derived necromantic device, the Palo *nganga,* we also find a dome-like container (usually a metal pot) containing an assemblage of ritually significant materials and objects such as dirt, bone and sticks representing once again the Kongo cosmogram, therewith creating a small universe inside the pot. What is important for this discussion is that, like the *bovéda,* a cross or crucifix is included in the *nganga's* constitution (as is the case of *nganga Cristiano*) in order that it may sanctify the microcosm contained therein before God.

---

40 Vega, Espiritismo in the Puerto Rican Community: A New World Recreation with the Elements of Kongo Ancestor Worship. Journal of Black Studies, 1999:349.

It is interesting to note that in a *nganga* the spirit is in fact bound to the pot with chains, fed blood and therefore is most thoroughly *'materialized'* – literally chained to this world like a *'dog'*. This absolute materialization is to ensure its ruthless efficiency and power. Whereas by contrast the transparency of the *bovéda* ensures the freer movement of the *muertos* and their ability to receive light, knowledge and clarity – virtues not all that desirable in a *nganga* spirit, considering that this would distance it from matter and undermine the ruthless potency of the famed Creole necromantic device.

Taking this into account we might view the *bovéda* and *nganga* as mirror images, at either side of material/spiritual binary – one transparent cool and filled with water, the other solid metal, hot and filled with dirt, blood and bone. A comparison that is all the more intriguing when taking into account the visual resemblance between the two devices and their functional relationship to the realm of the dead.

Community in This and the Otherworld

Conspicuously absent from most forms of Cuban and Puerto Rican *espiritismo* is any prerequisite for initiation. This is an important distinction in the religious continuum of the Caribbean, where so many of African-derived traditions place value on the initiatory process. Instead, an emphasis is placed on communal service in which the entire community moderates the orthodoxy of the religious experience. Therefore while the question of status certainly is one of importance in most African–derived traditions (because of the great emphasis on respect for one's elders), *espiritismo* boasts a flatter egalitarian model which, although recognizing mediums of different experience levels and aptitudes, instates no formal hierarchy among them. This is one of the reasons it grew so quickly in popularity in Cuba and Puerto Rico – being viewed as more spiritually democratic and therefore liberating adherents from the crushing weight of governmental and Catholic authoritarianism.

Even though the *mesa blanca* is understood to have a *'president'* for the duration of the *misa,* his function is closer to that of a timekeeper or master of ceremonies than that of a mediating priest. In some *espiritismo centros* and houses (such as our own in Amsterdam) the *'president'* function rotates weekly between the mediums. Instead of having a single clerical figure ministering, each medium has equal capacity to deliver messages, cleanse or address the participants as the *muertos* dictate.

Similarly, the format of the spiritual mass is mutable and can take a circular form in which every single participant in attendance acts as a medium sitting in the circle (this is the common arrangement in smaller *misas*). Alternatively, in bigger *misas* the room is arranged so that there is a congregation facing the front and a team of mediums up front who work the table. In this larger format, taking into account aptitude and willingness, congregants might be given the opportunity to work the table as mediums – receiving the valuable opportunity to serve their community and practice *caridad* (charity).

Espiritismo can only function in the context of community. Properly understood, *espiritismo* is a kind of psycho-spiritual social work. For the *espiritista* walking the path of lilies and water there is an obligation to his or her society, to the community, which naturally includes *both* the living and the dead.

For within the intricately interwoven pattern between incarnate and discarnate realms problems such as illness are conceived of as being rooted in the malfeasance of troubling spirits whom themselves are troubled by traumas experienced in life. These traumas can be soothed and healed with aid of other spirits through the intercession of the *espiritista*. This, in turn, can lead to healing and the resolution of all kinds of problems for the living. It is a framework in which the dead are *'both potential pathogen and the immune cell.'*[41]

Bibliography

Brandon, George (1993) *Santeria from Africa to the New World: The Dead Sell Memories.* Bloomington: Indiana University Press

Bettelheim, Judith (1985) *Caribbean Espiritismo (Spiritist) Altars: The Indian and the Congo,* in *The Art Bulletin,* 87: 312. College Art Association

Canizares, Raul (1999) *Cuban Santeria: Walking with the Night.* Rochester: Destiny Books

Kardec, Allen (ed. Gual, Candita) (2004) *Collection of Selected Prayers: Devotion manual and spiritualist prayer guide.* Universe.

Santo, Diana Espirito (2010) *Spiritist Boundary-Work and the Morality of Materiality in Afro-Cuban Religion.* Journal of Material Culture pp. 15-64. Sage

Santo, Diana Espirito (2010) *'Who else is in the drawer?' Trauma, personhood and prophylaxis among Cuban scientific spiritists'.* In *Anthropology & Medicine,* 17.3:249-259. London: Routledge

Vega, Marta Moreno (1999) *Espiritismo in the Puerto Rican Community: A New World Recreation with the Elements of Kongo Ancestor Worship.* Journal of Black Studies, 29:325. Sage

---

41 Santo, 'Who else is in the drawer?' Trauma, personhood and prophylaxis among Cuban scientific spiritists'. Anthropology & Medicine, 2010:250.

"*Death*" from *The Tarot of the Sidhe*
by Emily Carding, Schiffer 2011.

Don't Fear The Reaper: The Evolution Of The Death Card In Tarot

By Emily Carding

> *"Tarot Reader: Now we'll see what the future holds. (Turns over a card)*
>
> *Lisa: (gulps) The "Death" card?*
>
> *Tarot Reader: No, that's good, it means transition, change.*
>
> *Lisa: (relieved) Oh.*
>
> *(The Tarot Reader turns over another card)*
>
> *Lisa: Oh, that's cute.*
>
> *Tarot Reader: (gasps) The Happy Squirrel!*
>
> *Lisa: (timid) That's bad?*
>
> *Tarot Reader: Possibly. The cards are vague and mysterious..."*
>
> ~ *The Simpsons, 'Lisa's Wedding'*

Not so very long ago it was the case that the sight, thought or mention of the *'Death'* card would provoke the sharp intake of breath and trigger all manner of panicked thoughts of an early demise. As the above quote from the ever-popular television show *The Simpsons* demonstrates, the idea that *'Death'* doesn't mean physical death, but rather change and transformation, generally a positive one, has now seeped into popular consciousness. This became clear to me on a personal level a few days ago when I sat down with some neighbours who knew practically nothing about Tarot. As they were curious, I got a pack out to show them and we started to look through the cards. When the Death card appeared, they both commented that, *"Death doesn't mean death, does it? Doesn't it mean endings or change or something like that?"* And that, strangely, made me wince. It made me sad. Why?

Regardless of their awareness or otherwise of the potential meanings and symbolism of the Tarot, most people will be able to call to mind something like the traditional portrayal of the Death card. Most Tarot decks, (and there are now literally thousands to choose from), show Death as a personified force that is eternally familiar, the scythe-bearing skeleton known as the Grim Reaper. The earliest known versions of this Tarot trump, taking us back to the

15th Century, show this personified force of mortality in his most unavoidable guise, an unrobed skeleton that hews down all from the mightiest king to the innocent child. There are many variants, even in the very early decks, but the skeleton or corpse is constant, an unavoidable *memento mori*, a reminder of what we all without exception are reduced to when the flesh and material existence rots away. From the very first decks the card is numbered 'thirteen' and would often go unnamed, as though to name it would be to somehow attract it.

One of the best examples we have of an early Tarot is the Visconti deck, which hails from Italy, around the year 1450. There are a number of fascinating distinctions to be found in the Death card of this particular Tarot. The figure of Death himself appears as a decaying corpse rather than a completely skeletal figure. Though there is some flesh remaining on the bones, his torso has been rent open and we can see that his organs are missing, only his spine and ribcage can be seen. Around his head is tied a white bandage, the excess of which is blown around his head by an invisible breeze. In place of the more familiar scythe that can be seen in most consequent decks of this period, he holds in his left hand a graceful longbow.

Despite this grisly description, the Visconti Death is fairly approachable, (as animated corpses go). There is no sense of violence, he stands on a fertile landscape and wears almost an apologetic smile upon his face. With an inviting landscape of blue hills behind him, he is a welcoming sentry to a strange land. It has been suggested by a number of authors that the bow, as a long-range weapon, may have symbolised the dangers of the plague, a threat that was very much in the forefront of the public mind in this period. Of course Tarot symbolism did not develop in a vacuum and was, as it is today, influenced by popular culture and art of the time. Most commonly cited as one of, if not *the* main inspiration behind early Tarot is Petrarch's poem, *'I trionfi'* or *'The Triumphs'*. However, Petrarch's description of Death does not evoke quite the same image as we see in the decks of that period, describing only *"a woman shrouded in a dress of black"*. There was also a tradition of Ancient Rome, which thrived in Renaissance Italy, (home of the earliest known Tarot trumps), of the Triumphs as a costumed procession, and this was almost certainly an influence.

A more well-known Tarot from roughly this period, this time from France, is the Tarot de Marseilles, on which many modern decks are based. This deck brings us a Death who wields the familiar scythe, with some ferocity. The scythe is a symbol of Saturn, and hence may be seen to represent time, limitation, and of course the resulting child of those two factors, mortality. However, the agricultural metaphor should not be overlooked, as this Death is on his feet amidst blue and yellow foliage growing from a black earth, amidst which are strewn the heads, hands, feet and bones of a King, (he is wearing a crown, a symbol of the ego), and a pauper dressed in rags.

A strange harvest indeed! This has been rightly taken as a demonstration that Death does not discriminate between rich and poor or differing social status. Ego, however mighty, will fall at his hands, and under his influence all are equal. We are all connected through our mortality. It may also be interpreted as Death bringing an individual harvesting of our life's work, the final *'deadline'* as it were, if you'll pardon the pun. There is also the possibility of growth from death, as we know that corpses that rot in the earth feed the plants and creatures of that earth as they decay. On this card the hands and feet are almost indistinguishable from the grass and vegetation. This Death, like the Visconti, is unrobed, though he is partially clothed and still has a nose, so not quite skeletal. (No *'my Death has no nose'* jokes please.) His nakedness implies there is no hiding from Death and certainly he will not hide from you. We can see this as the result of a time of history when Death was very much an unavoidable part of daily life for everyone, regardless of their position in society. In fact when we look at the most influential historical Tarot packs, it becomes hard to see where the popular image of the Death card as a mysterious black robed spectre hails from, yet this is what springs to mind when most of us think of this card. Have we clothed him with our subconscious fears? Or is he more distanced from us now in our modern times of healthcare and advanced treatments?

These earliest Tarots may have been depicting mystical concepts and symbolism, or at the very least personified forces at work in people's lives, but divinatory meanings were not assigned to them, (as far as we know), until the 18th century. Whether there is any significance to the observation or not, it seems to be the case that once the cards started to be used for divinatory purposes, the Death card would more often appear clothed. It may be stretching a point to suggest that when faced with the prospect of actually having to confront the issue of Death in a reading situation with a client, people preferred their reaper to have a slightly more modest appearance, putting one layer of separation between their reader and the grisly reality of death.

The earliest examples of cartomantic meanings for the Death card are given to us very handily by Paul Huson in his excellent *Mystical Origins of the Tarot*, where he shows that *Pratesi's Cartomancer*, (1750), *De Mellet*, (1781) and *Court de Gebelin*, (1773-82) all interpret the Death card very literally as just that: death.

This seems to have remained the case until in the mid-19th century the influential occultist Eliphas Levi superimposed his knowledge of the Kabbalah and the Hebrew alphabet onto the structure of the Tarot, along with more mystical interpretations, bringing us the possibility of *'rebirth'* with his interpretation of Death. Eliphas Levi believed that Tarot had its ancient origins in Egypt, but since he also believed the Kabbalah to be Egyptian in origin, it all worked for him. To be fair, it does all work remarkably well, with subsequent figures and esoteric groups throughout history all bringing their own interpretations to it. The attributions with which most students of Tarot are familiar with today hail from the late 19th century writings of founding members of The Golden Dawn, (who were heavily influenced by the work of Levi), which is where the concepts of transformation and initiatory gateways are first connected to the Death card. It is also when the suits of the Minor Arcana became more firmly associated with the four elements. The teachings of the Golden Dawn, which incorporated large amounts of symbolism from Christian mysticism, were of course the basis of that most famous of decks, the Rider-Waite-Smith.

Considering that the Rider-Waite-Smith, (generally referred to as the RWS for brevity), is the most influential and replicated deck of modern times in terms of imagery and symbolism, it is interesting to note that our popular image of the Grim Reaper does not appear, other than the fact that Death is indeed portrayed as a skeletal figure on horseback. Pamela Coleman-Smith's Death wears black armour, not a robe or shroud, and wields neither weapon nor farming implement:

"The veil or mask of life is perpetuated in change, transformation and passage from lower to higher, and this is more fitly represented in the rectified Tarot by one of the apocalyptic visions than by the crude notion of the reaping skeleton..."[42]

It is fascinating that Tarot is perceived by the masses as being somehow sinister and certainly connected with witchcraft and paganism, yet the Bible is at the core of its symbolism. The RWS Death carries a black banner with a white rose, a symbol of life and rebirth. Though he does not bear arms, figures from all walks of life fall before him. In the distance, the sun rises between two pillar-like buildings, promising new life. However, despite the fact that the mystical concept of rebirth and transformation is now associated with Death, Waite still gives a very traditional divinatory meaning: *"End, mortality, destruction, corruption"* and goes on to say, *"Also for a maid the loss of marriage prospects"*. With this last addition we can see that Tarot truly is a reflection of its time, or certainly the society surrounding the creator and author of any given deck.

One deck that certainly bears the stamp of its creator in this way is the highly popular and influential Thoth deck, created by Aleister Crowley in collaboration with the extraordinary artist Lady Frieda Harris. This deck, which proves to be the most popular to this day with occultists and magicians, was created between the years 1938 and 1943, a period when one could suggest the powers represented by the Death card were at large in the world, both on a literal and metaphysical scale. The power of both the time and Crowley's teachings are more than apparent in Harris's portrayal of Death, a dynamic force of transformation and release. Once again, there is no sinister robed figure in sight. In this card we see a black skeleton

---

42 Arthur Edward Waite, The Pictorial Key to the Tarot, 1910.

caught in dance-like motion as he seems to be reaping living bubbles of energy. He wears the crown of Osiris, implying rebirth, fertility and life. There are geometric lines of force extending from his dance, and any space remaining in the card is taken up with representative symbols of the astrological, alchemical and Kabbalistic attributions.

The astrological sign associated with Death is Scorpio, represented by no less than three symbols on this card. Firstly the scorpion, which Crowley tells us stands for the powers of Scorpio in their *'lowest form'* and is logically placed at the very bottom of the card. The next is the serpent, which Crowley calls *"The Lord of Life and Death"*, and finally the eagle, which is Scorpio in its most exalted state. Crowley also relates these stages to the alchemical process of putrefaction. This is of course a complex subject that warrants an essay in itself, but essentially refers to the release of energy from dissolving physical matter that allows new life to emerge: a spiritual rebirth. The final symbol that remains is the fish, which relates to the Hebrew letter Nun (fish). To think about the symbol of a fish in connection with cycles of death and rebirth brings to mind a number of things. We can consider the symbol to relate to the Christian mythos, as the fish is a symbol of the followers of Christ and indeed Christ himself, as is noted by Crowley in *The Book of Thoth*. It also brings to mind the journey of the salmon as it instinctively returns to the place where it was spawned in order to die. All of these symbols are connected within the Death card and the twenty-fourth path on the Kabbalistic Tree of Life, connecting the Sephiroth Netzach and Tiphereth. The noted esoteric author and teacher Naomi Ozaniec captures the essence of this path nicely when she says:

"It is through the Imaginative Intelligence that the victory of Netzach becomes the shining Beauty of Tiphereth. This is, as the birth of Bodhicitta, the realisation of mystical consciousness, the emergence of the holographic mind and the birth of continuous consciousness."[43]

Although Crowley puts little emphasis on divinatory meanings of the cards, it is interesting to note that even in what he would have perceived as the most mundane use for the cards, the emphasis has now moved away from physical death completely:

"The universe is Changes; every change is the effect of an act of Love; all Acts of Love contain Pure Joy. Die Daily.

Death is the apex of one curve of the snake Life: behold all opposites as necessary complements, and rejoice."[44]

These concepts of death, rebirth and transformation are indeed powerful when used and understood in their proper context and with the knowledge and awareness of the significance of the whole process on an esoteric level. But what happens when these ideas are misunderstood, watered down, and packaged prettily for the masses?

---

43 Naomi Ozaniec, The Aquarian Qabalah, 2003.
44 Aleister Crowley, The Book of Thoth, 1944.

From the late nineteen-eighties onwards there has been a massive increase in Tarot deck creation and publication, to the extent that where there were very few choices and little availability of decks before the seventies, there are now literally thousands to choose from. This is no bad thing on one level, as there are decks of all artistic styles, and of symbolic content and themes to suit everyone. Although Tarot is often ignored by the art world, it does in fact provide the perfect vehicle for any artist to share their world view, as the whole world is contained within the cards. The art, by its very nature, reflects the artist and a true artist is in return a mirror for their times. However, for every deck that is thoughtfully crafted by artists and authors who have studied and assimilated an understanding of the symbolism, there are dozens more created by people whose understanding of the symbolism does not run deep, as they simply impose their chosen theme over the established symbolism of the traditional decks such as the RWS, Thoth or Marseilles. This results in a watered-down *'pop'* version of Tarot, and through a kind of *'Chinese whispers'* effect, the meanings start to lose their power. This brings me back to the conversation with my neighbours and why I was surprised to find myself feeling a little saddened that though they knew nothing of Tarot, they knew that Death meant *'change'* and not physical death.

"LORD, WHAT CAN THE HARVEST HOPE FOR, IF NOT FOR THE CARE OF THE REAPER MAN?"[45]

If you were to go out onto the street, (or onto Facebook, the virtual equivalent), and ask people who were in no way familiar with Tarot to picture the Death card, you would most likely have described to you a black-robed, skeletal figure wielding a scythe, his face concealed beneath his hood. This image of the Grim Reaper is so firmly embedded in our popular consciousness that they would not necessarily have seen Ingmar Bergman's *Seventh Seal* for example, or have read any Terry Pratchett, in order to have formed this personal impression. (Those who have read Pratchett would probably no longer see any threat in the image of the Grim Reaper, who, reflecting the author's own attitude to death, is portrayed more as an old friend who welcomes you into whatever afterlife you choose to create for yourself.) Yet as we have seen, most traditional packs bring us a naked skeletal Death, a Death that you must face full on in order to grow. What do we stand to lose if we deny ourselves this opportunity? It is the same on an individual level as it is on a global level. We deny ourselves the opportunity to truly evolve, for though the Death card does indeed represent change and transformation, the deepest levels of this transformation are only reached through the initiation of facing death itself, as a mortal and mystical force.

The Death card is number thirteen out of twenty-two Major Arcana, all of which are gateways to unity, harmony and completion. It is only just over halfway through the journey, certainly not the

---

45 Spoken by Death. Terry Pratchett, Reaper Man, 1991.

end! As the heroes of the Fool's journey of each of our lives, we must face this gateway if we are to meet with our higher selves, (XIV - Temperance), liberate ourselves from material attachment and addiction, (XV - The Devil), evolve beyond our ego, (XVI - The Tower) and unite with the cosmic powers of XVII - The Star, XVIII - The Moon, XIX - The Sun and XXI - The Universe itself. This is why we cannot simply dismiss the Death card as *"only meaning change"*, because without facing the possibility of Death, the transformation is not achieved. If Luke Skywalker did not face the Reaper in the form of his father, Darth Vader, he would certainly never have become a true Jedi. If Harry Potter had not faced the reaper in the form of the dark wizard Voldemort, (who like the early Death card is *'he who shall not be named'*), but instead was merely facing a change of school, then J.K. Rowling would not have made her fortune. And if Jesus had just given up on the whole preaching and being a fisher of men lark, escaping his crucifixion, well...the world would be a very different place indeed. On a global level, humanity needs Death to mean death. As a race we are in serious need of the spiritual evolution that this card represents. We need initiation, and as all that have been through any effective magical initiation will know, you face the real possibility of death in order to be reborn. Now I'm not suggesting we revert to looks of horror and hissing through our teeth like a builder about to give an over-priced quote every time we turn over the Death card in a reading, but that we acknowledge that in order to be reborn, some part of ourselves must die, we must say goodbye to our old selves. Let us pull back the hood of our Grim Reaper and meet his gaze, for the truth is that any breath of any day could be our last. If we, as Crowley suggests, *"Die Daily"*, then we open ourselves to the possibility of deeper awareness of life. If every day we acknowledge the fact that we will die, and it might be today, perhaps we will learn to truly live.

Bibliography

Berti, Gionardo & Tiberio Gonard (2002) Visconti Tarots. Torino: Lo Scarabeo

Crowley, Aleister (1978) The Book of Thoth. Maine: Samuel Weiser inc

Huson, Paul (2002) Mystical Origins of the Tarot. Vermont: Destiny Books

Huson, Paul (1972) The Devil's Picturebook. London: Abacus

Place, Robert M (2005): The Tarot, History, Symbolism and Divination. London: Penguin

Pollack, Rachel (2008) Tarot Wisdom. Minnesota: Llewellyn

Pratchett, Terry (1992) Reaper Man. London: Corgi

Waite, Edward Arthur (2008) The Pictorial Key to the Tarot. Stamford: US Games

Behind The Glasses Of Ghuedhe: Life In Death And Love In Both

By Kyle Fite

I step out of the car and flick on my flashlight. The air is chill and the graveyard menacingly moonlit, headstones spilling heavy shadows over the soft September soil. My companions and I are here on something of a *'psychic quest'*, following up on a lead from some ouija work done earlier this evening. I'm aware that I've entered territory presided over by the Baron, his cadaverous consort and cohorts from beyond the veil.

The goal is to locate and commune with a particular person whose name was telegraphed through the board. The several of us divide up and go shining our lights at the rows of marble monuments, searching for our contact. We couldn't hope for a better atmosphere. The graveyard is old, lichen crawling across many of the pock-marked stones. The night is dead silent and there is a bit of a sinister air about the place, intensified for each of us as we wander further away from the car and into the dark.

I'm ready for some terror, itching for that electrical exhilaration which emerges at such crossroads between the worlds. Any moment that bolt of fear will be shot from the shadows, sending the mind into a hypersensitive state whereby we gain a glance into the larger picture of what we are - and may become.

We're tripping through the Gates of Death. I'm keyed up. Feeling *'Voodoo'*. Ghost hunter persona activated.

And then my flashlight hits a portrait of a young boy, etched into a headstone upon which the love of Mom and Dad - and Grandma and Grandpa - is proclaimed. At the base of the stone are placed several small toys and action figures.

The sought after spookiness is blasted away and there is nothing at all left to fear. I sit down on the damp ground and simply stare as my guts begin to grind. My own son is the same age as the buried boy. I can understand - but will not pretend to feel - the parent's grief. The most powerful talismans are right before me, mass-made in plastic. I don't touch them. They're too sacred.

Off in the distance I can hear the voices of my companions. Our mystic mission now seems as superficial as a scavenger hunt.

Perhaps I missed the muffled thumping on a casket lid down the aisle or the hollow hissings circling in some luminous mist about a burial plot. Maybe I failed to see the flickering form of an earth-bound spirit next to the ancient oak tree as I rejoined the gang. I certainly didn't find our friend from the ouija chat. That's alright. I was too focused on what the Baron had decided to show me. And I wouldn't forget.

~~oOo~~

What is death? As humans, we have an intrinsic fascination with its *'emblems'*. I remarked recently to a friend that death and sex, Thanatos and Eros, seem bound together on some deep level of the psyche which gives rise to our fashions and fetishisms. From the popularity of wearing small silver skulls accentuating some sexy funeral black to the painting of eyelids and reddening of lips on a paper-pale face, we evoke the images of the dead and fuse them into our hot mammalian lives. The primordial need to reconcile our most basic life urges with the observation of our mortality is easily enough understood. But the dead do not explain death. The death-masks we wear facilitate a false familiarity.

~~oOo~~

"Samedhi Gate" by Kyle Fite, 2010.

Now I am dreaming. It's a strange adventure where a nefarious pimp seduces two women who I try to protect. His presence is ambiguous and compelling. He is a black man in a white suit, smoking a stogie. The girls cannot resist his charm and end up driving away with him. Later on, I am driving down a freeway and see the girls, pole-dancing off to the side of the road. There is the man again, putting them to work, laughing as his cigar dangles from his lower lip. Suddenly, an accident occurs. A station wagon ahead of me has just smashed headlong into a tractor trailer. I get out and run to the crushed car in the event that I might help. Crawling in from the back, I discover an infant in a car seat. Its body is severed in half and yet it is still alive. I carefully cradle the baby in my arms and pour all my love into its fractured frame. The end is near and I am helpless to help. I can only hush it to sleep, singing a gentle lullaby. All the while, the smoking man watches.

I wake up and know the man was Ghuedhe, loa of sex, death and the protector of small children. Like the Baron, he is teaching me. It is a week later and I am standing beside a hospital bed as a very sick friend elects to remove her ventilator and other life support apparatus. The sepsis her body has been fighting is now beyond cure and the end is inevitable. She wants to go without a tube in her throat. She wants the opportunity to say goodbye to her family and friends.

I feel awkward and surreal. All I can muster is the word *"Hey..."*

"Hay is for horses," she replies, always one for the quick joke. She's made this joke many times before. This will be the last.

I wanted so much to help but could only hold her hand. An hour later pain meds are given and she closes her eyes for the last time.

Did I mention the Ghuedhe are fond of laughter?

~~oOo~~

My earliest recollection of dealing with death was the passing of my grandmother. I was very young at the time and my family had driven in for the funeral. Of course, my parents had explained things to me and answered my blunt questions about death. So it was with great surprise that I saw all my relatives weeping and sombre. I saw my Grandfather sobbing like a child and was stunned. I was too young to question pat parental platitudes and simply believed that, as I was told, Grandma had *'gone to Heaven'*. I couldn't fathom why anyone was sad when she had essentially departed for Disneyland In The Sky and would be waiting for us to join her.

~~oOo~~

My life shuttled on, through school and college and marriage and a baby boy. People around me would receive their own tickets to the tomb but it wasn't until my Father died, after an unsuccessful operation for an arterial aneurysm, that I felt what my family's faith couldn't shield from my Grandfather's heart.

I would see my Father for the last time at the hospital where he died. I was kindly granted a viewing in some antiseptic morgue and his body bag was unzipped. Reality was becoming a blur around me and I felt as if everything was turning to static. I gently brushed his hair with my hand but his skin was like cool clay and my last visit with the man who raised me straddled some sickening line between the familiar form and the finality of the grave.

A knife would plunge into me repeatedly for weeks on end. I wept until my tear ducts dried up and I could do nothing more than dry heave in sudden spasms.

As I began to come back into myself and, once more, acclimatize to the land of the living, I would realize that this experience - and all the pain which trailed after it - was my father's final gift to me. It was a program downloaded onto the hard-drive of my soul. And it had begun to run.

~~oOo~~

When my father passed, I was already a long-time student of esotericism and the occult. I had cycled through various schools, each teaching their own metaphysical schema and explaining, often in a neat and tidy fashion, exactly what happens to the human being after death. I had sought to expand my consciousness into realms beyond that which our corporeal senses equip us to know. Meditation, astral voyaging, dream work. I had extended myself far enough into the subtle spheres to know there was much more than my '*body-suit*' operating in time and space. But my grasp on the ultimate destiny of the human being beyond bodily life was found wanting as grief swept over me and no theory or speculation could provide comfort.

It was at this time that I began '*talking to the dead*'. Some deep intuition was stirred within me as I dealt with my sorrow using the only tools I had. Helpless to bring back the dead and unclear as to what was really happening on the other side of the veil, I simply reached out from some place that seemed to be in my chest and directed its energy towards my father. It was a type of projection but also a harmonizing with his basic energy and through this '*beam*' I was able to communicate beyond words. I would do this again and again and then bring this practice to the many other loved ones who would die thereafter. I was amazed when I recently sat with a Palliative Doctor as she discussed with the siblings of a friend how they might cope with the imminent death of their sister. In clear and simple terms, without imposition of any theology or metaphysic, she described to them the process my father's death had spontaneously evoked in myself, asserting that an energy link could be formed through a projection and harmonizing - and that, through this, the needed love and support could be given... and received.

~~oOo~~

I would become very interested in the work of E. J. Gold after this time, especially his ideas on video-gaming as a form of '*Bardo-*

Training'. In fact, it was through Gold's work that I first encountered the term Bardo. This would lead me to the *Tibetan Book of the Dead* (after it led me to play QUAKE for endless hours). The TBD led me to look up an old friend who was a Buddhist and soon thereafter I was studying Chogyman Trungpa and sitting in meditation with the local Shambhala group, identifying myself as a *'Buddhist'* even though I kept on with certain occult studies. All of this was very powerful and wonderful for me. Meditation was opening me up to insight into the reactionary nature of the mind and I was amazed at how the Tibetans actually had developed a *'Science of Death'*. This was no vague and wispy ploy to control through comfort. It was precise, frank and bestowed compassion even as it confronted the ultimate dissolution of personal identity. This was transcendental and progressive action.

I then received a phone call one morning from a frantic friend. Apparently something had happened to the World Trade Center and I turned on the TV. Death was witnessed, indiscriminate and no respecter of persons, bringing down more people than the mind could fathom in a mere moment. My Buddhist quiescence cracked like rotten floorboards before the impact and weight of panic, fear and outrage. Shortly thereafter my personal life was thrown into upheaval and I was once more pushed off balance, slammed with grief and forced to face the inevitable and painful changes of a life whose nature - as well as destiny - is impermanence.

Bardo training with QUAKE was great fun. Panic could be stilled enough to steady aim and launch a grenade into a zombie's guts. I learned a lot from QUAKE. My skills of concentration, visualization and my work with dream states improved. I fortified the astral body and clarified some of its perceptive centres. But we also have an emotional body and this, too, is part of our unseen life. We take this with us into the Bardo and its limitations are preyed upon, leading us to either illumination or dissolution and rebirth. And, if there was one thing I was learning from Gold and Trungpa, it was that the Bardo isn't merely a holding station for the deceased. We are lost in its Labyrinth right now. It is extreme stress and upheaval that wakes us up to this condition. However, that same stress and upheaval can make navigating its corridors and hallways almost impossible.

Some situations may require quick wits and a double-barrelled shotgun. Others will ask for much more: control over the emotions; the ability to discern between illusion and reality; a connection to a higher frame of mind from which an aerial view of the assault on one's personal life might be seen in a more strategic and spiritually inclined perspective.

A marine stepping through an interdimensional slipgate led me into the Bardo. But there are trap doors beneath trap doors and the Bardo Run goes far beyond a computer screen.

~~oOo~~

Celebrities die and I feel very little, even as the internet lights up with momentary tributes and gossip. We've divided up people in the world and accord a greater importance to those who are known by many than the unknowns who live amongst us. We make a special crisis over a universal fact and replace our revulsion with the next bout of media entertainment. In some ways, this keeps our awareness of death compartmentalized and controlled. We can feel shock and sadness but need not have our lives shattered by it. After all, we didn't really know the pop star found on the hotel room floor. We can return to our lives as needed and get on with what the Tibetans call the *'Animal Realm'*, a Bardo of instinctual reactions and somnambulistic patterns.

I know people who won't attend funerals as it is *'too upsetting'*. Fear has dictated a circuitous route in the labyrinth of life and the hour of passing creeps steadily from behind. Diversion, excitement, anxiety and malaise all keep the mind from attending to the small yet persistent ticking built into the bio-machine. Yet that timeline, along which we race, is the backdrop for our shot in the physical universe, our flash in the pan. We'd better look long and hard at the situation we're in lest our lives implode in the twinkling of an eye and become a testament to a herded animal life instead of the Voyage of a Soul.

I've walked alongside death long enough to see a certain meaning in the sweep of the scythe, a meaning present from the headlines of tabloids to the obituaries of a small farm town newspaper. I could add to the anecdotes above and tell you how my best friend's heart stopped beating at the age of 30 and how I gave a eulogy for him to a family I had never met (and who he didn't particularly like). I could tell tales of helping a funeral director hoist a *'big and tall'* corpse from the bathroom where a toilet bowl heart attack stole from the world one of the kindliest spirits I've known. Death, smeared in sweat and fever, at the local Hospice centre. Flatlines at the hospital. Passing conversation in the hallway: *"Remember so and so? She suddenly died last week..."*

And every one of these deaths is overshadowed by that little boy's headstone in the graveyard where Samedhi put his hand on me.

~~oOo~~

My pursuit of the occult world has only grown in momentum. The Great Mystery of Death underpins many of my studies and explorations. I am hardly unique in this. However, extending knowledge into this *'Great Unknown'* does not seem to hold the ultimate answer we desperately desire. I recall Dr. Frankenstein, whose grotesque experiments were born of a reaction to loss and sorrow. He wished to evoke a power whereby suffering need not be. There are occult schools that teach the building and fortification of one's astral self that life and consciousness may continue even after the inevitable bodily decay. This is one step away from the ill-directed desire to preserve the body itself. Hope is held onto, Death's cold gaze evaded. Cryogenics has shifted from Sci-Fi to a lucrative service. Vampires are in vogue. Modern medicine will at least circumvent the slew of illnesses that dropped frontier folk like flies.

Are we running ahead, towards life, or running away, haunted by the most ancient of fears while being hunted by its progressing pace? Perhaps more importantly: is there an alternative to running in either direction?

~~oOo~~

All of my encounters with death have left their own unique scars on my heart. At the same time, each one has been a Gift. To fail in recognizing this would be a horrid ingratitude. Each life I have loved and lost has reminded me, for a brief incandescent moment, that I, too, will die - and yet am still alive. The utter inescapability of my death makes it more certain than any other event. In fact, it is so certain that I sometimes enter into the Gnosis of it having already occurred. It is a done deal. I'm already dead. This is not imagined. It is known.

This awareness most often comes to me at night, when I wake from dreams. I am once more conscious as a bodily being and yet still connected to my sleeping self. It is a strange *'Interzone'* where I suddenly know that I am already wiped out of existence and forgotten. Yet, somehow, I am still here. My awareness is like a rubber band, pulled across an abyss, immersed into its final destiny and then snapped back. I am reborn into Time. It is a Miracle. It is being raised from the dead and returning to the land of the living.

In Voudon, there is the Mystery of the Zombi. This often has dark and sinister associations. The Zombi is seen as something of puppet, a being whose personality has been expunged and whose post-mortem animation is directed by some alien force. A Zombi is *'bad'* and, certainly, no one wants to be one.

My own understanding of this symbolism may differ from popular conception. I have already spoken of the lwa, Ghuedhe, the Lord of both Sex (which is to say Life) and Death. In his *Grimoire Ghuedhe*, Voudon Master Michael Bertiaux includes a question and answer section, specifically addressing the Mysteries of the Zombi. I wish to cite a portion of this here:

"Q: Is it true that the dead are perfect in...Universe G (that is, Universe Ghuedhe), that they are really in the Resurrection?

"A: That is the meaning of the "life" in that universe.

"Q: Was St. Paul, the Catholic writer of the Epistles, an initiate of them or one who knew of them?

"A: What more could his writings indicate so clearly?

"Q: But what of the decay of the dead bodies which happens to them in this world?

"A: That is the difference between the body inherited from Adam (the body in Universe A) and the glorified body which is the hope of the True Resurrection in Universe G."

I found this to be a tremendously powerful passage. The implication is a Resurrection (or waking up) of our own Spirits which may then re-inhabit the corporeal form. This is very close to what I had experienced in my own, quite literal, *"wake up calls"*.

The *'Zombi'* is not a wretched creature, bereft of soul. Rather, the Zombi is *infused* with Soul! It typifies the Soul-Self directing action as opposed to the animal self on autopilot.

There is much more to this Soul-Self than the awareness of how miraculous its position in time and space is. The cognizance of mortality leaves the consciousness with nothing to define its existence save its own eternal nature beyond the vicissitudes of change. All of our experiences with death and dying have been leading us to this singular point. We have been shown that our natural tendency towards filling our minds with anything but this awareness is linked intrinsically into an attachment to the illusion of permanence. The real confrontation with the meaning of our mortality is not through the sorrow of loss or the stark experiences of watching others die and decay. It is through our own death, consciously and wilfully invoked, while still in the body. This is not some morbid meditation on an imagined dissolution of form. It cuts much deeper than that. Form is shown to be a projection of mind. Therefore, mind is entered to cut into its core.

Death is not the subsequent rotting of the flesh-frame. It is a moment where radical change in consciousness occurs. The practice of meditation evokes this change without waiting on the demise of the body. The result is two-fold. One achieves ever-deepening degrees of awareness of a universal consciousness on the transpersonal level, and one allows that same consciousness to enter the human form with greater degrees of freedom to express itself.

This consciousness is free of fear for it apprehends the illusory nature of existence and therefore the illusory nature of what we think of as *'death'*. The trouble is that we arrive at this Gnosis by cutting a route through the layers of mind which shrink in fear at the suggestion that their points of reference are not real in any permanent sense. More so than the scare of skeletal spectres, the fear induced by confrontation with impermanence is almost unbearable. It threatens not just the mortal life of the individual but the basic assumptions underpinning reality itself. One must willingly step onto a carpet knowing that it will ripped out from under the feet with no floor beneath.

Mammalian survival instincts recoil at the thought of this. We are hardwired toward self-preservation. It is through this tenacious drive that we continue to reproduce and human life on the planet continues. But why? What is the purpose of this outward flowing into the future? We can look back into our known history to see human awareness evolving. Simplicity moves towards sophistication, superstition towards sobriety. It has been a long-standing and arrogant conceit in our religions that proclaims *'Man'* to be chief amongst living beings. We are declared created in the *'image of God'* and our dilemma is not one of growth but acceptance and subservience to *'correct'* belief. The facts indicate otherwise. We are at an awkward and uncertain phase of being. Half animal, half spirit. We are pulled in two directions. Our momentum pushes us beyond the limits of our present incarnation and our evolutionary make-up shackles us to the tendencies which brought us to this point, tendencies which now oppose our ultimate destination. There is a vast difference between the evolutionary aberration of suicide and the action taken by Thich Quang Duc, the Vietnamese monk, who burned himself to death on June 11, 1963. Thich Quang Duc understood the nature of impermanence and shot an arrow into the public mind which would not miss its mark. The photo of his burning body is now famous. It also provokes the questions: how and why would a human being do this to himself? He cannot be written be off as an unstable mind. His Buddhism attests to a super-sanity. It is, perhaps, a sanity our own madness would prefer to evade. Thich Quang Duc knew that his life was a portion of the Universe whose nature is perpetual change. He also understood the pulse of life and what it is moving towards. On behalf of that Greater Life, he exposed the Roman Catholic persecution of Buddhists, the perpetuation of cruelty and insanity.

We fear death and yet we often come up empty handed when it comes to something worth dying for. Death is the price of Life. It is prearranged and built into our system ere we are conceived. If we do not have anything worth dying for, what is it we are living for?

~~oOo~~

Life and Death are glibly said to be two sides of the same coin. But, as we look at the endless changes that underlie all we conceive of as substantial, we see that our field of awareness is one of Being and Non-Being. Our bodies, continuously built up from a basic DNA platform, are being washed down bathtub drains every night. Seven years pass and all cells have been replaced. The person who lived then is no more. We have effectively died and been cremated. What was is no more. What is, therefore, shall no longer be. And just as our bodies are replaced with new and intelligent life, so shall our Being move into Continuance, even beyond the event we label *'Death'*.

It is my perspective that by going beyond our attachments and more deeply into the awareness of Life Itself, we confront crisis and come into a more fearless and compassionate, creative and vital path of action. We don't attain to a oneness with the Universal Mind. We enter consciously into the Oneness that has always been.

That having been said, we do not shed our skin-sheath to find some conclusive repose in a Nirvanic state. We are human. Our illumination and elevation does not preclude the nature of what we are. Our emotions, our loves... these things remain with us - and they make us what we are as part of the Plan.

In Aleister Crowley's religion of Thelema, the morbidity and repulsion surrounding death is traded for the idea of the *'feast'*. One's passing is the *'Greater Feast'*, a celebratory event connected to the great joy of life's continuity. As I see it, Joy and Sorrow are also two sides of a coin. If the grim and sombre view towards death holds us down from our Utmost, so may the opposite view. I do not feel compelled to rise above the loss of loved ones by denying my pain at their passing. *"It's my party... and I'll cry if I want to."*

A dear friend of mine simply said that the difficulty of death is found in the fact that we, the *'living'*, are left to *'miss the loveliness'* of those we've lost.

I felt this truth when I sat on the damp graveyard grass before the headstone of the little boy I wrote of at the beginning of this essay. The greater the loveliness and the deeper the love, the sharper the pain. As Morrissey sings in *"Mama Lay Softly On The Riverbed"*:

"Life isn't much to lose

It's just so lonely here without you."

Will we be back for another go on the Terra via some Reincarnational Route? For me, this is not the question. Rather, I want to know: what Reincarnational Route brought me here... now? It's not an issue of *"will I come back?"* It's a matter of *"I'm back... again... now what?"*

We connect to God by God connecting to us in this moment. There is no other moment. If God reaches into us, we may rightly call it *'Grace'*. This evokes within our hearts a deep gratitude, a flowing of compassion through our lives. This current calls up pains we'd rather anesthetize. It calls up love we didn't know we could transmit. It shatters us and in doing so it shatters the scales which have shielded our eyes from the glory and goodness which is at the heart of our Being.

~~oOo~~

When I attend funerals, I find that I must touch the body laid out so nicely in the casket. On one hand, I am confronting the stark reality of death's heaviness. I never think that she looks like she's sleeping. She's DEAD. And as my hand touches hers, I confirm this. But at the same time, I feel something of the reading of the *Tibetan Book of the Dead*, which is really called *The Book of Liberation through Hearing in the Bardo*. The body, now well chilled and lifeless, remains a link to the mind which journeyed through it. By means of this link, I give the best of what I am. I have not forgotten. I still love you. I give you this love and will continue to do so. You don't go into the Beyond alone. I'm a part of you and you are a part of me.

I'm not trying to comfort myself in this. There is no comfort. I open to the pain and let it move through me. I open to my doubts, my confusion. Let the carpet be ripped from beneath me. Let me fall. All that matters is sending the love I have. And as I fall into an abyss of uncertainty, I send it with all I have.

~~oOo~~

All I have written is to be read by the living. These words could only be written by one who is alive and, at the same time, they will soon be a testament to one who has died. It is my deep hope that you, the reader, might find something of value herein, something which helps escort you further on the path, even if it be a city block. Our lives are meant to be ALIVE. My dissolving body returns to the earth and feeds its endless processes of growth. My internal world of thought and feeling likewise returns to its Source. As the dust of my body feeds the energy of earth life, may the thought and life imbued in these words feed the Heart of the Child growing through our experience on this plane.

Death and Life may be two sides of the same coin but they come together to evoke Love in this world. We will love in both sorrow and joy. The scriptures do not lie when they proclaim that *'God is Love'*.

~~oOo~~

I now turn to Ghuedhe. We go awry if we think of him in terms of our humanity. We also make a great miss if we divorce his nature from our humanity. Ghuedhe is a Bodhisattva. He doesn't fit the bill of piety. Life, however, is not pious. It is real.

Ghuedhe is in our flesh. He is in our longings and desires and all that makes us human. At the same time, he is outside of this. He is the negative space around our temporal lives. Ghuedhe will come crashing the party, playing up every offense, obscenity and opposition. He is a Gift from God for he is here to bring us into balance. One lens of the glasses he wears is punched out, and the other inscrutable.

When we have been pushed, pulled and punched into what we've denied, we are then given the picture of the Child. We can see, with a clear vision, the sacrament of life, the potential bristling within the boy, the bright beginnings behind the eyes of the girl.

The details will take care of themselves. We are liberated when our compassion flows into the little ones - for we find in them ourselves. We then become ourselves.

~~oOo~~

I pour rum into a glass and raise it to Papa Ghuedhe. I raise it to Baron Samedhi, Lord of the Dead. I raise it to Mamman Brigitte, who has taught me more than can be conveyed in words.

I raise this glass to YOU, dear reader. Already maimed and claimed by the scythe, already a denizen of the grave, you LIVE. I drink to what you will do, to the love you'll send forth.

I drink to you going beyond yourself and into your SELF.

I give my heart to Papa Ghuedhe - and, in doing do, I give my heart to *you*.

~~oOo~~

THE DEATH OF BAPHOMET

BY JULIAN VAYNE

As you are reading this you are dying. The little knot of energy in the universe that constitutes you is fast winding down. Watched from the perspective of evolutionary time your own little life is a tiny fluttering of biology. Watched through the eyes of geological time we hardly register at all. Compared to the titanic entropic droop of the universe stumbling towards its heat death (assuming the Standard Model of cosmology for the moment to be true) we are as nothing. Yet we certainly feel ourselves to be something. On the immediate scale of humanity our lives, and therefore our deaths, loom large. No culture fails to speak of death. No religion fails to have sometimes fairly detailed instructions about what death means, how it should be prepared for and, critically, what comes after death.

I posed the question 'so *what do you think happens when you die*' to a number of my magickal colleagues recently and was intrigued by their broad agreement about what happens in the processes of death and dying. This essay is inspired by those conversations.

Let us return to the utter unimportance of our own deaths, at least in terms of the Big Picture of the universe. Unless a bold new physics emerges that tells us a new story (and that of course is by no means impossible) we can assume that our own perceptions, our lives and indeed life as a whole, emerges in a relatively brief window of opportunity. Sandwiched between the big bang and the long echo that will follow, as all energy becomes evenly distributed across the universe, we exist. Those tiny quantum fluctuations in the first few moments, when space and time were new, have given rise to little islands of possibility. We can detect these in the uneven appearance of the cosmic background radiation (CBR) photographed by our spacecraft. The fact that the very earliest observable signature of the early universe holds such inconstancies means that, rather than being spread out in dull uniformity, denser zones of nascent reality formed. Dust clouds expanded, stars came on, planets aggregated and fell into stable orbits. On at least one of these worlds the complex chemical interaction we call life begins. From tiny chaotic butterfly flutterings in the primal Kia, we arise.

This mathematical oddity, this outpouring of increasing complexity in a cosmos that is otherwise running out of steam, can be imagined as Baphomet. The apparently anti-entropic emergence of the ten-thousand things. But if Baphomet is, in one sense, the life-force then that force is both framed within death (the big bang and big crunch) and peppered with death throughout. Indeed so pervasive is death that biology rides on its back. The teeth that bite, the claws that catch; single celled organisms absorb their neighbours, mycelium the size of cities creep beneath the surface of the soil, spiralling vultures descend the thermals and settle to feed in the towers of silence.

The first point that a number of magicians will point out is simply this; given the grand scheme of things why should the death of a human be any more significant than the death of a house fly? Many religions of course claim otherwise. They claim that humans are special, that they are imbued with souls, spirits and all kinds of complex post-mortem shenanigans happen when we shuffle off this mortal coil. But why should this be the case? Does the death of a dolphin, a dog or Drosophila melanogaster matter more or less to the universe than that of a human? This of course isn't to say that humans as a species can't do some quite remarkable things, but dying really isn't an unusual behaviour.

Death is welded into the bald fact of our biology. Though there are a very few multi-cellular species (notably *Turritopsis nutricula,* the potentially immortal jellyfish) which can cheat, or at least (in principle), stave off death for considerable periods, as far as we are aware everything alive must die. In the case of humanity it is our understandable fear of death that feeds our desire for life-extension strategies, after-life realities and cryogenic suspension. But it is also the impermanence of life that inspires other aspects of our spiritually. Many forms of Buddhism and Hinduism, with their desire to go beyond the narrow confines of self, embrace death. Christianity is the classic cult of death, growing from the same sandy soil in which the pharaohs were buried, its afterlife promised to the faithful by the bloody sacrifice of God in human form. In praise of this post-mortem paradise great cathedrals are built.

Do magicians hanker after an after-life? Well not those I spoke to. The idea of any *'final state'* seems rather silly in terms of the magical world-view. Everything is process, everything is cycle, everything changes, nothing is static. The atoms that constitute our bodies are recycled. Why should it be that, for no obvious reason, an ape that walks upright on a tiny planet gets to attain some endless non-corporeal state - with the same form of consciousness as when they lived - once dead? The whole premise seems as preposterous to most occultists as resurrection in the body seems to those who refuse to believe in the literal transubstantiation of the mass.

Yet this wide-angle view does seek to trivialise the embodied experience of death for the individual, it's obvious cultural significance or indeed reduce conscious awareness to some inconsequential epiphenomena of our chemistry. This is because many magicians take the view that the universe is imbued with, or perhaps even created by, a panpsyche, a world soul. Consciousness is implicit in all aspects of the universe. In a simple sense this is the observer effect noted in physics, that observation in some way creates the observed. Consciousness does not merely arise out of the physical structure of the cosmos; it is a fundamental quality of reality, much as space and time are. Indeed many occultists take the view that consciousness is the container of reality. Personally I suspect this view is amenable to scientific enquiry, and that it is by understanding the inconsistencies in reality that the CBR alerts us to, that we might come to know more. The *'random'* nature of reality (which gives rise to fractal complexity) is probably the field in which a panpsychic physical model of the universe might be developed.

So when we die our consciousness does not, in the panpsychic sense, end. If consciousness is an intrinsic property of the universe, ubiquitous as gravity (indeed it may be *the* underlying fabric of reality) can it really be said to die? Perhaps the *'I'*, as Spare put it, is *'Atmospheric'*. This notion of the panpsychic universe may also explain an observation that Carl Jung and his student Marie-Louise von Franz explored in her work *On Dreams & Death*. Namely that the unconscious mind does not behave as though it is going to end. Although it may send signals to the consciousness (in the forms of dreams and synchronicities) that the bodily life is coming to an end, it does not indicate that it in itself, nor its expression as archetypal forces, will be terminated.

But what can we say about the personal experience of death? The natural position of the magician, as you might expect, is that of radical uncertainty. We simply don't know the details of how it feels to die, and what - if anything - happens to awareness after death, and occultists tend to fully acknowledge the contingency of their beliefs. Their views are informed by both ancient soul-lore (such as the complex views of post-mortem experience described by Germanic or Egyptian myth) and contemporary ethnographic and scientific exploration. We certainly know that in near death experiences (NDEs) there are narrative elements that are common to many accounts. This isn't any more remarkable than the discovery of form-constants in the entoptic images produced by hallucinogenic drugs or other trance practices. We have a common biology, and while this may be interpreted in the light of different cultural values (I see the horned god/dess Baphomet, you see the Devil), what happens in a NDE is broadly similar across cultures.

A wide variety of researchers have looked into the NDE. Ornella Corazza provides a good summary of current research in her book *Near-Death Experiences: Exploring the Mind-body Connection*. NDE commonly includes elements such as an imagined journey. Corazza compares research into NDEs from western cultures with studies conducted in Japanese, Indian, Chinese & Melanesian cultures. The form of the journey seems to be culturally dependent but whether it is imagined as a road through the mountains, a ride down a river or, as is most common in the west (and in the *Tibetan Book of the Dead*), travelling through a tunnel towards a bright light, some form of apparent movement happens. These narratives are not rare events; in fact NDEs happen in around 45% of cases of people who have a brush with death (this figure is over 80% in children). So whatever is going on subjectively is a consistent effect, though clothed in the iconography that makes sense to the individual.

Experiences of meeting entities are common. These may be ancestors, supernatural or mythic beings. Again we see, unsurprisingly, what we expect to see. Extrasensory perception and out of body experiences (such as seeing one's body on the operating table, as though from above) are also cross-cultural. A sense of peace and oneness with the universe is common. Less frequent, but also reported, is abject terror. In many NDEs there is a point at which the individual is sent back. They may be told that they must return to their body by a mythical being or simply know that they cannot (yet) go on. For a small number there is the experience of a life review, as memories long lost from conscious recall re-emerge. For many there is the experience of entering, or sometimes seeing in the distance, a beautiful landscape.

Various methods can be used to simulate the NDE. To the magician these are great allies since they literally prepare us for death. Although by no means identical when scrutinised phenomenologically these experiences provide us with the flavour of what it is like to die. Electro-stimulation of the temporal lobe, prolonged isolation, DMT, nitrous oxide and ketamine all contain NDE-like elements. Corazza's research includes recording people's visions in the ketamine state and looking at these in relation to NDE accounts. There are certainly differences but also significant similarities. This is hardly surprising as Karl Jansen in his ketamine research suggests that the endogenous chemistry of the dying brain stimulates and suppresses similar neural systems to those which ketamine affects.

Ketamine is also increasingly used in pain management during palliative care in the west and therefore familiarity with the state may be of even more importance to the magician. It could well be that this drug will be the last exogenous experience one has before death begins. Knowing the psychic territory from which one might enter the beyond would make sense in terms of being able to let go into death successfully. Letting go is the critical ability for navigating psychedelic drugs, especially at high doses. It would also make sense to deploy this approach when we die. Since most pain is not pain in itself, but is instead generated by our anxiety about our pain, to make death less painful we need to relax. It may be romantic to rage against the dying of the light but when your number's up it will make no difference. Better to focus one's intention on opening fully to the experience. Once you've taken a hit of a powerful psychoactive such as Dimethyltryptamine (DMT) there is no going back. Attempting to hold onto sober reality will only create cramping, collapsing, cruelly twisted visions (which will come anyway no matter what you do). Perhaps if we close up at death it is then that ghosts are spawned. Maybe it is also in this way that cases of apparent reincarnation occur. Tragic deaths seem to produce both. In these instances could it be that somehow elements of non-localised consciousness become locked into reality? Either embedded in stone, as haunted houses, or translated into newly forming brain tissue as memories of a previous life. Certainly there are little boys who awake crying, feeling the flames melting their skin and pilot's jacket as a World War II bomber comes crashing down. These cases are ubiquitous and not only in cultures that believe in reincarnation. I asked my magician friends about this. One said *'yes that has a reality'*. But this is no simple transcendentalist model where we are therefore seeking to be liberated from that pesky Samsara wheel. Rather this reincarnation is just another aspect of the process of death-consciousness-life. It represents simply one of the many outpourings of our vast, mysterious universe. And while cases such as those documented by psychiatrist Ian Stevenson in his *Twenty Cases Suggestive of Reincarnation* do occur, they do not always lead us back to a world of suffering or seem to be connected by traumatic death. Sometimes children are re-born into the same family and surrounded by the love they had once before. Sometimes they turn out to be the new Dalai Lama.

One conjecture about death is that of the eternal moment. The distortion of time is common to many trance states, certainly this occurs with many psychoactive drugs and also perhaps with dying. One model of psychoactive action proposes that these drugs alter the usual *'refresh rate'* of the perceptual systems in the brain. This leads to trails of light, like time-lapse ghost images, emerging from our waving hands as we dance. The perceptual grids that mark the edge detecting elements of our visual system pile up upon each other. This leads to the complex grids and morphing visuals that accompany many psychedelic states. Inside our minds time becomes stretched out; thirty minutes may seem like many hours, and an hour like an eternity. Eventually at the high point of a psychedelic trip this piling up of perceptual data (from both the senses and inner awareness) feeds back on itself, generating an experience in which time stops and everything in awareness becomes simultaneously connected to everything else. Where once there were fractal patterns created by the mathematical interpenetration and recursive layering of the inputs into consciousness, instead white noise and often the white light appear. We hang for a moment, outside the circles of time, in a formless realm. This is the ineffable, timeless peak of the trip.

The chemistry of death contains many processes that could produce such visions. Death of course means that all the cells begin to break down and the resultant chemical soup contains a wide variety of interactions, which we are, as yet, unable to model very satisfactorily. One thing we do know is that during hypoxia, ischaemia, hypoglycaemia, temporal lobe epilepsy and other NDE inducing events, the neurotransmitter glutamate comes rushing out. This glutamate flooding stimulates the N-methyl-D-aspartate, (NMDA) receptors in the brain, over activating NMDA receptors resulting in neuro (*'excito'*) toxicity. This process is very similar to the blockade of NDMA created by ketamine. NDMA has a critical role in synaptic plasticity and memory. Subjectively we may experience this chemical change as our memories crowding into one another, we live all moments we have ever lived in the death trip.

Perhaps as we travel through our mythic reality towards the point of no return we have such a moment when time stops. The electro-chemical cycle of the brain breaks down as death happens and our awareness (viewed from a perspective outside the dying mind) ends. But our last subjective vision, whether it be of the universal light of peace and love, or alternatively of the horror at being extinguished, lasts forever. There may be no afterwards because we are dead; our narrative stops with this last unending experience of heaven or hell. Being open to this experience, and having magickally practiced it, may mean the difference between which of these realms we inhabit forever.

Yet our treatment of the bodies of the dead may also be important, not least to the decaying consciousness. One of the great uncertainties of NDE is whether cognition and the formation of memories can happen after the electrical activity in the brain ceases. This could be an acid test for the *'hard problem'* of mind/body dualism but gathering the evidence is, to say the least, tricky. What is surely the case is that even after electrical activity in our tissues ceases there are still deeper percolations of chemistry going on. Awareness may be contained to some degree in these final fluctuations. In many cultures mourners sit by the corpse, praying over it, dressing it, opening windows and turning mirrors to the wall. The lingering awareness gutters and dies like a candle but isn't finally snuffed out until days after we stop breathing. The work of the living is to help the dead rest in peace. Our bodies, which are themselves formed of elements created in dying stars, also dissolve back into the earth. Whether we choose burial by sky or water or earth or air, the story, in the long term, is the same. We are taken up as nourishment for new life, over millions of years our organic traces may be folded deep within the earth, subducted into the fiery darkness. Our last gasp of air floats free, charged molecules of what once upon a time we would call *'me'* may even evaporate into space. The way we treat the bodies of our dead says so much about our culture. Certainly it is one of the primary ways that the archaeologists of the future will attempt to re-construct what and how we believe. The spirit of our society leaves clues to its nature in the scattered mortal remains of its members.

Why do we die? At the roots of death is the fact that in the ancient earth there existed, as well as bacteria, viruses. These strange structures, tiny shapes that lock into cells, sometimes confer evolutionary advantages. But they can also alter the chemical cascade of life and become *phages*: disease. They feed on the DNA-coded energy expressed in the cell's life and destroy it, multiplying and spreading. Aeons before multi-cellular creatures existed, our bacterial ancestors came up with a strategy. They deploy caspase-1 enzymes that race through the cell, killing it. In this way bacteria could die rather than let the phage spread. Uninfected cells would remain, some generating resistant progeny. In time the viruses would also mutate but once the tactic of death was established it could help life stay ahead of the game. Death is a strategy for life, and this applies at the most fundamental level of biology, not only when we get to the level of lions eating zebra. The life-force, Baphomet, has taken death inside itself, just as billions of years ago the first eukaryotic cells emerged and absorbed the mitochondria to be their power-house, and hidden in those mitochondria was the mechanism of the capase protein. Death waits coiled in the heart of all our cells.

So death is always with us. Like Castaneda says, *'always at your shoulder'*. Whether it is the *memento mori* on your desk, or the skin of your hands as you hold this book, we are always facing death. So is there a moral in this story? Does this magician's view of death tell us how we should live? Perhaps it tells us that death is vital to life. This may not stop us fearing death, or grieving; these are natural human processes. But it does help us see death as part of a larger story, as part of the narrative of Baphomet. And that tale is of a universe that, despite its apparent hurtling towards entropy like an unstoppable juggernaut, also rises up into consciousness. It tells us that at every moment this awakening happens, as matter switches on awareness. It tells us that we should live both as though we were going on forever and, at the same time, as though any moment now we are going to...

"The Nurturer (Queen) of Wands", Baron Samedi, by Nic Phillips.
From *Sol Invictus the God Tarot,* Schiffer, 2007.

Papa Gede, Petit Gede: Spirits of Death in Haitian Vodou

By Sophia Fisher

For Mimi, 30th October 1931 – 13th July 2011
With thanks to Sosyete Gade nou Leve

"With the Haitian, death is not a man dying, or a used-up, unloving body; it is an entity, a positive power in nature. Death is Papa Gédè."[46]

Out of all the Vodou Lwa the Gede family is said to behave the liveliest, yet it is comprised of the unclaimed dead. Papa Baron, father of the Gedes, is called upon to protect children and aid women in labour – the spirit of death is associated with birth. At the beginnings of ceremonies in 21 Divisions Vodou, Baron del Cementerio (Baron of the Cemetery) *'mounts'* or ritually possesses his servitors in the manner of a corpse: laid out rigid on the floor, his face is covered with a black cloth and the atmosphere is sombre. Later in the ceremony Papa Gede arrives in the form of a snide, black-hatted comedian, gyrating provocatively and smoking two or three cigarettes at a time. So the Gede family forces us to face the fact that we too will die, but often causes us to laugh - this apparent paradox is of central importance to their mystery.

This essay seeks to explore the relationship between Papa Gede [47] and his servitors- those people who, like myself, have chosen to serve the Lwa (*'loa'*) by giving them sacrifice, which can take many forms - not least of which is that most precious commodity, our time. I will consider the origins and appearance of Papa Gede in Haitian and Dominican Vodou, his message and the symbols placed upon his altar, and how and why he acts in certain ways. I will also look at the lessons we may learn from his behaviour during the 'possession performance' central to these religious traditions. [48] Along the way I consider the role of Baron as Divine Judge and Gede's place as

---

46 Crosley, pp. 98

47 In this essay I will refer to Papa Gede, particular Gede spirits such as Gede Mazaka who are seen as separate entities to Papa Gede, and the Gede family, as well as the Barons who rule them. Some say all Barons are one Baron and all Gedes are one Gede, and that that Gede is Papa Gede. Alternate ways of spelling include 'Guede', 'Guedeh' and 'Ghede', all of which may be accented. I have chosen the shorter form 'Gede' for this piece, but have kept the original in any quotations where alternative spellings are used.

48 The use of the word 'performance' emphasises "the theatrical quality of visits from the Vodou spirits" and does not imply "playacting" (McCarthy Brown, 2001:6 fn 2).

taboo-breaker, healer and guardian of children, and the ways in which he is both cherished and denied.

Something like a holy trinity is invoked in Vodou: *les Morts, les Marassa, les Mystères.*[49] The Lwa are mysteries, *les invisibles*, and have many layers; it is impossible to ever fully explore their depths and as each servitor enjoys a private relationship with his/her Lwa, many experiences cannot be placed into words. This essay is necessarily a personal endeavour. All mistakes are my own.

As might be expected, I cannot pursue the attempt without delving into some dark territory. The affectionate relationship many servitors have with Papa Gede – speaking to him in the manner of a friend, father or brother - can only be partially understood from the Western perspective where death is sanitised and hidden in care homes and hospitals and many people have never beheld a corpse, much less helped in laying out the dead as generations passed would have done. Most have watched overtly violent depictions of death on film and television, however this leaves us unprepared for the 'real thing'. Open coffins are rare and funerals seem generally grey and sombre (of course there are exceptions), and our cultural attitudes to death reflect all this. Western magickal practitioners live in a society where death is something to be dealt with privately, cleaned up quickly and set aside; and many Pagan underworld deities, Hades, Hel, Erishkegal and so on, seem to be dealt with in correspondingly sombre ways. Serving Papa Gede, then, can be somewhat refreshing.

I conclude the essay with the smallest spirits in the Gede family, the Petit Gede –child-spirits of the dead. In Vodou we acknowledge them by treating them much as we would living children. The death of an infant or small child, thankfully much more rare than it used to be (it is still common in developing countries), has become a taboo subject rarely confronted in our culture. Yet it happens and, when it does, society (if not the grieving family) seems to want to forget about it as quickly as possible. It is an uncomfortable idea and we would like to believe that we have all the answers in the form of medical science to avoid it. Other cultures with access to less advanced medicines have had to find ways to deal with this sad event since it occurs more frequently. Without acknowledgement of the dead, the living cannot heal.

Introducing Papa Gede

Even those unfamiliar with Vodou will probably have some knowledge of the Gede spirits. If not, it may help to consider Papa Gede and Baron Samedi alongside other deities. Deren compares Gede to Wotan, one-eyed God of the dead, since Gede has only one lens in his sunglasses (when asked, he declares it better to see into

---

49 The dead (Ancestors), the Marassa (divine twins), and the mysteries (spirits).

the realms of the living and the dead and therefore keep an eye on his food).[50] Saint-Lot associates him with Dionysus:

"both symbols of life and death...associated with the phallus, the emblem of reproduction. Both have a penchant for mirth, orgies and a debauched life. Although contrary to those for Gede, the Dionysus rites conveyed excessive sorrow, they both generate an atmosphere of excitement...Both occupy a low rank in the eyes of their fellow gods."[51]

Vodouisants have synchronised Gede with the Catholic saints Gerard, Expedit and others.[52] Meanwhile, those familiar with Breton mythology may recognise certain motifs in the legend of Ankou, the grave-yard watcher who protects the cemetery and is comprised of the soul of the first dead person of the year[53] (in Haitian Vodou the first dead male to be buried in the cemetery becomes the Baron of that place, and the first dead female becomes his wife, Brigitte; both are placed in a similar role to the *Ankou* as protectors of and spokespeople for the dead).

Those of a certain age may recall the use of Gede/Baron-like imagery adopted by Papa Doc Duvalier, *"internationally known for appropriating iconography from Vodou"*, who focussed his self-image particularly on Gede, creating a persona *"through visual motifs of the Gede lwa...[and] donning the characteristic dark vestments and hat of these spirits and their leader, Baron Samedi"*. [54] It was originally this image of *'Papa Doc'* (prevalent in world news at the time) that made the trappings of Gede so hauntingly familiar in the public sphere; his image also informed the character of Baron Samedi in the 1973 Bond film *Live and Let Die*, which remains recognizable to later generations.

The now archetypal image of Baron Samedi, a tall black man or skeleton done up as a traditional undertaker/freemason (complete with top hat and cane), is a modern take on the hooded, scythe-bearing Angel of Death. Even Death's character in Gaiman and Dringenberg's comic book series *'The Sandman'* is depicted as a sassy young Goth girl wearing an ankh pendant and top hat, and it seems that the Baron image is more popular than his classical counterpart. The debonair but grisly character can even be located in Disney films, where he is reproduced after a fashion in the heroic Jack Skellington (*Nightmare Before Christmas*) and villainous Dr Facilier (*The Princess and the Frog*).

---

50 Deren, 1983:108 footnote.

51 Saint-Lot, 2004:149.

52 The symbols found in Catholic saint images are a shorthand for the Lwa: St Gerard Majella, for example, is sometimes depicted with a cross and skull, both symbols of Gede.

53 Anatole le Braz, The Legend of Death cited at http://en.wikipedia.org/wiki/Ankou

54 Ramsey, 2011:250.

Appearance and behaviour of Gede

Satyr-like Papa Gede is satirist extraordinaire. The insurmountable Lwa swears, drinks, struts, smokes, makes rude gestures and even ruder body movements, then shrugs a bony shoulder and turns away: *what are you going to do*, he might as well drawl in characteristic nasal tones, *kill me again?*

Most of the Gede in possession speak as if holding their noses (one Gede I met had a deep and throaty Brooklyn accent, and some do not speak at all). This is believed to be symbolic of the common treatment of cadavers: the noses of the dead were stuffed with cotton wool. However, it could also be the result of a more obvious irony: the Haitian upper-classes speak French, not Kreyol, and such could be mockingly reproduced with a nasal twang. Equally, the rustic Haitian is said to speak in more nasal tones than his city cousins: Kouzen Zaka, Lwa of agriculture, speaks in such a way, and it may be that Gede reveals his origins here (they are said to be brothers). As so often with the Lwa it could be that all or none of the above is true.

The Gede family almost always insist upon darkness: most will wear sunglasses if available, while others *"wear top-hats, bowlers or straw hats decorated with crepe, ancient frock-coats or threadbare dress-coats... mourning dresses and black or mauve veils"*.[55] Even the cleanest and most dapper apparel seems to quickly debauch itself once presented to Gede, displaying peculiar stains and unexplained rips; and many who serve will find themselves the mysterious recipients of walking sticks, black hats and sunglasses with one missing lens. The pale face of Death as depicted in Western imagery everywhere from the operatic world to Bill and Ted's chess scene is more than satisfactorily mirrored by Gede, who uses copious amounts of talcum powder scattered on the face of his *'horse'* (the person he has possessed) and many of the fine black satin scarves I have presented to him have since turned grey.

Haitian Vodou ceremony is attended by entire families from children and breastfeeding mothers to elderly village patriarchs. All are welcome to witness Gede's licentious behaviour, rubbing his *zozo* (penis – improvised by a walking stick) against various skirts and ordering couples to make babies *"for Guinen"*. He asks the men to demonstrate the size of their appendage along the length of his cane and offers an upgrade if he thinks it too small. He screams out *"Koko!"* (slang for the female genitalia) to which the required answer is always *"Zozo!"*: a puerile entertainment that often causes the entire congregation to collapse into fits of hilarity. Gede smokes two or three cigarettes at a time, flicking ash over other spirits' offerings, and shouts disgusting jokes that, even in Kreyol, cannot be misunderstood except by the naïve.

---

55 Metraux, 1989:114.

"Their language, too, is full of the unexpected. They distort the commonest word or substitute others with filthy connotations. Lunettes (spectacles) becomes doubles languettes (double clitoris), rum becomes pissetigue and clairin becomes claleko. They have a fine repertoire of obscene songs which they sing with a stupid look..."[56]

Papa Gede is associated with spiritual cleansing as well as physical healing (it's arguable than one cannot be properly achieved without the other), yet is stripped of all constraining social taboos by virtue of being dead. Seemingly less *'elevated'* and certainly *'earthier'* than other spirits, *"Gede appears as some nasty, degraded old drunk at a bar. But Gede is not degraded. He is simply above all notions of morality...He laughs at our secrets because death renders our secrets laughable."*[57]

Of course Gede adores prudes, whom he mocks excessively: *"Thus he introduces men to their own devil"*. Ideas of romance are satirised as nothing short of the erotic cloaked in the pretence of morality: *"'I love, you love, she loves. What does that make?' (Chorus, drawn out) 'L'AMOUR.'"*[58] The urgent desire to copulate is, Gede would argue, the driving force of the human race – indeed all of life – and we may moralise all we wish; we are animals in that regard. By taunting our pretensions towards the romantic (particularly where we deny our inherent eroticism) and by constantly emphasising the physical act of love, Gede plays his message up against public pretence and self-deception. There is no lying to the dead, who see everything.

For Gede, sex is medicine; it is also crucial, for without sex, there is no procreation, and without birth, there is ultimately no one to die - in fact, no Gede! The legacy of children, or that of making some other reverberating contribution to the world, is important to those who feel that, even if there is no heaven or afterlife, a person can continue to live on in others' memory. That is why family stories, the mouth-to-mouth transmission of one's own legend, are so important; it is an offering to those who have passed that can live on in our tales.

Gede and Erzulie

At a ceremony some years ago, Papa Gede's nasal voice appeared out of thin air to monopolise the song of Maitresse Mambo Erzulie Freda Dahomey, our 'Goddess of Love': *"Ezili Fre li Fre li Freda, O Maitresse Fre, li Fre li Freda, Ezili o! Li pa manje moun anko, inosan Bondye va gade ou,"*[59] turning the lyrics with a flip of sardonic Kreyol into a moment of irony rather than the touching declaration of love

---

56 Metraux, 1989:113.

57 Glassman, 2000:115.

58 Both quotes from Deren, 1983:103.

59 "Ezili Fre li Fre li Freda, O Mistress Fre li Fre li Freda, Ezili O! She doesn't eat people anymore, God beholds her as innocent"

we intended. At another fet, he boasted of *"fucking the Virgin Mary"* who is synchronised with Freda. Perhaps he seeks revenge, for *"legend has it that, although she seduced many other gods, she rejected Gede whom she believes is beneath her."*[60] Papa Gede and Erzulie Freda are indeed polar opposites, and it might be worthwhile to consider some of her attributes in order to better understand his.

> *"Ezili O the house needs sprinkling*
> *If there is no water, sprinkle perfume..."*

As suggested by the song above (which reminds me of the saying falsely attributed to Marie-Antoinette, *"Let them eat cake"*), Maitresse Freda is the epitomy of purity, innocence and romance to a degree that would be impracticable for most people. She represents love, beauty and purest idealism and it is very difficult to keep her happy. Her demanding sense of etiquette and cleanliness (she walks only on a white sheet, appears when all is pristine, and cannot abide swearing or strong liquor) means that she will rarely appear after the 'dirty' presence of Gede. Her alluring coquetry (Erzulie frequently persuades young men to marry her) and abiding sense of romance are anathema to him, who mocks all pretensions to affected ideals. Erzulie often weeps for love.

Where Gede's colours are deep purple and black, Freda is served with light pastels - pink, baby blue and purest white; where his offerings are cigarettes, coffee and Piman (peppered rum), she enjoys delicate cakes iced in the appropriate colours, cool spring water and gently scented floral bouquets. Things that *'heat you up'* – smoking, drinking alcohol, having sex – are strictly forbidden not only around Freda, but many other spirits in the *Rada nachon* (Rada nation) which is known to be *'cooler'* or *'sweeter'* than the other divisions. To honour these Lwa, practitioners will avoid such activities prior to a Fet, and that may explain the sense of relief when Gede's section is finally reached close to the end of ritual; it is as if everyone can finally *'let their hair down'*.

Uninvited

Practitioners of *Sevis Guinee*[61] – many but not all of whom choose the label Vodouisant – treat the Lwa with the respect due to an elder, calling them *'Papa'* or *'Mama'* where appropriate. We are all children in the eyes of God; the Lwa (who are not deified, but classed in a similar role to saints or angels) are still elevated enough to be our elders, and this is true even of those commonly represented as children such as the Marassa. Just as a child has a duty to respect the parent, so the parent is obliged to guide the actions of his child, protecting them where necessary; thus to call the Lwa, as well as

---

60 Saint-Lot, 2004:142.

61 Service of Guinee, the spirits or spiritual world. Guinee is a reference to the African homeland that slaves hoped to return to after death – it was thought to exist on an island beneath the sea.

one's spiritual godparent [62] *'Papa'* or *'Mama'* is not mere formality but a declaration of reciprocal duty.

Whereas we extend this title of *'Papa'* to Gede, he is sometimes treated more like an uncouth *'bad uncle'* than a paternal protector. And in some cases he may be only grudgingly accepted as a Lwa at all. It would be safe to say that in certain ceremonies Papa Gede's presence is tolerated rather than enjoyed; it does not help that he persists at appearing at the most inopportune moments, often uninvited or well before expected (much like death itself) and with such incorrigible behaviour! He is perpetually hungry, stealing food and cigarettes from the congregation[63] as well as other spirits, and many Lwa would rather promptly depart than share the people's attention with him. He leaves calling-cards – a cigarette butt in warrior spirit Ogou's rum, most disrespectful – and does his best to ruin moments of ceremonial pomp.

Admittedly, Gede often gives back what he has stolen: one story I heard involved Baron and Brigitte in mutual possession, the Baron playing card tricks as he passed through the crowd, and somehow, magically, pulling dollar bill after dollar bill out of thin air! Murmuring uncomfortably, the congregation began to imagine itself witness to nothing short of a miracle: where did the money come from? Yet Brigitte, moving along behind her husband, had been pick-pocketing them as she went, passing the proceeds to Baron who proceeded to play the part of benefactor. Relieved laughter greeted discovery of this con: the people expected nothing less, and as their money had been more or less returned, no serious harm was done.

These stories – many of which are passed along by word-of-mouth, one practitioner to another – can serve as exemplary tales, taking the place of myth to illustrate the nature of the Lwa. While a mythology involving the characters of the Lwa does exist, it seems largely absent in comparison to other religions, at least in the public sphere. It is as if the spirits prefer to demonstrate their character *'in person'* rather than being held down to an outdated legend or folktale. This allows them to evolve as time passes, and it also permits the appearance of new Lwa – hence the truism that no Houngan or Mambo can ever name each and every spirit served in Vodou. In some cases, a Lwa is known to only one family or village; in others, a Lwa popularly served at one time slowly falls out of favour and is forgotten over the years.

'They say Papa Gede is not a Lwa!'

Despite his disreputable behaviour, Papa Gede must not be ignored. He is just as important as any of the other spirits and has just as much to teach us about the nature of our world. He seems to

---

62 The Houngan or Mambo who guides us through the djevo, initiatory chamber.
63 Deren, 1983:104-107.

rather grumpily remind us of this in the following song cited by Courlander:

Gédè-vi ya wé ago-é!	*Papa Gédè is a loa!*
Gédè -vi ya wé!	*When they are sick they say*
	Papa Gédè is a loa!
	When they are well they say
	Papa Gédè is not a loa![64]

Interestingly from the folk point of view at least two other versions of this song, both using similar melodies and words, seem to have evolved over time. The first from the Alan Lomax collection emphasises the singer's loyalty to a variety of Lwa, not all Gedes. The recording, sung with obvious affection by a *rèn chante* (queen of song) named Francilia at the town of Carrefour Dufort, is translated as follows (with thanks to Kim Huggens for sharing it with me):

> "Gedevi Yawe, Gede Nibo
> Gedevi Yawe
> Papa Gede is my lwa
> Loko Atisou is my lwa
> Gede Nibo is my lwa..."[65]

The second, found on the Dominican band Boni Raposo's album *Afro-Caribbean Chants and Drums* seems to return us closer to the original meaning, calling:

> "Gedevi ai eh, Gede!
> Gedevi ai eh,
> Gede Nib'ho is a Lwa!"

The version goes on to name a number of Gede spirits from Brigitte to Gede Fatras, reminding us that these spirits too are Lwa and worthy of respect.

Origins of Gede

"Vodoun permeates the land, and in a sense, springs from the land. It is not a system imposed from above, but one which pushes out from below. It is a thing of the family, a rich and complex inheritance from a man's own ancestors...You cannot readily destroy something with such deep and genuine roots."[66]

Some say that the Gede family derive their name and perhaps their *racine* (root) origin from a long-extinct African tribe. Deren suggests that Baron Samedi, rather than being named for the weekday associated with death, Saturn's day (Saturday), is actually named for *"the Indian Zemi which connotes...the spirit of the dead, the*

---

64 Courlander, 1939:85.

65 Alan Lomax in Haiti CD 7: Francilia, Ren Chante. Track 29, "Gedevi Yawe, se lwa mwen" 1936-37.

66 Courlander, 1939:7.

soulless living";[67] that is, the Zombie.[68] It has been posited that the African roots of both Gede and Baron are less important than their native Haitian roots; that is, the indigenous Taino and Carib cultures who lived upon the land of *Ayiti* (which means *'mountainous')* prior to Columbus.

These cultures were almost (but not quite) erased from history, killed off very quickly in appallingly high numbers by previously unknown illness brought by their invaders, slavery (they were forced to work to death on their own motherland) and suicide. Yet some fled to the inaccessible mountains on the island and their descendents are likely to have come into contact with later Maroons (escaped African slaves). The origins of Haitian Vodou are certainly not pure African, and Gede is not the only spirit to enjoy offerings specific to the native cultures such as *"cassava, an Indian bread"*.[69] A full (though dated) argument is given in Appendix B of Deren for anyone interested in pursuing it; others are sure to have considered this further.

In a sense, all Lwa are (or at least once were) dead, for the theology of Vodou describes how they originate from the realm of the ancestors:

"Upon death, the aspects of the soul separate...the Gwo Bon Anj [Big Good Angel, an aspect of a person's soul] is returned to the immortal Waters of Ginen, where it joins with the community of the Ancestral Dead. After a year and one day, reclamation rites call the Gwo Bon Anj back into the community of the living, where it offers guidance, advice, understanding...[and] can become a Lwa eventually..."[70]

Deren describes how the Lwa are not merely deceased spirits complete with all the memories and caprices of their former life. In the slow process of becoming Lwa, the spirit-personality moves beyond itself:

"As his [the deceased person's] contemporaries die off, and with them all immediate first-hand memories...there is left...only the distilled, depersonalised, almost abstract essence of the principle that especially characterized him. Thus, in time, the person becomes principle. And yet – what once was so real, so substantial, cannot be permitted to end...the principle must become person...In time, the ancestor becomes archetype. Where there was once a person, there is now a personage...What was once believed, is now believed in...The ancestor has been transfigured into a god."[71]

---

67 Deren, 1983:70.

68 Metraux describes the Zombi as "recognised by their absent-minded manner, their extinguished, almost glassy eyes, and above all by the nasal twang in their voices – a peculiarity which they share with the Guédé" (Metraux, 1989:283).

69 Deren, 1989:283.

70 Glassman, 2000:19.

71 Deren, 1989:28-29.

Yet the Gede are *not* believed to have come into existence via the rites of reclamation. They are instead the unclaimed or forgotten dead whose descendents either could not or would not perform the ceremonies required to reseat the *Gwo Bon Anj* into its rightful place within the community. Rather, Baron chooses (for what reason no one can know) to reclaim them into the bosom of *his* family (hence being the *'father'* of the Gedes). They are still Lwa, but have become so perhaps more immediately; hence the exceptionally lively personality many choose to display, and their particular enjoyment of the freedom of being unconstrained by previous communal norms. They have not forgotten the social fetters of life and taboos exist to be broken!

While they may retain certain attributes of their previous existence, these spirits are still required to take on many of the characteristic aspects of the Gede family – a perfectly upright and teetotal spinster in life, for example, may return significantly altered if she becomes one of them. The Gede spirits are ambiguous; existing outside the realm of hierarchical structure and communal expectation which can continue *even after one has died*, they are the vagrants, the wanderers, the uninvited, unwanted or unidentified souls who now (with Baron's patronage) can continue to pester and benefit the living.

How many Gede?

Just as the numbers of the world's dead cannot be counted, so too the vast ranks of Gede can never be known. Some are specific to a locale, others travel extensively outside Haiti, stretching far beyond New York and Little Miami (where many Haitians emigrated); and of course there are new Gede all the time, as Metraux's "*Guédé-fait-que-paraitre*" (Gede who just appeared) reminds us. Metraux alone named eighteen different Gede over just two pages: "*Guédé-brave*" (Brav Gede), "*Captain Zombi*, or *Captain Guédé*", "*Guédé-double*", "*Guédé-souffrant*" (Suffering Gede), "*Guédé-z-araignée*" (Zaranye, the spider),[72] "*Guédé-t-pe'té*", "*Guédé-fatras*" (Gede Fatras),[73] "*Linto*", "*Guédé-caca*", "*Guédé-antre-toutes*" (Gede among all), "*Pignatou-Guédé*", "*Madame Kikit*", "*Guédé-vi...* (vi means *'children'*)", "*Guédé-usu*", "*Guédé-loraye*" (Gede the storm),[74] "*Guédé-ti-wawé*" and "*Guédé-masaka*".[75] In McCarthy Brown, Papa Gede draws himself up and insists upon his *'full title'*: "*Msye Gede, Ti Malis Kache Bo Lakwa, Papa'm Te Rekonét Mwen, Gwo Zozo...sil vu ple* [Mister Gede, Little Mischief Hidden Near the Cross, My Father Acknowledged Me, Big

---

72 In possession, this Gede moves fast, scuttling like a spider: spiders can be messengers of any of the Gede however, not just Gede Zaranye.

73 The garbage-man Gede: he moves through the crowd with a large refuse sack and disposes of that which we no longer need.

74 Gede Loraye: "a woman of small stature who reveals herself during storms"

75 Metraux, 1989:115-116.

Cock...if you please]!'" [76]   With other names such as *Gede Koko Inspecté* (Gede Vagina Inspector), *Gede Plumaj, Ti Mazaka,* and so forth, plus the Barons, many more can be added to this list!

In many cultures the image of death personified is specifically masculine, and you may have noticed that many of the Gede are males: exceptions to this rule include Maman Brigitte, who is today more prevalent in New Orleans than Haiti; the girl Gedelia, who is associated with St Therese *'the Little Flower'*, and the midwife/abortionist Gede Mazaka (the latter is sometimes viewed as male-dressed-as-female or both male and female at the same time). Quite why there are not more female Gede is not known, although new Gede appear all the time. In 21 Divisions, the Dominican tradition of Vodou, the place of Brigitte is taken by the indubitable Baronessa, and the sister of Papa Gede, a spirit associated with Saint Martha the Dominatrix commonly known as Filomena Lubana, is also an important Lwa who works with Baron and enjoys some traditional Gede colours and offerings, though she herself is not a Gede spirit.

Many women I know feel greatly drawn to these feminine spirits of death: their woman-knowledge and the particularly guttural jokes they may enjoy speak to us on a body-level more so than the corresponding jibes of the Gede males. In fact the closest goddess I might ever compare Maman Brigitte to is Baubo, the Greek belly goddess with nipples for eyes and a vulva for her mouth:[77] both have been known to use the feminine body as a source of amusement and corresponding healing for the soul.

Divine medicine

Although a spirit of the dead, Papa Gede *"should not be confused with the souls of the dead, or with ghosts";*[78] there is a very different form of service to be taken for one's Ancestors. But certainly Gede has divine powers over death and is strongly associated with it. And yet he is very much alive; he is a powerful healer too. It is one of the paradoxes of Vodou that the Gede are often more immediate and vibrant than other spirits and frequently called upon to *save* life; it is also no paradox at all since they are, by and large, closer to humanity, and more likely to remember what it is to be alive as well as what it means to die.

"People feel close to Gede because he is earthy and because he portrays a phenomenon utterly natural and human: sexuality, fertility, life...[But] Gede's real dimension resides in the dichotomy of his

---

76 McCarthy Brown, 2001:357.

77 Refer to Clarissa Pinkola Estes, Women Who Run With The Wolves: Contacting the Power of the Wild Woman (Rider, 1998)

78 Metraux, 1989:112.

character. If he is cheerful and funny, he is at the same time very serious, in essence..." [79]

In our Sosyete, Brav Gede (a suave Gede associated with gambling) frequently makes up a luck bath for the congregation. This involves combining whatever discarded items were left lying around during ceremony - cigarette butts and corn kernels from the floor, libated coffee, herbs, and other ingredients of questionable content. Somehow this bath always smells good and unfailingly, it works; but what could be more symbolic of the intrinsic message of Gede than the idea that decaying rubbish, even if ceremonial, should be cleansing; that there is a form of purity in the lowest of items, especially those that come from the earth, which is everyone's place of origin, initiation or beginning, and yet also the place of decay, corrosion and ultimately transformation. Gede's utter lack of pretension and imminent practicality inform the viewer about one of his greater mysteries, though we cannot understand it fully as long as we live.

Herbal medicine is strongly associated with the Gede family, some of which are indeed referred to as *'Doctor'*; they are said to be particularly helpful in the case of sexual and reproductive problems, although they can also cause these as a form of punishment. If not actually curing (or causing) such issues, the Gede are known for giving advice - often quite loud and public advice – on sexual matters. There is something deeply cathartic about this if we can overcome our initial embarrassment at our secrets being so publically exposed!

The Gede can also appear in dreams, including in matters of medical emergency: Gede Mazaka once appeared to me in the form of a cobwebbed, withered grey old tramp, proffering a bowl filled with tiny fleshy things which turned out to be tonsils. Shortly after that my son had an overnight stay in hospital for the first time, his tonsils being inflamed; as horrible as the dream was, I recognised its importance as both warning and confirmation that Gede was looking after us.

Danse macabre

"But death leads everyone into the dance: from the whole clerical hierarchy (pope, cardinals, bishops, abbots, canons, priests), to every single representative of the laic world (emperors, kings, dukes, counts, knights, doctors, merchants, usurers, robbers, peasants, and even innocent children). Death does not care for the social position, nor for the richness, sex, or age of the people it leads into its dance..." [80]

On first making his acquaintance one was either delightfully engaged or else seriously offended by Gede: if offended, some may have wondered why we deal with him at all. Yet no one can do

---

79 Saint-Lot, 2004:149.

80 Source: http://www.lamortdanslart.com/danse/dance.htm

without Gede, we all die, and for every one of us a personal death awaits: from this comes Gede's widespread appeal and horror. Out of all the spirits, the tribal backgrounds of Gede (his roots in Africa, indigenous Haiti and elsewhere) seem perhaps less crucial to our understanding of him since death itself (as opposed to our *culturally informed treatment of it*) is universal.

Although it is often said that someone's death was unfair or before its time, the *fact* of death is truly egalitarian in two important ways: it can happen to anyone at any time however much we try to ignore it, and sooner or later, it will happen to everyone. And so, if people are afraid of Papa Gede, those same people are terrified of Baron: the former is dead, but the latter is death itself.

Divine judgement

Although Vodou theology sets out a detailed explanation of the many parts of the soul and suggests that each has its place to go upon death, the religion as a whole is largely concerned with more practical considerations. The Lwa involve themselves in correcting people's behaviour less out of consideration of the soul's prospects in the next life, and more in the ways in which it can cause harm now, both for the individual and the community. Vodou spirits seem primarily concerned with the present.

This of course reflects the fact that the average Haitian lacks Western luxuries, and indeed may lack such basic necessities as food, water and a place to live. To spend time contemplating the next life when struggling to eat in this one would be vastly unhelpful. Maslow's Hierarchy of Needs places such philosophising at the top of the pyramid while more physiological requirements are prioritised at the base.

According to Desmangles, there is actually no agreement amongst Vodouisants that an afterlife exists:

"Although many Vodouisants believe, similar to Catholic belief about the soul, that the ti-bon-anj in Vodou is judged by Bondye [God], this belief is not held everywhere in Haiti. It exists primarily in the cities where the proximity of Catholic churches has influenced Vodou's theology. In the remote mountains... many Vodouisants believe that after nine days, both the body and the ti-bon-anj are dissolved in the navel of the earth."[81]

Despite this, the Gede and particularly the Barons can and do take upon a role similar to that of divine judge – if not in the afterlife, then certainly in this one. One song expresses:

> *"Baron Samedi hold that man!*
> *Don't let him go!*
> *Don't let him go, heavenly judge, hold that man!"*[82]

---

81 Desmangles, 1992:75.
82 Courlander, 1939:88.

In contrast to the behaviour of Papa Gede, the Baron is known to act *"more on the tragic side of life"*.[83] I have heard it said that Gede is about 90% tomfoolery, whereas Baron is serious for the majority of the time. In matters of justice, where people feel truly wronged and wish to see the wrongdoer punished, he is the Lwa to approach. A pair of scales, universally representing the powers of justice, is one of his symbols.

The black hat of Baron puts us in mind not only of the undertaker but also of the black cap of British judges when historically decreeing a verdict of execution. Meanwhile his general attire and certain other symbols used on his *veve* (sacred symbol) and in connection with him are said to be Masonic. The rites and rituals connected with the Order of Freemasonry frequently allude to the necessity for upright citizenship; if you look carefully, you can discover various Masonic images in Vodou symbolism, while the wearing of *"black in the Masonic ritual is constantly the sign of grief"*.[84]

The top hat - which is especially pertinent to representations of Baron - has in the past been associated with *'fat cat'* capitalism and the upper classes and was therefore a target for comical satirists. Neither can class, status or financial clout save a person from becoming Baron's chosen object of ridicule. My godfather, guesting at a ceremony in Haiti, witnessed this. The Lwa not only accused a prominent local businessman (whose wife was present at the time) of infidelity, but in the face of the man's firm denial chose to march the entire congregation down the street, straight to the front door of his mistress. The businessman died not long afterwards. It does no good at all to attempt to fight death, Gede knows every skeleton in your cupboard, and indeed, false contradictions can only make his behaviour worse.

Memento Mori

In truth, everything Gede says and does is gravely serious (pun intended), and if he is taken to one side, he may choose to drop the banality altogether and proscribe great wisdom. With his symbolically hedonistic excesses, Gede teaches the catharsis of the celebration of life even – especially - in the face of its tragic endings. His party is the Jazz funeral or Irish wake, sombre *and* celebratory, for in celebrating the life of the departed we also acknowledge our own mortality.

Many Vodouisants recognise the figures of Gede, and especially Baron and Brigitte, in the beautiful shrines of *Dia de los Muertos*,[85]

---

83 Crosley, 2000:98.

84 W.Bro Kenneth J. Tuckwood, 'Masonic Colours & their Symbolism'. Source: http://www.kinggeorgelodge.com/downloads/education/tdf005-masonic_colours_and_their_symbolism.pdf

85 The Mexican 'Day of the Dead' falls at the same time as the Haitian 'Fet Gede', 2nd November, All Soul's Day (but also the month of November generally). A similar brand

where skeletal children, dead gamblers, and little papier-mache Corpse Brides and Bridegrooms link hands in tiny brightly-painted boxes. Feasts for the dead are held, family tombs are decorated, and the entire carnival is a profusion of colour and gaiety; sugar-candy skulls are distributed as *memento mori*. The lives of those who have passed are celebrated at the same time as each member of the community acknowledges their inevitable end amidst much jubilation and merriment. What could be more Gede than that?

Gede's sardonic humour is an elegant way to deal with the fact that every living being must die, indeed the whole world will pass away. *"Death is for the dead and living is for everyone else"*:[86] we are all fading moment by moment, time is not our friend, and what better reason to enjoy the world while we have it? Every discarded opportunity is a death; every choice involves the loss of that which was not chosen, the road not travelled, people never met.

Death has already won, we all lay down in the earth sooner or later as food for the worms. It is only a matter of time (which Gede has in abundance): *"no one can elude him, who is master of both life and death"*.[87] This, Deren suggests, is also the reason why Gede, *"ruler of men...[is] probably the most lonely...[and so is] the most interested in the trifling, intimate details of men's daily life."*[88] More than any other spirit, on a primordial level - the basic drive to survive - we can never truly accept him; he is the most feared of all Lwa and consequently the most isolated even as he is closest to us. Gede breathes down our necks all the time.

Gede's children

It is said that no one can die until Gede agrees to dig his grave, that Baron will only take people when it is their 'time'. Others dispute this. Yet both Baron and Gede are said to have powers of great healing, and may even be able to pull us back from the brink of death.

Courlander recalls a song for Papa Gede during which women, praying for his protection, placed little coins on a white plate especially set out for the purpose:

Gédé main l'a'gent;	*Gede take the money;*
Gédé Nimbo main	*Gede Nimbo take the*
l'a'gent;	*money;*

---

of celebratory disorder ensues in Haiti during this month although it is less popularly known than the Mexican celebration.

86 From Death is for the Dead, a poem about having AIDS, by River Huston. Source: http://www.positiveside.ca /e/V6I3/Death_e.htm

87 Deren, 1983:103.

88 Deren, 1983:111.

M'apé ba rou l'a'gent	I shall give you money
p'ou ga'dé zenfants!"	to guard the Lwa's
	children![89]

One of the saints associated with Papa Gede, Saint Gerard Majella is known as the intercessor for children, the unborn and particularly women in labour. Birth can prove fatal, especially in circumstances of disease or poor hygiene; where a child is born death is always close by, and while in the Western world he usually leaves empty-handed, even in our more *'developed'* circumstances that is not always the case. Historically, if mother and child survived the birth, a large percentage of children would die sometime in the first five years of life. They still do in developing countries. Haitians proverbially say "*Tout moun fet pou soufri, tout moun fet pou mouri (Everyone is born to suffer, everyone is born to die)*". And it is still the case that:

"*The average life expectancy [in Haiti] is alarmingly low, and the infant mortality rate alarmingly high; in some parts of Haiti, half the children die before their first birthday...[yet] Haitians are not, on the whole, a depressed or morose people. Gede's humour is their antidote.*"[90]

It is no surprise that Baron, in his role as protector of children and the unwanted, should have included child-spirits in the Gede family. Gede Mazaka, midwife and abortionist, is representative of the sovereignty death holds even in the womb. The loss of a child, whether *'wanted'* or *'unwanted'*, can be particularly hard to deal with, and is perhaps more likely to be set aside or forgotten than any other kind of death.

When dying soon after birth or when aborted, miscarried or stillborn a child may never be given a name or funeral (looking through personal family history, it is common to find *'Baby Boy'* instead of a name – not all lived long enough to be baptised). In the UK no registration of death is required for *'miscarriages'* which occur during the first 24 weeks of pregnancy (and of course the same applies to abortions which *must* occur under 24 weeks by law). Citizens Advice suggests that many funeral directors, crematoriums and cemeteries may not charge fees for arrangements in the case of stillbirths (which occur after the first 24 weeks)[91] though some families may feel a funeral was inappropriate. Others might wrestle with a sense of guilt – did they cause the stillbirth in some way? - or as if society doesn't see the baby as having *'really existed'*. This is particularly true in the case of miscarriage, where even doctors use such terms as *"third time lucky"* as if talking about a lottery ticket – language which would never be used after the death of a child.[92]

---

89 Courlander, 1939:87.

90 McCarthy Brown, 2001:375.

91 Source: http://www.adviceguide.org.uk 'What to do after a death'

92 Moulder, 2001:87.

In the eyes of the law which thrives on exact definition, clear lines are drawn between miscarriage and stillbirth, foetus and embryo – yet for the families involved the loss is more than just a cluster of cells. According to Moulder, there is a difference in the way medical professionals treat a *'mother'* who has lost her child and a *'woman'* who has suffered miscarriage or stillbirth. Some women found it easier to use the term miscarriage.[93] Others feared to ask about disposal of the remains which usually (before 24 weeks) involved hospital incineration;[94] some had to actively fight for the right to bury their child.[95] Yet a funeral (formal or otherwise) can aid the acknowledgement of loss, and a name (even if only ever used by immediate family) turns *'it'* into a little person and may aid the healing process.

"Such life, I'm told, is not life

And grief unreasonable.

But I felt that lie

Within."[96]

Gede is a Lwa called upon for help in cases relating to problematic births and sick children. He takes this role very seriously: I have heard of him thwarting attempts at a termination, and he is also described as appearing in a labour ward to aid one of his petit right in the middle of contractions.[97]

One particular story of Gede as healer was witnessed in Haiti in the late 1940's by Maya Deren. The child lay dying: all attempted cures, medical and herbal, had failed. Laying the child on a tomb, Gede anointed her with a *"life fluid"* that came from *"between his legs...It was not urine. And though it would seem impossible that this should be so, since it was a female body which he had possessed, it was a seminal ejaculation...And though there is no reasonable way to account for this, the child lived."*[98] Symbolically, this describes more perfectly than words can say the dynamic interflow between death and the progenitive force epitomised in all persons of the Gede family. To have turned to the spirits for help in the face of this crisis is not as ludicrous as some cynics might feel given the high mortality rates in Haitian hospitals up to the present day: to be sent to hospital was almost a death sentence in itself, even supposing one could afford the fees.[99]

---

93 Moulder, 2001:59.

94 Moulder, 2001:64.

95 Moulder, 2001:66.

96 Moulder, 2001:58: a poem written by 'Sharon', who suffered miscarriage at thirteen weeks.

97 McCarthy Brown, 2001:372.

98 Deren, 1983:114.

99 In the 1960's, Haitian immigrants to the United States were described as having a different but equally valid fear when going to hospital: possible deportation. McCarthy Brown, 2001:72-73.

Petit Gede

Death is never satisfied. Gede is said to be ever-hungry, even famished, and one particular Lwa is known for biting chunks of flesh from his horse during possession, much to the anxiety of the congregation who will do their best to distract him from this activity with more palatable gifts. Not all spirits are *'safe'*. Of course viewed contextually all the Lwa are hungry: in a typical group ceremony for the spirits, we provide most of the following: coffee, peanuts, corn, rum, wine, perfume, beer, fruit, tobacco, sweets, bread, fizzy drinks, beans, rice, meat, flowers, cakes, cigars...all of which excludes particular gifts of note.

But the Gede are known for their hunger. And any parent who has ever watched the almost never-ending capacity of a toddler for sweets, ice-cream and other things that are *'bad'* will understand the idea that the hungriest Gede may very well be the Gede children. Of them not much is known, but Gede Ti Mazaka (*'Little'* Mazaka, who may or may not be related to the Gede Mazaka mentioned earlier) in Haitian Vodou and Guedecito in 21 Divisions are two served in our house. Both are *'masked'* by the image of Santo Nino de Atocha, the child Jesus carrying basket and crook – although the figure of John the Baptist as a child (also with crook) has been used as well.

In service, we acknowledge the child Gede and treat them as we would any children on a special occasion: they are given candy, peanuts, toys and fizzy drinks, and on one occasion an entire *'pizza'* comprised of cookie-dough base with red and black liquorice, sugar sprinkles and jelly bugs as *'topping'*. While the Marassa also appreciate sweets (and like any pair of siblings, must always have exactly the same amount in their bowls to be contented) in my experience the Gede children seem to favour Halloween-type goodies over regular confectionary. That is to say: oozing jelly bugs, liquorice spiders, chocolate eyeballs, black, white and purple jelly beans, candy sticks that look a bit like cigarettes from a distance... Gede altars can frequently take on the appearance of a trash-heap, complete with mould – Gede never wants to throw anything away because he's *"not done with it yet"*. I once had to put up with a plate of melted sweets topped with a deflated purple balloon so ancient it had cobwebs on it for over a year before I finally persuaded the Petit Gede to accept a replacement offering.

Ti Mazaka would like to be treated as one of the older Gede (he is seen as Brav's little brother). I envisage him as a young and scrawny child, around eight but thin enough to look younger. He is dressed like his brothers but the black coat and hat are far too big for him and he may if lucky have borrowed someone else's sunglasses for the occasion. He is famished and dirty. He would like to drink the rum and smoke Brav's cigar, but he can't reach. Perhaps one of his older brothers will sneak him a cigarette. He is more Artful Dodger than Oliver Twist. He steals, plays nasty tricks and tries to be like his brothers. This includes strutting and repeating their language, albeit with a child's understanding: hence the boastfulness of having a big red penis in the song below. Papa Gede uses innuendoes and satire but Ti Mazaka, being only a child, imitates him coarsely:

> *"Ti Mazaka bay nou chans la,*
> *petit gede genyen yon gwo zozo...*
> *Zozo a tout wouj nan menm moun yo!"*[100]

This representation of child-spirits may seem a little grotesque to us; however we must remember that certain rules are followed by all the Gede, such uncouth behaviour is a *'signature piece'* of the family and it is not beyond the bounds of possibility that a young boy would attempt to emulate his older brother in this way. Another petit of the Gede family is Linto, who seems to represent a much younger child:

"He induces puerile behaviour in those he 'rides'. They walk clumsily, with a certain stiffness, like a baby who scarcely knows how to use his limbs. They babble and weep for food. The company treats Linto like a little child and teases him good-humouredly."[101]

Two things may be learned from the representation of Petit Gede, especially in regards to our treatment of them. We have previously spoken of the Lwa as *'Papa'*, *'Mama'*, *'Met'* (Master) or *'Maitresse'*, as spirits whose protection we wish to invoke. We are all the Lwa's children (a *'child of Gede'* is a servitor with particular links to, or pathos with, Papa Gede) but at the same time they are also dependant on us. Servitors are protective over the petit - giving them sweets and cola, for example, instead of the usual rum and cigarettes – and the relationship is both affectionate (the understanding is that by feeding Linto we feed all lost children) and reciprocal (we cannot exist without them, nor they us). That the company would treat Linto *"like a little child"* is not disrespectful but a recognition of who he represents: we are protective of him precisely *because* he is a baby, while still taking the place of Lwa.

Vodou is a democratic religion in terms of its spirits: all manner of men and women seem to be included in the pantheon, and no one has charted the territory entire. It is no surprise, then, that child-spirits are incorporated, but an additional purpose is achieved: just as a woman may feel drawn to share her burdens with Brigitte as a more feminine image of death, so a mortal child may find the symbolism of petit Gede particularly pertinent to himself. The child-Gede are said to make excellent playmates (manifesting as *'imaginary friends'* to those who may later discover the Lwa) and are perhaps less frightening than some other manifestations of Gede. Having said that, most children seem to love Baron quite as much as he loves them, and children seem to connect with Gede on a very real level more quickly than some adults, whose preconceived ideas of propriety may stand in the way.

---

100 "Ti Mazaka give us some luck, Child Gede has a big penis...The penis is very red when it's in peoples' hands!"

101 Metraux, 1989:116.

In conclusion

It is touching, sad, and perhaps a little frightening that Haitian Vodou should incorporate child-spirits within the Gede family: given the infant mortality rates previously mentioned it is also not very much a surprise. But this adoption of Petit Gede serves a purpose for any Vodouisant regardless of culture, and means just as much to those of us serving in the West as it does for the Haitian.

There is a saying that a death in a family is soon followed by a birth. While preparing this essay I experienced that personally, for at the same time that my grandmother 'Mimi' was passing away my husband and I discovered we were pregnant. It was in the midst of much joy and sorrow, fervent prayers, hope and loss that the essay was written. In this juxtaposition of opposites - tears and laughter, a beginning and an ending - nothing could be more appropriate to Papa Gede, spirit of life and death.

Bibliography

Alcide Saint-Lot, Marie-Jose. Vodou: A Sacred Theatre – The African Heritage in Haiti. Educa Vision Inc., 2004.

Courlander, Harold. Haiti Singing. University of North Carolina Press, 1939.

Crosley, Reginald. The Vodou Quantum Leap; Alternative Realities, Power, and Mysticism. Llewellyn Publications, 2000.

Deren, Maya. Divine Horsemen: The Living Gods of Haiti. McPherson, 1983.

Desmangles, Leslie G. The Faces of the Gods: Vodou and Roman Catholicism in Haiti. University of North Carolina Press, 1992.

Glassman, Sallie Ann. Vodou Visions: An Encounter with Divine Mystery. Villard, 2000.

McCarthy Brown, Karen. Mama Lola: A Vodou Priestess in Brooklyn. University of California Press, 2001.

Metraux, Alfred. Voodoo in Haiti. Pantheon, 1989.

Moulder, Christine. Miscarriage: women's experiences and needs. Routledge, 2001.

Ramsey, Kate. The Spirits and the Law: Vodou and Power in Haiti. University Of Chicago Press, 2011.

THE TRUTH ABOUT ZOMBIES, *OR*: HOW TO SURVIVE THE ZOMBIE APOCALYPSE

BY KIM HUGGENS

Originally presented as a lecture at the Glastonbury Occult Conference, March 12th, 2011.

It has been asserted that every interesting person in the Western world has formulated a plan for the inevitable Zombie Apocalypse. Perhaps it's the looming doom of 2012 that has turned our minds towards an apocalyptic way of thought, and perhaps it's modern civilization's apparent obsession with staving off death and ageing, that makes the threat of a specifically Zombie-themed apocalypse so fascinating and simultaneously terrifying for so many of us. The image of the undead, hungry for human flesh and brains, roaming a post-apocalyptic wasteland searching for the last few survivors to convert with harrowing efficiency into another mindless monster, is one that haunts so many people in the modern age.

But how can the interesting occultists out there know how to implement their plans for the Zombie Apocalypse without first understanding the magical, mythological and medicinal mechanics of the Zombie? The answers lie in the traditions of the Zombie in the context of Hoodoo Conjure, Haitian Vodou, and the ancient Graeco-Roman sorcerers (with brief mention of the Norse and Chinese undead too!) From necromantic rites and the dredging of a soul out of Hades, to psycho-spiritual Zombie effects and ethno-botanical studies, we will discover that surviving the Zombie Apocalypse requires more than a just shotgun and people who run slower than you.

In examining these traditions, in highlighting their similarities and differences, we may also begin to work out what it is about the Zombie in our nightmares and fascinations that just won't go away.

We are probably all familiar with the filmic image of a zombie found in movies. The list of zombie movies runs to the hundreds and includes all-time classics such as *Dawn of the Dead* (1978, dir. George A. Romero), *The Evil Dead* movies (1981 and 1987, dir. Sam Raimi), and *I Walked With A Zombie* (1943, dir. Jacques Tourneur), modern action flicks with added totty in *I am Legend* (2007, dir. Francis Lawrence) or any of the *Resident Evil* (2002-2010) films, and modern comedy spoofs of the movie genre such as *Shaun of the Dead*

(2004, dir. Edgar Wright) and *Zombieland* (2009, dir. Ruben Fleischer). Most of the movies give us a very clear image of the zombie in one of two forms:

A shambling, slow, mindless, base creature with a need for braaaaaains... It is often partly decomposed, having once been dead and usually buried. Sometimes these zombies are given their origins in the cult-like activity of some *"voodoo"* group, as in *I Walked With A Zombie*, or they are the dead, risen from the earth in *"When Hell is full the dead will walk the earth..."* style.[102]

A fast, effective hunter with a hunger for blood, flesh or brains, more akin to vampires yet still sometimes retaining the typical appearance of a rotting or emaciated corpse. Often these kinds of zombies were never buried, usually created not through reanimation from the state of death, but through an infectious spread of disease, as in the movie *28 Days Later*. In films such as this the bite of a zombie – like the bite of a vampire – spreads the highly contagious disease, or even contact with the blood or body fluid of a zombie could cause infection.[103]

Despite the fact that these are conceptions of zombies gleaned from a study of the zombie movie genre, they allow us to explore the various traditions of zombies throughout the world. The first category bears relevance to studies of zombies in the Hoodoo and Vodou traditions, in that the first stage of the zombie creation process involves burying the victim/corpse (here I use the term *'victim'* as we will discover that the issue of whether the zombie was ever truly dead in these cases is debateable.) The second category can also bears relevance to the Hoodoo tradition, as it refers to a disease, mutation or change in mental state, which in Hoodoo may be caused by entheogens or other toxic substances as well as certain amounts of social and mental control. We'll also find that the second category shares some features with the Norse idea of zombies, called *aptrgangr* or *druagr*, whilst the Graeco-Roman idea of reanimation of the dead poses a few problems for the traditional conception of zombies.

Perhaps most importantly, the zombie image is one that is so recognizable not because the zombie is undead: there are plenty of other undead monsters out there, such as vampires, wendigos, and ghosts. Rather, they are so recognizable because they are mindless.

---

102 It is actually a common mistake to attribute the statement "When Hell is full the dead will walk the earth..." to the Bible. It does not appear anywhere in the Bible, but first appeared in George A. Romero's original Dawn of the Dead movie. It is believed that Romero did, however, have a Christian eschatological agenda in relation to the zombie film genre.

103 Because of this, some have suggested that this genre of zombie film has become more popular due to increased awareness and fear since the 1980's of sexually transmitted diseases, which are passed in the same way. It might be suggested that the zombie of yesteryear holds the same taboo as sexually transmitted diseases do today, yet both are spread via a necessary human function – in this case, death and sex, or Thanatos and Eros.

Unlike other monsters and undead creatures, the zombie cannot think for itself, has no feelings, no passions, no desires, does not feel pain and has lost all remnants of that which made it human. Even Dracula could feel love, even a ghost can feel sadness, even a wendigo in its animalistic state can feel bitterness. A zombie feels nothing and thinks nothing, and perhaps this is the real reason it holds such terror for us, living as we do in a society that values freedom of speech and individual thought so highly.

Traditions in Which Zombies Appear

There are a large number of traditions in which the zombie appears, but the four I shall be examining in this paper, for brevity's sake, are the Graeco-Roman tradition, using literary evidence from both magical texts and the Greek and Latin dramatists; Hoodoo practice and the Vodou tradition in Haiti, using an array of modern studies, case studies, eye witness account and folkloric/religious beliefs; the Norse tradition in which literary evidence from the many sagas gives us an image of the undead; and finally the Chinese tradition of the Jiang Shi, informed mainly by folkloric tales and superstitions.

Dead Men DO Tell Tales: the Graeco-Roman Zombie

Unlike the other traditions, the Graeco-Roman zombie is created only for a short period of time and for a specific purpose (although the Hoodoo zombie is often given a purpose, it is usually longer lived.) Created by sorcerers to gain information otherwise forbidden to the living, it was believed that the reanimated corpse of a man could give oracles regarding the future, since the state of death enabled the dead man's spirit to see all of time. As such, these zombies were usually created from the freshly dead, often on battle fields where it would have been easier to find freshly dead corpses, and their souls are reinstalled in their bodies, though their bodies are unable to act of their own accord except in the manner in which the sorcerer chooses, e.g. to speak. In this, the Graeco-Roman zombie is almost the opposite of the Hoodoo zombie – the former is given back its mind and soul so that it may give information, but its body is merely a vessel and not otherwise used; the latter has its mind and soul removed, leaving the body vacant, at which point it is put to use at whatever menial task or labour the sorcerer dictates.

In some cases the Graeco-Roman sorcerer much preferred the recently dead, pulled back into its relatively fresh corpse, over a long-dead ghost dredged up from the depths of Hades. After all, surely it was less work to pull back a spirit that had only just started its journey to Hades, than to pull one back that had long ago become comfortable amongst the shades.

"But the obvious method, in view of the fact that there is such an abundance of fresh death around us, is to raise a single body from the Thessalian plains so that the mouth of a corpse only recently dead

and still warm may make utterance with full voice. We will not have to cope with a deathly shade, its limbs dried up by the sun, squeaking indistinctly to our hearing."[104]

Undead Enslavement: the Haitian Zombie

This particular zombie tradition is probably the most recognizable and influential of them all; it inspired the first zombie movies, and has drawn the most research, debate and fascination. The word 'zombie', Wade Davies suggests, comes from the Kongo word 'nzambi', meaning 'spirit of a dead person', however it could mean 'god'. The debate concerning the origin of this term has not yet reached a conclusion, as highlighted by Ackermann and Gauthier in 1991.[105] In this tradition the zombie is mindless and soulless, their body being controlled by the *bokor* (sorcerer) that created them. There are many possibilities as to how they are created, and the book *The Serpent and the Rainbow* is an interesting exploration of the journey to try and discover the infamous zombie powder supposedly used to create them.

Here, the victim of zombification is buried first. Whether they are dead when this happens or not is heavily debated, as case studies describe victims waking up in the coffins, having been buried alive, and many show signs of brain damage that could be caused by oxygen deprivation from such an act. It is often presumed that some sort of powder, drug, or poison is used to cause the victim to fall into a death-like state, like that used by the star-crossed lover Juliet in *Romeo and Juliet*, and that this tricks the family into believing the person dead. However, in some accounts the victim is dragged from being dead and fed a paste that induces the zombie state. The drug that is used still has not been truly discovered, as there are apparently many ways to make it, and of course any researchers trying to track it down are highly unlikely to be given the actual formula by practicing *bokors*.

In this tradition the zombie can also be created magically by a sorcerer, who raises the body back from the dead and takes a piece of the soul (specifically the piece that governs rationality and independent thought) away, and binds the zombie to his will; a variation upon this is to take the soul of a dying person as it detaches from the body just before death. However, in actuality Vodou distinguishes between two different kinds of zombie – the 'zombie astral' – somebody's spirit trapped or coerced into a jar and used for work by the *bokor*; and the 'literal zombie' – somebody who has had their *ti bon anj* (part of their soul that is their will and independence) stolen or bound in some way.

---

104 Lucan, Pharsalia, 6.588. 2008

105 Ackermann and Gauthier, "The Ways and Nature of the Zombie", in The Journal of American Folklore, (Autumn, 1991) vol. 104.414:467-469.

The zombification process is seemingly used as a punishment for wrongdoers or revenge upon one's enemies; this is particularly the case for those who have committed great acts of social violence such as rape or murder, and those cases in which the law is unable or unwilling to act. After zombification, the zombie is put to work by the sorcerer at menial labour,[106] much like the original African slaves brought to the New World would have been, and in this we might see the true terror in the threat of zombification for the Haitian: the enslavement both of the body and the soul. For a country and culture that fought and worked to gain independence and freedom from slavery, the zombie is a fate worse than death.

The extent to which the zombified state is drug-induced, magically-induced, or simply a form of folk belief mixed with brain damage from live burial, mixed with mental disorders, is greatly debated. But one thing's for sure: in Haiti, it is not being harmed by zombies that people fear, but becoming one.

Hopping Zombies Controlled by Post-it Notes: The Chinese Zombie

The strange phenomenon of the Chinese zombie, called the *jiang shi*, which shares many features with the traditional image of a vampire, is caused either as a result of premature burial (similar to the Haitian zombie above), or can be created when the soul fails to properly leave the body upon death due to a violent death, such as suicide or murder. In Chinese folklore it may also be created by Taoist sorcerers. It is these sorcerers that were charged with the transportation of corpses back to their homeland for proper burial, but it is said that to make the job easier they reanimated the bodies and taught them to 'hop'. They did this by writing spells in Chinese characters on small sheets of yellow rice paper, which were then affixed to the corpse's forehead. Whilst the original accounts do not mention what happens to the *jiang shi* in the event of the paper falling from their foreheads, more modern accounts and horror films in particular have the *jiang shi* becoming a crazy monster hell-bent on feeding off the life essence of anybody it could find.[107] In this they share features with the vampire who drinks blood, but also more traditional zombies that hunger for the brains of living humans. It can also be suggested that they share slight similarity with the Jewish legends of the golem, a magically constructed creature given life by a magician who writes the Hebrew word for *'life'* on its forehead; the only means of destroying a golem is to remove one letter from this word, turning it into the Hebrew word for *'death'*.

The *jiang shi* are variously described as appearing in different states of decay depending on how long they have been dead, with

---

106 However, in contemporary accounts, many zombies end up in an asylum, or living homeless on the streets or in the graveyards they were supposedly buried in.

107 Thus, control of the Jiang Shi depended greatly on sourcing a reliable glue. Modern sorcerers may find a stapler better suited to the task.

long tongues, sharp black fingernails, and blindness. Due to the fact that they are often in a state of rigor mortis or decay, they cannot walk properly so instead they perform a strange, hopping jump.

The Again-Walkers: the Norse Zombie

The Old Norse sagas have many mentions of a particular kind of undead creature called variously *aptrgangr* (*'the after goer'* or *'again walker'*), *draugr* [108] ("ghost"), and *haugbai* (*'mound-dweller'*, in this case specifically a grave mound or barrow). These undead are, depending on whether they are draugr, haugbai or aptrgangr, often physically animated corpses that live in their grave mounds or barrows and jealously guard their grave goods, attacking anybody that may try to rob their final resting place, or they are less corporeal beings able to walk through the stone and earth of their graves and walk about the land.[109] Whilst haugbai are rarely found far from their resting place, the draugr are sometimes found roaming the surrounding area, sometimes terrorizing the livestock. All aptrgangr are described in the sagas as being giant in size, swelling after death. In the *Eyrbyggja Saga,* Thorolf is described as: *"...uncorrupted, and with an ugly look about him... swollen to the size of an ox,"*[110] though it is clear that the swelling of the dead body is not caused by gases created during decomposition, as the same saga reports that Thorolf's body is so heavy that it had to be lifted with levers. The aptrgangr also had immense strength and power, sometimes demonstrating this by crushing people to death. One attack by an aptrgangr named Glamr leaves a shepherd *"...with his neck broken and every bone in his body crushed."*[111] Indeed, when a mortal hero enters into combat with one of these undead creatures, the fight is described as being difficult for the hero, with the *aptrgangr* offering a challenge beyond that of a mere mortal.

These undead creature share one typical feature of other zombies in that they hunger for living flesh, and will even attack and attempt to eat their own closest friends and family, forgetting their ties to them in life. When the mortal Asmund sits watch with his newly deceased friend Aran in his grave mound, along with live animals as grave goods, we find that Aran decides his old friend would be a tasty meal:

"During the first night, Aran got up from his chair and killed the hawk and hound and ate them. On the second night he got up again from his chair, and killed the horse and tore it into pieces; then he took

---

108 It must be noted that this word is not linguistically linked to the word "dragon", though both the draugr and the dragon in the Old Norse sagas share some features, e.g. they both jealously guard grave goods or treasure hoardes.

109 Such as is the Laxdaela Saga, where the aptrgangr Hrapp is being attacked by the mortal Olaf, and sinks into the ground where he is standing so that he may escape the combat. (Magnusson and Palsson, 1975:103.)

110 Palson and Edwards, Eyrbyggja Saga, 2006:187.

111 Fox and Palsson, Grettir's Saga, 1975:74.

great bites at the horse-flesh with his teeth, the blood streaming down from his mouth all the while he was eating.... The third night Asmund became very drowsy, and the first thing he knew, Aran had got him by the ears and tore them off... "[112]

Of course, these accounts seem to be in direct contradiction to the idea of a Norse afterlife such as Valhalla, demonstrating a difference in practice between folk belief and religious teaching. However, even in this version of a Norse paradise, the dead rise again, as at Ragnarok the warriors in Valhalla will fight on the side of the Gods against the legions of Hel. The idea of dead warriors coming back to fight on one side or another in a great conflict is one that runs through much of European mythology. Consider, for instance, the folklore of King Arthur, supposedly the *"Once and Future King"*, who in many legends around the British Isles is said to be sleeping in a secret cave along with his Knights, waiting for Judgement Day or Britain's hour of need; or take the story of *Branwen, Daughter of Llyr* in the Second Branch of the *Mabinogion*, in which the Irish use the Cauldron of Rebirth to reanimate their dead warriors during a battle.[113]

Zombification: How to Make a Zombie

If we're going to survive the Zombie Apocalypse, we should first find out how zombies are actually made. The different traditions differ greatly on this, yet in places share some surprising similarities. Broadly speaking there are four possibilities for the creation of a zombie: Magic, Mundane (Mind Control, Social Control, etc.), Medicine and a Mixture.

Magical Methods

The Graeco-Roman tradition gives us almost exclusively magical methods for creating zombies. In his *Pharsalia*, Lucan describes the witch Erichtho, called upon by the son of Pompey to give him an oracle regarding the fortune of the war he has entered into. Erichtho advises him that the easiest method to obtain this oracle, given that they are at the tail end of a battle that has left many freshly dead corpses, would be to reanimate a corpse and enquire the fortune from the reinstated soul of that dead man. So, Erichtho finds her victim:

"Eventually a corpse was chosen, one with its throat cut, and brought. She put a hook into a deathly noose round its neck and dragged the pitiful corpse, destined to live again, over the crags and rocks. Dour Erichtho stationed it under the high roof of the mountain cave she had dedicated to her rites."[114]

---

112 Palsson and Edwards, Gautrek's Saga and Other Medieval Tales, 1970:99-101.

113 Guest, Lady Charlotte, The Mabinogion. 2000

114 Lucan, Pharsalia, 6.624. 2008

She then calls to the chthonic gods, searching the shadowy realm of Hades until she finally sees the black shade of the man whom she wishes to reanimate, fearful to enter his mutilated body. Seeing his fear and sensing the reluctance of the chthonic gods, Erichtho screams threats to the Underworld, threatening to give away secret information:

"Tisiphone and Megaera, you who scorn my calling, do you not drive this hapless soul through the emptiness of Erebus with your cruel whips? Any moment now I shall call you up by your true names and make you stand as Stygian hounds in the light of the upper world. I shall pursue you through tombs, through burials, ever hanging on your heels, I shall drive you from barrows and keep you from all urns. You, Hecate, decaying and colourless in appearance as you are, are in the habit of showing yourself to the gods above only after first making up your face. I will show you to them and forbid you to alter your hell-face. I shall blurt out, Persephone of Henna, the meal that traps you beneath the vast weight of the earth, the agreement by which you love the sombre king of the night and the corruption you experienced that induced your mother to refuse to call you back. Upon you, Hades, worst of the world's rulers, I shall send Titan, the Sun, bursting your caverns open, and you will be blasted by the instantaneous light of day. Do you obey?"[115]

In most cases the threats are also made towards the spirit of the dead man that is being called up. A second incantation must usually be made, therefore, to goad it into agreeing to enter its body once more.

The dead man finally enters his body and speaks a prophecy, having learned everything from the ghosts in the Underworld; it is clear that he can feel the pains of his mangled body, his spirit and mind trapped in the body yet unable to die unless Erichtho says so. Upon finishing his prophecy, the witch does give him a means of dying forever so that his spirit would never again be called up from its rest by another unscrupulous witch or magician, and so he strides into a magically prepared funeral pyre and is released.[116]

Both Erichtho and the Bessa woman of Egypt raise the dead at points that are closer to Hades. Erichtho performs her rite in a dark, mouldy cavern that seems to have cracks that reach down to Hades, and the Bessa woman builds a fire on one side of the corpse of her

---

115 Lucan, Pharsalia, 6. 719. This formula of threatening the powers or gods is common to this genre of magical literature, and appears as much in the work of the dramatists as it does in the actual magical texts themselves.

116 It might be interesting for some to note that Neil Gaiman took inspiration for part of his Sandman graphic novels series from the character Erichtho, creating a witch named Thessaly, who herself performs a similar reanimation rite, but instead of using the entire body she slices off only the corpse's face, takes his eyes and his tongue, and pins them down so that they may speak, then calls the dead man's spirit back into his mutilated flesh. A Game of You, DC Comics, 1991.

son and digs a pit on the other, into which she pours offerings of milk, honey and blood – traditional offerings for the dead.[117]

Both witches perform their magic at night, and Erichtho in particular creates a shroud of *'double-darkness'* for her working. In fact, the place she chooses to perform the reanimation is so dark, so close to Hades, that Lucan makes reference to Homer's description of Aeneas descending to Hades:

"Within the cave is a morose darkness and gray mould, the product of protracted night. No light is shed except that which is manufactured with a spell. The air in the jaws of Tainaron is not as stifling as here. It is the dismal boundary between the hidden world and our own. It is such that the kings of Tartarus do not fear to let the dead pass to it. For, although the Thessalian prophetess does violence to the fates, it remains uncertain whether she is able to look upon the Stygian shades by virtue of drawing them up or by virtue of going down herself to them."[118]

The witches Erichtho and the Bessa woman put themselves between the worlds, both physically and spiritually. However, despite the fact that this is a magical method of reanimation, there is a possibility that a medicinal method is used in conjunction, as Erichtho uses herbs and creates a potion which she pumps into the corpse, though the ingredients in many cases are far more metaphorical than those we will see later may be used in Haitian zombie powder:

"In this was mixed whatever creature nature had produced under ill omen. Nothing was missing: not the foam of the water-fearing rabid dog, not the guts of the lynx, not the hump of the dreadful hyena, not the bone marrow of a deer pastured on snakes, not the ship-stopper [echenais], which detains a hull in the middle of the sea, while the east wind strains her cables, not the eyes of snakes, not the stones that murmur when incubated under a mother eagle, not the Arabian flying snake, not the viper born beside the Red Sea, guardian of the precious pearl oyster, not the slough of the still-living Libyan horned snake, not the ashes of the phoenix that settles itself upon an Eastern altar. After putting these common-or-garden and namable blights into her mixture, she added branches drenched in unspeakable spells, herbs on which her dread mouth had spat at the moment of their birth, and all the poisons she herself had contributed to the world."[119]

From the Haitian zombie tradition we get tantalizing glimpses of various magical rituals performed to create the zombie. Even Wade Davis, in his hunt for the ethnobotanical ingredients behind zombie powder, speaks about some sort of magical ritual. He interviews Clairvius Narcisse, a man who claims to have once undergone the zombification process but who later escaped his zombie captivity,

---

117 Heliodorus, 6.12-15.

118 Lucan, Pharsalia 6.642.

119 Lucan, Pharsalia, 6.667.

who says that he saw his soul floating above the grave, that a *bokor* didn't use any powder or poison on him, and that instead the *bokor* had used his power to call the soul back from its journey to the afterlife and put it back into the body:

"They called his name and the ground opened. He heard drums, a pounding, a vibration, and then the bokor singing..."[120]

Narcisse was, in fact, adamant that he was turned into a zombie magically and not through the use of a poison or drug:

"There was no poison; otherwise my bones would have rotted under the earth. The bokor sent for my soul. That's how it was done."[121]

In the magical method in Haitian Vodou, the *bokor* must separate certain parts of the soul from the body. The *ti bon ange* (*"little good angel"*) – the individuality and will of the victim - is removed and captured. The gros bon ange (*"big good angel"*) – the link to the Divine – must not be allowed to reach its reunion with God. The *bokor* must *"...prevent the transformations of the various spiritual components that would normally occur at the death of the body. First the ti bon ange – which may float above the body like a phosphorescent shadow – must be captured and prevented from re-entering the victim. One way to assure this is to beat the victim violently. Secondly, the gros bon ange must be prevented from returning to its source. Thirdly the n'ame must be retained to keep the flesh from decaying. The zombie cadaver with its gros bon ange and n'ame can function; however, separated from the ti bon ange, the body is but an empty vessel, subject to the direction of the bokor or whoever maintains control of the zombie ti bon ange."*[122]

Note that in this method the *ti bon ange* hovers close to the body so is easy to capture; in the Graeco-Roman sources, the ghost of the dead person is still only on the banks of the river leading to Hades, and thus easy to call back.

The Mundane Method: Mind Control, Fear, and Mental Illness

"But a zombie represented far more than a set of symptoms; if true, zombification was a social process unique to a particular cultural reality."[123]

Something that is regularly highlighted in the study of the Haitian zombie is the fact that more so than anything else, mental illness and fear seem to play a role in the post-zombification symptoms as well as the zombification process. One of the zombies encountered by Wade Davis – Francine Illeus - is described as having

---

120 Davis, Wade. The Serpent and the Rainbow, 1985:62.

121 Ibid., 1985:80.

122 Davis, Wade. The Serpent and the Rainbow, 1985:186. The "n'ame" is like the vital energy or essence that keeps life going, life force. Without it, the body decays.

123 Ibid, 1985:61

the symptoms of schizophrenia and catatonia, plus several other psychotic symptoms. Davis attributes this to brain damage, and it is easy to see how accounts of being buried alive (either with full consciousness or having been administered a poison or powder) would corroborate brain damage caused by oxygen starvation beneath the earth. Even were the victim removed from the grave before oxygen starvation began, it is easy to see how the psychological trauma – especially when fed by pre-existing social taboo and superstition – could cause mental illness that has effects similar to those of a zombie. The cultural and social control inflicted upon the victim of zombification cannot be ignored.

The case of Clairvius Narcisse, in Davis' study, exhibits some features of cultural and social control: he is basically kidnapped after being *"resurrected"*: he is immediately bound, gagged and beaten, his mind still functioning but his body unable to move or do anything. Narcisse later comments that it is the people who run the country that do this, and thus we find an element of political control or social punishment involved; the fear created by such a dynamic must be immense for anybody at the receiving end of it.

Davis makes the point that *"...just as an individual's sickness may have a psychosomatic basis, it is possible for a society to generate physical ailments and conditions that have meaning only in the minds of its people."*[124] So, for somebody in Haiti to be buried alive, put under immense psychological pressure and into a very vulnerable state, possibly starved of oxygen, and then dug up and immediately kidnapped or be on the receiving end of magical rituals, including drumming and singing, and in some cases a baptism with a new name[125] (effectively cutting them off from their previous life and putting them under the control of their new owner) it is easy to fall into the socially prescribed meme or role that they have been raised knowing intimately.

The function of the zombification process in Haiti seems to be a socially driven one, put upon individuals who have wronged a *sosyete* (society) member (usually the Bizango or San Pwel) in some way, and enacted as a form of internal justice via one's fellow *sosyete* members. Davis pinpoints seven reasons for which a person may be brought to a society tribunal, and recognizes that Clairvius Narcisse had fulfilled at least one of these criteria. Such a tribunal judges both the accused and the plaintiff in these cases, ensuring that nobody brings to tribunal an innocent man. Those at tribunal may be ill for some time, their *ti bon ange* being removed from their body to also be judged. He that is guilty then starts undergoing the zombification process – although as Davis points out, this process has already begun.

---

124 Ibid, 1985:136.

125 "For it is in the course of that intoxication that the zombie is baptized with a new name, and led away to be socialized into a new existence," Ibid, 1985:166.

Although no other tradition has recourse to such mundane explanations for the zombie myth or phenomenon, it strikes a chord with many people outside of Haiti. One could suggest that the prevalence of the horror surrounding zombies in the modern Western world relates to our fear of losing our individuality and our freedom to think, speak and act of our own free will. Yet at the same time as fearing this, many people voluntarily undergo a sort of zombification process, submitting themselves to media and political control that takes power out of their own hands, or placing themselves as victims of addictions that control their appetites in every way. Further, others can turn people into victims that lose (or feel they have lost) their ability to act independently or enact their will) through violent acts such as rape and child or spousal abuse.[126]

The Medicinal Method: Psychoactive Drugs & Ethnobotanical Studies

Whilst we do find herbal components and potions used in spells during the Graeco-Roman period, it is fairly certain that their application on corpses is limited if not completely ineffectual. PGM XII. 401-44 gives a list of the meanings of certain magical ingredients used in Egyptian magic, similar to those strange ingredients in Erichtho's potion for reanimation of corpses. Some of those listed are definitely poisonous or psycho-active, so could presumably be given to a living person to make them have a semblance of death, or a zombie-like mind-effect; however, they would need to be applied to a living person rather than a cadaver, and as we have already seen, the Graeco-Roman tradition from which this list derives only mentions reanimation of the already dead, not zombification of the living or at the point of death like the Haitian tradition.

Wade Davis did a lot of research into the possibility of a drug used to create zombies in Haiti, the folklore and legends being well-known and rife. Having studied various zombie accounts, Davis pinpointed the features the drug would need to have in order to match these accounts: it needed to lower the metabolic rate of its victim so that they could survive longer periods without oxygen when in their coffin, (although they would still in some cases sustain a certain amount of brain damage, their brain would not completely die); it would need to imitate death by making the pulse and breathing undetectable, cause the body temperature to drop rapidly and therefore bring a death pallor to the victim's face. Since accounts of Haitian zombies in the modern era often bear the feature of having a doctor or somebody familiar with the signs of death examine the

---

126 This is by no means saying that every person who has undergone such an experience is a "zombie", as many people find recovery, resolution and peace in overcoming the trauma of such acts, however in certain cases these acts cause hurt that runs too deep, and the victim is left in a state of powerlessness, their drive and will to act lost.

'corpse' and confirm death, this drug would need to fool such a specialist.

The administration of this drug is described in various ways. Sometimes it comes in powder form, on the threshold of the victim's doorway and therefore absorbed through the skin of the feet (in a culture where many people go barefoot). Sometimes it is blown into the face of the victim, therefore is possibly ingested through the porous skin on the face and the eyes. It may also be ingested orally by being used to spike food or drink. In some accounts a second drug is then administered after the victim has been dug up from their grave, and it is this second drug that reanimates them. However, there is much to suggest in Davis' research that any ethnobotanical drug administered to a zombie victim only goes so far as to immobilize or kill them; no powder is given to resurrect them – it is the magic that resurrects. It must also be pointed out that this medicinal method for creating zombies goes against the grain of the zombie image we have grown to recognize: these zombies are never dead, only seeming dead of under a powerful anaesthesia. Further, the drug seems to also induce a prolonged psychotic state of some kind.

When Davis began to research the medicinal method of zombie creation he used the term 'poison', which only confused the issue. Those he spoke to did not equate the concept of poison with the zombie-creating drug: their term for poison was "coup poudre." Equally, any such drug, even when both the researcher and his sources were on the same page, was not regarded as a poison at all, but rather a magical act:

"There is no poison. Narcisse came out of the ground. A poison would have left him where he lay."[127] One's first thought on this might be to state that this clashing of worldviews comes about because the Haitian has a more primitive understanding of science to the Western world; however, another perspective to take on the matter is not that the understanding is primitive but rather that they understand the inherent power in such a drug.

Davis was given a number of different formulae for the mythical zombie powder, many of them being dead ends (probably deliberate misdirection.) However, some of the ingredients had no psychoactive components in them whatsoever, and some psychoactive components that were discovered were found in some zombie powders but not others. Davis became convinced that one of the key ingredients is tetrodotoxin (from the puffer fish), though even this is inconclusive, elsewhere zombie's cucumber (*datura stromium*) is posited as the main ingredient. He also looked into the possibility that a large toad called *bufo marinus* was part of it, various lizards, sea snakes and fish. Interestingly, a large number of zombie powders contained parts of a corpse. Such an ingredient couldn't possibly

---

127 Davis, Wade. The Serpent and the Rainbow, 1985:84.

contain any active components whatsoever, yet it does highlight a key feature of necromantic practice as a whole that I have discussed elsewhere: death begets death.[128]

Some researchers have suggested that the zombie powder does not contain any pharmacological effectiveness at all, but rather contains ingredients that form part of a sympathetic magical technique.[129] Thus, ingredients are those that already bear some relation to death via virtue of their name, such as the aforementioned zombie's cucumber, or components gathered from a corpse or graveyard.

A Mixture

Whilst being relatively outdated, particularly in light of the research of Ackermann and Gauthier (1991),[130] Booth (1988), [131] and Kemp (1989), [132] Davis' research poses very interesting assertions about the zombie creation phenomenon. Although Davis set out to discover an ethnobotanical cause of zombies – a formula that could be recreated and administered – he pointed out that zombies, rather than just the symptoms of zombies, were a varied mix of social setting, cultural setting, faith, kidnap, ritual and drug.

Putting together all that he found, we have a rough idea what might go on in the zombie creation process:

The victim is given a drug that slows their metabolic rate and effectively *'kills'* them, often exhibiting certain symptoms, e.g. hypertension, pulmonary oedema, vomiting, hypothermia, rapid loss of weight, cyanosis and parasthesia. The slowed metabolic rate allows people around to think they are dead, pronounce them so, and for them to seek burial.

The victim, still conscious but *'locked in'* (compare this to *'Locked-in Syndrome'*), [133] hears/sees their relatives grieving for them, may be a passive observer at their own funeral, and is then buried alive.

During the burial some brain damage may start to set in.

The victim is keenly aware of what has happened, and carry with them immense social conditioning and stories of zombies.

---

128 Huggens, Kim. "Nefarious Occult Dealings: necromancy, ghosts and spirit expeditions in the Graeco-Roman, hoodoo and Vodou magical traditions" in The Conjure Codex, Hadean Press, 2011.

129 Ackermann and Gauthier, "Ways and Nature of the Zombi", in The Journal of American Folklore, (Autumn, 1991) vol. 104.414:466.

130 Ibid.

131 Booth, William, "Voodoo Science," in Science (Washington) 24, pp. 274-276.

132 Kemp, Mark, "Chemistry of Voodoo", in Discover 10, pp. 26-28.

133 For a vivid account of Locked-In Syndrom, see The Diving Bell and the Butterfly by Jean-Dominique Bauby.

In magical thought the *bokor* will capture the *ti bon anje* of the victim as it hovers around the corpse cadaver for several days after physical death.

The magical ritual is performed to raise them; they are pulled out of the ground, drugged again, baptized with a new name, bound, gagged, and kidnapped. (Even though some may question the validity of magical ritual, the social weight carried by the one performing such a ritual, and the act itself, impresses upon those party to the process that the victim is to be treated in a certain way – the social community generates a role and meme for the victim to step into, and perpetuates it.

Given that the victim is probably suffering from some sort of mental breakdown at worst, or fear induced shock at best, they are pliant and easy to manipulate. Add to this the understanding of the victim of the unquestionable power that a *bokor* or magical ritual wields, and the truth in the zombie concept, and they conform to the expected role.

Afterwards, the victim has the knowledge that he is being punished for wrongdoing by his community and those that hold social power. He knows also that he can never reclaim his former status, property or position in society: even though he has been brought back from the dead, he is dead to society and his old life. Thus, his will is broken further, and even if he later regained freedom from the zombie state it is debateable whether he would reclaim his *ti bon ange*. He therefore becomes one of the lost and the rejected of society, which explains why so many modern zombie cases are found living homeless on the streets as beggars, or in cemeteries in self-imposed exile, or in hospitals being treated as mental patients.

The Mindless Walking Dead?

The filmic image of the zombie paints a picture of the undead as the mindless walking dead, however this image is limited in its portrayal. As we have seen, in the Graeco Roman tradition the reanimated corpse is not usually buried before the zombification process; they talk and have minds and are simply the soul returning to the body. The fresher the cadaver the better, so there is not rotting flesh and a voice returns more readily to the recently deceased lungs (a zombie film director on a limited budget would be better off portraying the Graeco-Roman zombie!). These undead beings are called upon for information, since they have an intimate knowledge of the future, present and past by virtue of their exposure to the Underworld. They are also not malevolent towards the living, retain some memory of who they were in life, and do not hunger for living flesh or brains. They simply long for death again.

The Haitian zombie could better be described in a similar fashion to the filmic image: it is buried first (possibly alive), and is mindless, controlled by its creator. Depending on accounts, the Haitian zombie either has no soul, or its soul is bound to its creator and out of its own power or liberty; it is in a form of slavery. However, Davis' account of Clairvius Narcisse raises an interesting point: Narcisse escaped being a zombie when he rebelled against his captor (the bokor that made him) and killed him with the hoe he was using to work the fields. This suggests that either the Haitian zombie is not completely mindless, or it retains some part of its soul, or that the process of regaining one's liberty and soul as a zombie is understood in Haiti to require first an act of liberty. Just as death begets death, so freedom begets freedom.[134]

Yet some Haitian zombies do seem to be mindless, or have a seriously damaged mind, as in the case of Ti Femme, whose 'zombie' symptoms are the same as catatonic schizophrenia. It would remain to be shown if the zombification process caused the symptoms of catatonic schizophrenia, or if catatonic schizophrenia is classed as zombification in itself.

The Chinese *jiang shi*, of all the above descriptions of zombies, appears to be closest to our Western Romero zombie: they are mindless, controlled only by the sorcerer's wishes and magic. They are empty bodies, their will and mind gone, but their motor functions and animalistic parts still present. Hence, when the control of the sorcerer breaks, they go on a bloodthirsty rampage. Similarly, the Norse *druagr* seem to have lost a part of their soul – the part of the individual that is their morality, their compassion, their humanity – as they are reported as willingly eating their closest friends and relatives without recognizing them.

Some might suggest that it is because zombies are mindless that they desire to eat brains. But it seems that in most accounts it is not the brain-mind that the zombie is missing, but rather the heart-mind, the mind that makes us who we are; it is part of our soul, a part of our will and our ability to act consciously and with self-awareness, it is our liberty. The vampire drinks blood and lusts after it because the vampire itself lacks life and that is what blood represents; the zombie longs for brains because in most cultures the brain is the seat of the soul and is certainly the organ with which we make decision, enact our will, and demonstrate our freedom both of thought, speech and action.

Preventing the Zombie Apocalypse

Prevention is better than cure, they say; so how can we prevent the dead from rising? The various zombie traditions hold the answer.

The ancient Norse had many methods for preventing their recently dead from becoming undead, most of which were performed just before burial. Whilst some of them seem closer to ghost laying,

---

134 It might also be suggested that the rebellion, action and subsequent liberty of the Haitian zombie is strikingly similar to the Haitian slave revolution of 1791-1804 in which the Haitian slaves rose up against their captors and eventually achieved freedom.

or preventing a spirit from returning to its old home and causing trouble, there are some obvious actions performed upon the corpse that are aimed at preventing it from being able to use its body again.

"*...in old-fashioned homes [certain antique practices] were very carefully followed; a pair of open scissors laid on the dead person's chest, small pieces of straw laid crosswise under the shroud. The great toes were tied together so that the legs could not be separated. Needles were run into the soles of the feet, and when the coffin was carried out, the bearers, just within the threshold of the door, raised and lowered it three times in different directions so as to form a cross. When the coffin had left the house, all chairs and stools on which it had rested were upset, all jars and sauce- pans turned upside down, and when the parson in the church- yard prays for the rest of the dead, he is supposed to bind the dead to the grave with magic words, to keep him fast.*"[135]

The 'corpse-door' studied in the paper from whence the above quote came is a feature found in certain old Danish homes. This corpse-door was a bricked-up opening in the external wall of the house, which could be opened up specifically for the removal of the coffin for burial and quickly sealed back up again afterwards. It was believed that the spirit of the deceased could find its way back to its home from the burial ground, but only by the way it had come; thus is the corpse-door was bricked up, it would be unable to re-enter the house. However, to be safe the coffin was still carried feet-first rather than head-first from the house, to ensure the deceased did not get a good view of the path from the house to the burial ground. Compare this, and the above practice of raising the coffin up and down several times and to different directions, all of which formed a cross (a common symbol for blocking or confusing), with the practice of the Tana Toraja people of Sulawesi, Indonesia, in which not only is the coffin shaken violently, but on its way to the burial ground is taken on an unfamiliar route through the forest to ensure the spirit of the deceased cannot find her way home.[136] The cross is further formed by the pair of open scissors laid upon the chest of the deceased, and the straw cross.

That the big toes of the corpse are tied together, and needles driven through the soles of its feet, suggests a fear that the corpse would physically walk again, as well as its spirit.

The practice of mutilating the body in some way to prevent its rising again from the grave is found in Haiti:

"*It is to prevent such a fate that family members may kill the body of the dead a second time, sometimes plunging a knife into the heart of the cadaver, sometimes severing the head in the coffin.*"[137]

---

135 Feilberg, H.F. "The Corpse-Door: A Danish Survival," in Folklore 18 (1907), p. 366.

136 For a documented practice of this, see Episode 1 of Around the World in Eighty Faiths, BBC Two, 2009.

137 Davis, Wade. The Serpent and the Rainbow, 1985:26.

This is similar to some vampire-prevention practices in which the corpse is buried with a wooden stake through its heart, or decapitated with its head buried between its feet. Similarly, the ancient Greeks would sometimes perform a process on their dead enemies called *'armpitting'* which would prevent the *nekydaimones* (dead spirits) of their enemies (killed in battle) from returning to plague them. [138] Of course, this demonstrates that the ancients were already aware of one of the main rules of surviving the zombie apocalypse: Double-Tap. [139]

The modern, filmic zombie image is far from the *'real'* zombies of the previously discussed magical traditions. Instead, they are a product of our fear of social control, of becoming mindless automatons to the system, or being at the mercy of such mindlessness and having our freedom taken from us. In this sense, preventing the zombie apocalypse is simple: stop watching television, think for yourself, take responsibility for your actions, exercise your liberty and don't lose parts of your soul to external factors.

How to Survive the Zombie Apocalypse

Should all the above fail, and our society turn into a broiling milieu of undeath, the zombie traditions also have safeguards in place to help us survive.

The Graeco-Roman tradition suggests that we should learn to contact the chthonic deities of the Underworld so that we can remove the souls from the walking corpses and send them back to Hades where they belong. The Haitian tradition advises that we put the undead to work at menial tasks. In Haiti this might be working the fields, but in our society perhaps the civil service or call centre work would be more appropriate. Should we suspect a magical cause of the zombie apocalypse, we are best advised to track down the magician that created the zombies and kill him/her (occultists and stage magicians alike might wish to go into hiding should the apocalypse come...)

It is also wise to get on good terms with the Vodou lwa Baron Samedi, Baron Lakwa, Baron Cemitye or Papa Ghede, as *The Serpent and the Rainbow* records that certain rituals performed for the Baron could cure a person of being a zombie.

Of course, we could always take up arms and combat the undead with weapons – but the choice of weapon we use should be a careful and well-informed one. Whilst many modern films prefer baseball bats, chainsaws, SMGs, and Molotov cocktails, the Norse tradition dictates that only iron weapons could harm the *druagr*, and this only when certain other things are done: specifically, the hero must decapitate the creature, usually with a weapon taken from its own burial horde, and sometimes in order for the creature to stay dead

---

138 See Ogden's note on this practice in Magic, Witchcraft and Ghosts in the Greek and Roman Worlds, pp. 162-3.

139 Zombieland, dir. Ruben Fleischer, 2009.

the hero had to jump in the gap between the head and body before the corpse hit the ground; or walk around it three times anti-clockwise, or pierce its heart with a wooden stake.[140] In some instances it might be worth burning the corpse and burying the cold ashes in the remains of the barrow.

Conclusion

Forewarned is forearmed, and armed with this new knowledge of how zombies are made, how the rise of the undead can be prevented and combatted, we should all be better equipped to deal with the impending Zombie Apocalypse. Knowledge is power, after all, and remember: when the Apocalypse comes, the geeks shall inherit the earth. Which includes most occultists.

Bibliography

Ackermann and Gauthier (1991) *The Ways and Nature of the Zombie*, in *The Journal of American Folklore*, vol. 104.414:466-494.

Booth, William, *Voodoo Science*, in *Science (Washington)* 24:274-276.

Byok, Jesse (trans.) (2009) *Grettir's Saga*. Oxford University Press

Davis, Wade (1985) *The Serpent and the Rainbow A Harvard Scientist's Astonishing Journey into the Secret Society of Haitian Voodoo, Zombies and Magic.* Simon and Schuster

Dickie, Matthew W. (2001) *Magic and Magicians in the Graeco-Roman World.* Routledge

Feilberg, H.F. (1907) *The Corpse-Door: A Danish Survival*, in *Folklore* 18.

Gaiman, Neil (1991) *Sandman: A Game of You.* DC Comics.

Guest, Lady Charlotte (trans.) (2000) *The Mabinogion.* Harper Collins.

Homer, *Odyssey*, trans. Rieu, E.V. (2003) Penguin Classics.

Huggens, Kim (ed) (2010) *Vs.: Duality and Conflict in Magick, Mythology and Paganism.* Avalonia Books.

Huggens, Kim (2011) *Nefarious Occult Dealings: necromancy, ghosts and spirit expeditions in the Graeco-Roman, hoodoo and Vodou magical traditions,* in *The Conjure Codex,* Hadean Press.

Kemp, Mark, *Chemistry of Voodoo*, in *Discover* 10:26-28.

Lucan, *Pharsalia (Civil War)*, trans., Braund, Susan H. (2008) Oxford Paperbacks.

Luck, Georg (2003) *Ancient Pathways and Hidden Pursuits: Religion, Morals, and Magic in the Ancient World.* Ann Arbor: The University of Michigan Press.

Luck, Georg (1985) *Arcana Mundi.* John Hopkins University Press.

Magnusson, Magnus and Palsson, Hermann (trans.) (1975) *Laxdaela Saga.* Penguin Classics.

Ogden, Daniel (2002) *Magic, Witchcraft and Ghosts in the Greek and Roman Worlds: A Source Book.* Oxford University Press.

---

140 Saxo Grammaticus, Vol. I:150 and Vol. II:89.

Palsson, Hermann & Edwards, Paul (trans.) (2006) *Eyrbyggja Saga.* Penguin Classics.

Palsson, Hermann & Edwards, Paul (trans.) (1970) *Gautrek's Saga and Other Medieval Tales.* New York University Press.

Palsson, Hermann & Fox, D.H. (trans.) (1975) *Grettir's Saga.* University of Toronto Press.

Pinckney, Roger (1998) *Blue Roots: African-American Folk Magic of the Gullah People.* Llewellyn Publications.

Yronwode, Catherine (2002) *Hoodoo Herb and Root Magic.* Lucky Mojo Curio Company.

TRADITIONAL CRAFT AND THE CULT OF THE DEAD

BY MICHAEL HOWARD

In modern traditional witchcraft the nature and role of the witch-god and witch-goddess as chthonic deities of life and death and psychopomps, or guides to the dead, is very important. Both deities have dual aspects, both bright and dark, and it is their dark side that connects them to death and the underworld. In fact both deities have the position of rulers of the underworld or the 'land of the dead'. They also act as intermediaries between the dead and the living and between the netherworld and Middle Earth or the material world. For this reason some have described traditional witchcraft as the 'cult of the dead'. In the words of the modern cunning man Andrew D. Chumbley, *'The Great Sorcerer draws Power from his own Death. Now!'*[141] and Shani Oates, the present Maid of the Clan of Tubal Cain, has said that the rituals of her tradition are a preparation in life for the passing of the practitioner to the spirit world.

The twin faces of the witch-god are the Lord of the Greenwood in summer and the Lord of the Wildwood in the winter. In his summery aspect he is symbolised by the foliate or leaf mask of the Green Man or Jack-in-the-Green. This ancient fertility image can be seen carved in pre-Reformation churches and it dates back to the Roman art found on tombs of the first century CE symbolising rebirth.

Sometimes these foliate masks or faces have a deadly aspect with tendrils curling from their mouths, forcing them open in a death-like grimace. They suggest *'the worms that push out of a corpse's eyes'* or *'the roots of the churchyard yews'* and represent physical decay.[142] To those who saw this image when they attended church services it was a grim reminder of their own mortality and death. This was occasionally illustrated in an even more explicit manner by carvings of a human skull with leaves and plants growing from it. A classic example of one of these so-called foliate skulls dates from as late as the 18th century and can be seen on the Sadford and Challoner Memorial in Bristol.

Kathleen Batsford, a 20th century folklorist who was a renowned expert on foliate masks, has connected this death-head image with a 17th century painting by the Italian artist Giovanni Francescio Guereino. It depicts two shepherds in an idyllic pastoral landscape

---

141 Chumbley, Opuscula Magica, 2011:49.
142 Harte, The Green Man, 2001:10-11.

contemplating a human skull resting on a piece of crumbling masonry. On the stonework is carved the words *Et in Arcadia Ego,* meaning that even in Paradise there is death.[143] This fact is illustrated by the biblical myth of the Garden of Eden and the Fall of Adam and Eve.

In the seasonal cycle of vegetation and agriculture the Green Man is associated with spring (the Vernal Equinox or May Day) and summer (the Summer Solstice and Midsummer's Day). At Lammastide at the beginning of August however he is transformed into the harvest or corn spirit, represented in English folk song and folklore as the anthropomorphic character John Barleycorn. The corn spirit allegedly inhabits the last sheaf that is cut down in the fields at the end of harvest. John Barleycorn symbolises the divine king sacrificed by Sovereignty, the goddess of the land, to bring fertility to the land and his spilt blood ensures that there will be good healthy crops the following year. It connects the witch-god in both his bright and dark aspects with the seasonal agricultural cycle of the planting of the corn, its growth and eventual harvesting. Sometimes the last corn sheaf is called the Maiden or the Hag indicating the goddess of the land.

On a symbolic, esoteric and spiritual level this seasonal cycle of growing and decay is a metaphor for the human cycle of birth, death and rebirth or reincarnation. As John Matthews says:

"In ancient times the earth was thought of as the Mother of all living things, she who gave life and received it back again through the interment of human remains, through blood sacrifice, through the ritual of spilling human seed upon the earth, and through the yearly replanting of the corn."[144]

In traditional forms of witchcraft this process of eternal return is symbolised by the leaf face of the witch-god as the Green Man, the foliate skull and the legend of John Barleycorn (Cain).

Behind the verdant mask of Green Jack lurks the stag-skull mask of the Lord of Death and the Wild Hunt who rules the year from Hallows (October 31st) to May Day. The god is sacrificed with the silver sickle of the Dark Goddess at Lammastide and at the Autumn Equinox or Michaelmas he journeys to the underworld, the Land of the Dead, the realm of the Old Queen, who is the goddess of death and fate. He crosses the alder bridge or is taken by the ferryman in his boat across the water to the Castle of Roses or the Hollow Hill *'beyond the setting sun'* in the west. The symbolism of the Hollow Hill lends itself to one of the titles of the traditional witch-god as the Lord of the Mound. This mound can be seen in physical terms in the landscape as a prehistoric burial chamber or cromlech, or by an artificial or natural hill such as Silbury, Glastonbury or Merlin's

---

143 Batsford, The Green Man, 1978:126.

144 Matthews, The Quest for the Green Man, 2001:75.

Mount in south-west England, Arthur's Seat in Edinburgh or Tara in southern Ireland.

Glastonbury Tor in Somerset is an archetypal and symbolic example in a physical locality of the underworld as the Hollow Hill. In prehistoric and medieval times the Tor was an island surrounded by water and marshland. Originally it was known in Welsh, the language of the ancient Britons, as *Ynys Wydrin*, the Glass or Glassy Isle, or as *Afallon* (Avalon), the Isle of Apples Trees, the traditional sacred fruit of the underworld and the goddesses in pre-Christian mythology, like Holda who ruled it. The so-called *'Silver Branch'* was an apple branch with blossom and silver bells on it that was given to the queen of the faeries by mortals as a passport to enter the Otherworld.

Anciently Glastonbury Tor was regarded as a *'faery hill'* and the Island of the Dead, one of the entrances on the material plane to Faerie, the Otherworld or the underworld. In the Arthurian cycle of legends the once and future king is taken to Avalon at the end of his life to be healed of his wounds. He is conveyed there in a barge by three queens and one of them is Arthur's half-sister, the mysterious enchantress and *femme fatale* Morgan Le Fay (the Faery). With her company of nine maidens she is the guardian of the healing well at the base of the Tor. Nine is a magical lunar number and some traditional Crafters regard Morgan as an aspect of the witch-goddess.

Morgan (meaning *'woman from the sea'*) is another aspect of the Queen of Faerie. She is personified as a young woman robed in green velvet riding upon a white horse with silver bells on its bridle. In the Scottish folk ballad of *Thomas the Rhymer* he encounters her one May Day morning while sleeping under a hawthorn bush. After they make love all day, she carries him off on her horse. They travel down to the underworld and after a terrifying journey arrive at her castle. Thomas stays there for seven years (the reign of the divine king) and before he returns to Middle Earth the goddess grant him the *'silver tongue'*, the gift of verbal or poetic eloquence, and the power of prophecy or prediction.

In Christian times when the new religion came to Glastonbury the anchorite Celtic saint Collen decided to make his home on the slopes of the Tor. Unfortunately he was trespassing on the realm of its owner and occupier, Gwyn ap Nudd, the Welsh deity who was one of the Children of Don, the ruler of Annwn or the underworld, the king of the faery folk, a leader of the Wild Hunt and today is one of the traditional forms of the god of the witches. It is inevitable that the saint and Gwyn, who the Christian Church regarded as the demon-king, would eventually meet and that conflict would ensue between them.

One day St Collen heard a knock at the door of his hermitage. On answering it he was confronted by a faery messenger from Gwyn requesting a meeting on the mist-shrouded summit of the Tor. Collen refused and the messenger returned two more times, the magical three again, repeating the request. On the third visit he threatened the saint that if he did not attend the meeting it would be the worse for him. Finally Collen reluctantly agreed to meet with his adversary and armed with a flask of holy water and clutching a crucifix he walked up the hill.

On the summit of the Tor the saint was astonished to find the largest and fairest castle he had ever seen in his life. It was occupied by a company of the strongest and best armed warriors, a band of skilled musicians and a herd of fine horses ridden by handsome young men and beautiful maidens. In fact there was everything on top of the hill that one would expect to find in the earthly court of a powerful and rich mortal king.

Collen was invited into the great hall of the castle where Gwyn ap Nudd sat on a high-backed chair made from gold and upholstered in silk. The faery king invited the saint to join him for a meal, but Collen was wise enough to know if he ate the elven food, tempting as it was, he would be trapped forever in the Otherworld. Instead the wily saint threw the contents of the flask of holy water over his host and made the sign of the cross. The demon-king and the castle and all its gay occupants immediately vanished in a cloud of sulphurous smoke.

In the medieval Welsh legends collected by Lady Charlotte Guest in the nineteenth-century and given by her the generic title of *The Mabinogion,* there is a reference to Gwyn ap Nudd. It illustrates his role as the dual-faced god of the seasonal rituals of the Wheel of the Year and his relationship to the witch-goddess. The story tells how Crieddylad, the daughter of King Ludd, and Gwythyr, the son of Greidawl, were to be married. However Gwyn lusted after Crieddylad and he kidnapped her to be his bride instead. Despite the fact he was going up against a god, Gwythyr was so in love he gathered his war-band and sought to rescue his beloved from Gwyn's clutches.

When King Arthur heard what was happening he intervened in the dispute. He summoned both Gwythyr and Gwyn to his court and ordered them to make peace. It was agreed that Crieddylad would live at her father's house and every Beltane (May 1st) until Doomsday her two suitors would fight for her hand. Whoever won the combat would have her company for the year. This annual combat could be the origin of the mythical roles of the God as the Holly King and Oak King in some forms of modern traditional witchcraft, each ruling half of the year as the Lord of the Greenwood and the Lord of the Wildwood.

In winter the God is the Lord of the Wild Hunt and the leader of the Mighty Dead, or ancestral spirits, and the Hidden Company – those witches who have passed to the spirit world and yet have elected to remain earthbound to act as teachers and guides to the living. The mythos of the Wild Hunter with his pack of demonic hell-hounds hunting for the souls of the newly-departed is an important aspect of traditional witchcraft. It provides an essential link between Middle Earth, the material world of mortals, and the spirit world that can be used by the traditional witch to access and communicate with the Other Side.

The Wild Hunt is usually described as a cavalcade or procession that includes goblins, elves and faeries, woodwoses or arboreal spirits, the spirits of those who have suffered a violent or unexpected death and criminals (especially those who have been hanged), miscarried babies and unbaptised children. In south-eastern Europe it was believed that the souls of unbaptised children became *'storm demons'*. They appeared in the shape of birds such as crows and owls, small black children, dogs, cats, mice or chickens and brought destructive gales, hailstorms, illness and death in their wake.

They are connected with other entities who accompany the Wild Hunt known as *'shadows'*. These are malevolent spirits of the dead who appear in either bestial form or as human beings with the heads of dogs, goats and donkeys. They can be seen by those who possess the Sight at crossroads on the night of the new moon. Other spirits of the dead associated with the Hunt are suicides whose wailing as they cross the night sky is sometimes confused by listeners with the howling of the wind.[145]

The Hunt is led by the Wild Hunter who is variously described as a pagan god-like Gwyn ap Nudd, Odin or Woden, Judeo-Christian figures such as Cain the first murderer or the archangels Gabriel or Michael, the Devil or sometimes a mortal personage of royal blood such as the Holy Roman Emperors Charlemagne and Barbarossa, the biblical King Herod or King Arthur, a famous human hero like Sir Francis Drake or a local evil nobleman whose soul is condemned to hunt for eternity.

Odin has many aspects and one of them is the god of the glorious dead who perished in battle. These departed souls of warriors become part of Odin's *Wuothiserheer* or:

"...Furious Army that travels across the night sky with the winter storms. Almost paradoxically this nocturnal procession or cavalcade of the living and the dead is believed to promote the fertility of the land and a sighting of the Wild Hunt is the portent of a good harvest."[146]

Odin's other roles as the master of the runes, restless wanderer, spirit traveller, sorcerer and god of ecstasy relate indirectly to his leadership of the Wild Hunt. He is sometimes described as the *'god of the crossroads'*. This was a liminal place in the landscape which was sacred to Hekate, the Greek goddess of the witches, and where witches gathered and executed criminals where buried. In African-American magical beliefs it was where you met the Devil (possibly originally the African god Eshu) at midnight and he taught you skills like playing the fiddle or guitar or winning at gambling.

---

145 Pocs, Fairies and Witches in South-east and Central Europe, 1989:17.

146 Hasenfratz, Barbarian Rites: The Spiritual World of the Vikings and Germanic Tribes, 2011:98.

Through his position as the Wild Hunter Odin or Woden repeatedly breaks down the rigid structure of normality. In doing so, he simultaneously makes room for the new, the unheard of, and the uncommon, and for movement and change.[147] This has always been the traditional attributes of the god of the witches as the trickster and opposer of divine authority.

A female deity can also lead the Furious Host and these are usually pagan goddesses with some association to death, the underworld, the dead, the moon and witchcraft such as Diana, Hekate and Holda. In the tenth-century CE the *Canon Episcopi* condemned *'wicked women'* who, allegedly deluded by the Devil, believed they rode at night with *'Diana, goddess of the pagans'*. These night-riders were popularly known as *'good women'* (i.e. witches). Traditionally the female leader of the Hunt stole the souls of unbaptised children and punished naughty ones or anyone who did not leave gifts out for her during the liminal Twelve Days of Yule from Christmas to Twelfth Night. Any housewife who dared do spinning or weaving during that period also faced the goddess' wrath and would be cursed with illness or death. This illustrates the witch-goddess as Fate and the ruler of the destiny of human beings.

The witch-goddess is also dual-faced and she has her dark and bright aspects as the Lady of Life and Death, the Creatrix and Destroyer. She can appear as both a beautiful young woman or an old crone or ugly hag and is both the giver and the taker of life. In her bright aspect she is often traditionally represented in the summer season, especially on St John's Eve or Midsummer Eve (June 23rd) as the Queen of Elfhame ('elf home') or Faerie.

However, as we have seen, at Lammas she takes on the more sinister role of Sovereignty or the goddess of the land who is responsible for the death of the divine king or sacrificed god. In this role she grants the kingship of the land *'to whom she pleases'*, providing of course that he is a worthy candidate for the position. In a sacred grove near a lake in Italy sacred to Diana it was said that every seven years two men fought in combat for the right to be her priest. Significantly the winner held the title of *Rex Nemorensis* or *'the king of the woods'* until he was challenged by a new rival.

The mythical personification of the witch-goddess in modern Traditional Craft includes such folkloric and pagan deities from biblical, classical and Northern European mythology as Diana, Hecate or Hekate, Holda, Lilith and the Norns or Wyrd Sisters. The first of these is Diana, the Roman goddess of the forest, hunting and the moon. Catullus's *Hymn to Diana*, dating from the first-century CE, describes her as the queen of the underworld and Diana Trivia, the ruler of the crossroads, where witches and executed criminals are traditionally buried. Diana shares this title with Hekate, the Greek goddess of the dead, the underworld and witchcraft who rules

---

147 Ibid., 2011:99.

over places where three or four roads met. In fact Virgil described Hekate as *'the three faces of the maiden Diana'*. Hekate's other titles include the Queen of Hell and the Mistress of Witches. King James I in his 16th century anti-witchcraft book *Demonologia* (1592) said that Diana is the *'queen of the fairies'* and was worshipped as such by contemporary witches.

Both the Greek Hekate and the Roman Diana are associated with hunting hounds and with the legend of the Wild Hunt. As we have seen, Diana leads the *'good women'* in their nocturnal rides and Hecate's presence is announced by the howling of dogs in the night. Black dogs are also traditionally sacrificed to her. Apollonius of Rhodes stated that Hekate was accompanied by *'death spirits, devourers of life, the swift hounds of Hades who, hovering through all the air, swoop down on the living'*.[148]

Frau Holda, a Central European or Germanic goddess of winter and darkness, was also associated with witchcraft and the Furious Host as the nocturnal supernatural procession of the dead. According to the famous German collector of fairy tales Jakob Grimm: "*Hoselberg [mountain] is at once the residence of Holda and her Host [the Wild Hunt] and a trysting-place of witches.*" Grimm identified Holda with the goddess Freya in Norse mythology and Lady Goda in Shropshire folklore. Goda was a female leader of the Wild Hunt known as the faery queen and a local version of the witch-goddess who took a human husband. The medieval Church may well have confused the Germanic Holda with the classical Diana.

In the 11th century CE Bishop Bernard of Wurms condemned women who had been *'deceived by the Devil'* so they believed they rode on wild animals at night with Holda. In such medieval accounts the names of Holda, Hekate and Diana are interchangeable.[149] The ancient Germans believed Holda was the wife of Woden (the Germanic form of Odin), a male leader of the Wild Hunt. In 1630 a male witch called Diel Breull of Calbach Hesse in Germany confessed to travelling in spirit form to the Venusberg Mountain where he met with *'Dame Holda'*. He described her as a *'fine woman from the front but from the back she is like a hollow tree with rough bark'*. This is a metaphorical description of the bright and dark aspects of the witch-goddess. In 1582 the wife of the archbishop of Salzburg's counsellor was arrested and charged as a *'night traveller'*. It was said that she had travelled to the Unterberg Mountain where she met with the goddess of the witches called Herodias and her retinue, who included faery ladies and mountain dwarves.

In British witchcraft accounts there are references to witches, male and female, travelling to the *'hollow hills'* or faery hills, often associated with prehistoric burial mounds. There they meet with the queen of the faeries and she teaches them herbal knowledge, healing

---

148 Argonautica, 4.1.

149 Wodening, Holda and the Cult of the Witches. The Cauldron, 2010, no. 128.

and divination. One notable case was of John Heydon of Somerset in the 17th century. He was a well-known astrologer in London and had to flee the capital for his life to the West Country after making predictions about the death of the dictator General Oliver Cromwell. In Somerset Heydon claimed to have encountered a green-robed woman at a faery hill. She revealed to the astrologer that she was the queen of the faeries and took him to a *'glass castle'* where she taught him esoteric lore.[150]

Another form of the witch-goddess in traditional modern witchcraft is Lilith, misrepresented and demonised in Judaic propaganda as a night-stalker and succubus who suffocated babies in their cots and preyed on sex-starved men giving them erotic dreams. As one rabbi said: *"One may not sleep alone in a house for whoever sleeps alone is seized by Lilith."* Although not officially a recognised leader of the Wild Hunt, Lilith was the first wife of Adam and according to rabbinical sources with him she *"begot ghosts and male demons and female night demons."* In other versions she gave birth to or spawned elemental spirits, goblins and faeries.

Originally Lilith was also a storm or wind spirit in Sumerian and Babylonian mythology that took the form of a screech owl or dragon and also guarded the Tree of Life. In the Hebrew *Zohar* or *Book of Splendour* her creation is associated with the waning or dark of the moon. In the Middle Ages she was connected with Herodias or Herodiana, possibly the origin of Aradia, the goddess revered by the Tuscany witches in the nineteenth-century (see Charles Godfrey Leland's *Aradia-Gospel of the Witches,* 1899). Herodias was a name for the witch-goddess taken from the wife of the Jewish puppet-king Herod during the Roman occupation of Judea. Herod was, as we have seen, one of the nominated mortal leaders of the Wild Hunt and his wife may have taken a similar role. A medieval carving of Lilith in a German cathedral also shows her in the act of giving birth to a Green Man.

In Scandinavian mythology the Norns or Nornir probably originated in a single primordial earth goddess known as Urthr or Urdr who was the creatrix of life. She later became a triple goddess or triad of goddesses called Urd or Urdr (Fate), Verdanti (Being) and Skuld (Necessity). They were known collectively as the Nornir and they ruled the past, the present and the future. The Norns spin and weave the destiny of the human race, individually and collectively, and the whole fabric of the universe – the web of wyrd or destiny. The three witches on the blasted heath in Shakespeare's Scottish play are based on the Norns and they also appear in fairy tales as faery godmothers predicting the future of the new-born.

The Norns in Northern European mythology were associated with weaving and spinning and they can be compared with the Moirai or Fates. One of these Greek goddesses spun the thread (birth), another

---

150 Jackson, The Call of the Horned Piper, 1994:18, 20 & 22.

measured it (life) and one cut it (death). Therefore like the witch-goddess they have the power over life and death. In fact the modern traditional witch Robert Cochrane said that the true name of the witch-goddess was *'Fate'* and she was the primary deity of all witches.

In modern traditional witchcraft the symbolism of the web and weaving is connected to the spider, the totem animal of the witch-goddess as Fate. The cord as one of the working tools of the traditional witch alludes to the use of nooses, ropes and snares by the goddess of death to lead the departed on their journey to the afterlife. The so-called *'bog bodies'* excavated from peat in many parts of Northern Europe were found strangled with halters or nooses tightened around their necks. The Bronze and Iron Age people who carried out these human sacrifices believed that the bogs and marshes were entrances to the underworld, therefore depositing these corpses in such places with nooses was highly symbolic.

As a modern traditional witch has said:

"Goddesses such as Holda and the folkloric Goda are female leaders of the Wild Hunt who rode out on Walpurgis Night [April 30th] and Hallows Eve [October 31st], with a vast retinue of demons and beings of the Otherworld, to round up the souls of the dead and escort them to the afterlife. We see in these legends goddesses of absolute female power who are fulfilling their divine purpose as they see fit. They exist on the liminal boundaries guiding souls from one world to another. They are guardians, keeping all in balance, life and death in a continuous cycle, so that chaos cannot overturn order – they are not necessarily associated with the light, but with the dark and the underworld."[151]

To understand the role of the Wild Hunter or Huntress as aspects of the witch-god and witch-goddess we have to first understand the mythos behind the legend. By removing the Christian propaganda that has cleaved to it, one can see that the leader of the Host is the harvester of human souls. In fact he or she acts as a psychopomp or guide to the departed on their journey to the underworld – the Hollow Hill, the Isle of the Dead and the Castle of Roses.

Death is the final frontier and the Wild Hunter is the guardian and gatekeeper of the border between the land of the living and the realm of the dead. This can be clearly seen in the myth of Gwyn ap Nudd and his association with Glastonbury Tor. When Christianity took over from the old pagan religions a chapel to St Michael was erected on the Tor. In Judeo-Christian mythology the archangel was the guardian of the gates of Hell preventing the demonic hordes from invading the world.

What is the point of working with the gods and goddesses of death and underworld or indeed with the spirits of the ancestral dead? Necromancy, or the magical ritual of summoning and

---

151 Lucas, The Pale-Faced Goddess. The Cauldron, 2011, no. 141.

communicating with the dead, has always been about obtaining knowledge that is not available to the living. It has been widely believed that those who have left their physical bodies and are now in the afterlife on the Other Side have a superior knowledge and the power of prophecy. In traditional witchcraft as we have seen there is also a belief in the *'Hidden Company'* who act as guides and teachers to those who are still incarnated on the physical plane.

In practical terms, making contact with the ancestral dead, the Hidden Company and the chthonic deities of the Old Craft does not mean a nocturnal trip to the local churchyard to dig up a corpse and magically animate it. Many traditional witches work with a human skull as an oracular vessel. This may date back to the cult of the severed head in the Iron Age and before. Warriors collected the heads or skulls of their enemies because they thought they contained their spiritual essence, power and life force. In magical rituals they were then a way to summon back the spirit of the dead person from the afterlife.

Today human skulls can be obtained quite easily and legally from specialist dealers or on the internet. Alternatively, a wooden death's head carved from a magically suitable wood such as yew and blackthorn can be substituted. To prepare the skull it should be coated with oil of myrrh, which gives it a golden colour and a pleasant smell. Myrrh was traditionally a perfume used in the anointing and embalming of the dead. The bone head should also be anointed with a small amount of the blood of the user or users to form a psychic link. This can be obtained by either lightly cutting the skin with a clean athame or ritual knife or by using menstrual blood. Before using it for the first time in ritual wine, perfumed essential oils and incense can also be used to purify and consecrate the skull accompanied by appropriate charms, incantations and prayers.[152]

Another modern traditional witch, Evan John Jones, has described the magical employment of a human skull as he experienced it as a member of Robert Cochrane's covine in the 1960s. He said that before use the skull should undergo a ritual cleansing in the name of the four elements of fire, earth, air and water. This purifies the object and cleanses it of any association with its past owner so it can then attract any departed spirit.

The ritual cleansing consists of symbolically drawing the breath of the previous owner of the skull out of its nostril cavities, sprinkling it with earth and water and then passing it through the flames of a candle or a fire. This is done three times as that is a primary magical number with occult significance. Finally the skull is placed between two lit candles, life is breathed into it and it is libated with wine. It is then officially given a new name to complete the ritual of purification and consecration. Once this has been accomplished

---

152 Schulke, The Perfum'd Skull, The Cauldron, 2005, no. 116.

the skull can be utilised as a spirit vessel or oracle of prophecy and questions are asked of it by the assembled covine.[153]

In Traditional Craft, as in modern forms of neo-pagan witchcraft, Winter's Night, Hallows Eve or Hallowe'en is the time of the annual ritual when those discarnate spirits of the ancestral dead are invited to return and enter the circle of the living and the Wild Hunt rides the night sky. Although today Hallows is often seen, in both its secular and spiritual celebration, as the primary festival of the dead, it is one of three so-called *'spirit nights'* of the year. The other two are May Eve or Walpurgis Night and Midsummer's Eve, when it is believed that the veil between the worlds is thin. On these nights the faery folk and the spirits of the dead come out of the *'hollow hills'* to roam the countryside and scarecrows come alive in the field. Sensible, God-fearing people stay in their homes with the doors locked and the curtains drawn.

On Hallows Night the spirits of the dead are believed to visit their old homes or those of their relatives, descendants and friends. Food and drink were left out for them or an extra place was set at the dinner table for the ghostly guest or guests. In the old British custom of trick or treating, later taken to North America by Scottish and Irish immigrants, masks and costumes were worn by those going house to house begging for money and food. These were to disguise the wearer's identity, hence they were called *'guisers'*, and also to represent the spirits of winter, the powers of darkness and the dead. Originally the guisers were adults but when the custom was adopted in the United States it was taken over by children going out after dark and asking for sweets from their neighbours. If the treat was not forthcoming then there was a trick such as pelting the front door of the mean person with flour and eggs, tipping over their dustbins or pouring water through their letterboxes.

Before pumpkins were imported into Britain, country people used turnips and swedes to make their spirit lanterns. They were hollowed out and carved with a nose, slit eyes and a grinning mouth to form a goblin face and a lighted candle was placed inside. These *'Jack O' Lanterns'*, a traditional name for the witch-god, were then surmounted on poles or sticks for carrying. Sometimes the lanterns were placed in the windows of houses or on gateposts to ward off evil spirits, the faery folk and witches.

Jack O' Lantern or Will O' the Wisp was originally an elemental spirit whose ghostly light led travellers astray when they passed by marshes. They would see what they thought was a lantern guiding them and fall into the marsh and drown. In traditional Hallows rites today Old Jack O' Lantern is sometimes evoked as a wight or land spirit or as an aspect of the witch-god who can open the *'spirit paths'* or *'corpse roads'* (ley lines) across the countryside. This allows the

---

153 Jones, Witchcraft – A Tradition Renewed, 1990:134-43.

shades of the dead to return along them from the underworld to the land of the living.

In a typical Hallows rite practised in traditional witchcraft black candles are placed on the altar and in lanterns (sometimes made from pumpkins) around the circle. Either the altar or the stang (a forked staff placed upright in the ground representing the Horned God) are decorated with seasonal foliage such as yew, acorns, rowan berries and pine cones. Often two circles are cast to represent the world of the living and the realm of the dead. During the ritual the celebrants pass from one circle to the other symbolising the transition of the departed into the afterlife and the return of the dead from the Other Side. The witch-god and witch-goddess will be called on to attend the rites in their dark aspects as the Lord of the Wild Hunt and the Queen of the Underworld. The spirit paths or ghost roads will then be opened so that the Mighty Dead and the Hidden Company can be invited to join in the celebrations and partake of the houzel or sacramental communion of *'cake and wine'*.

Modern traditional witchcraft is not monolithic in nature. Attitudes and beliefs regarding death and the afterlife in the Craft vary from individual to individual and group to group. Some traditional witches accept the Eastern belief in reincarnation. Others believe that after the death of the physical body the spirit or soul returns to the Source from whence it came. In most cases however there is a firm belief in the afterlife and the spirit world and a two-way communication between the land of the living and the dead.

In the Robert Cochrane tradition the symbol of the double ended spiral or double helix represents the journey of the soul through the world and its eventual liberation from the cycle of birth, death and rebirth. The spiral symbolises the path of the reincarnating soul until it reaches that stage in its spiritual development or evolution when it no longer needs to incarnate in a physical *'coat of flesh'*. When that stage is reached *"...it then becomes part of and at one with the Godhead that is re-creating itself from all the fragments first used to seed the Earth in the form of individual souls."*[154]

During his time in Robert Cochrane's covine in the 1960s, John Jones was taught that the human soul's desire to survive the death of the physical body created a pathway or pathways into the Otherworld to an ancestral place where it awaited rebirth. In Cochrane's words:

"What we have created in thought we create in that other reality.' His belief was that when a witch died they would go to another place that 'both myself and those who have gone before me have created. Without their work it would not exist, it was their faith that built it and it is my believing in it that will secure my inheritance."[155]

---

154 Jones, The Roebuck in the Thicket: An Anthology of the Robert Cochrane Witchcraft Tradition, pp. 99.

155 Quoted in Ibid, pp. 70.

In Cochrane's tradition this *'other place'* was the Rosy Castle or Castle of Roses on an island in the western sea beyond the setting sun. This was the *'glass castle'* or *'four squared castle'* of the witch-goddess. Ancient beliefs state that the incarnated soul comes into the world at birth from the east, facing the rising sun. When the *'silver cord'* is cut and the discarnate soul leaves the physical body however it travels west towards the setting sun where the *'Land of the Dead'* or Paradise is located and awaits rebirth. Traditional witchcraft therefore can be seen as the cult of both life and death as symbolised by the witch-god and witch-goddess in their dual bright and dark aspects.

Bibliography

Batsford, Kathleen (1978) *The Green Man*. D.S. Brewer.

Chumbley, Andrew (2011) *Opuscula Magica – Volume 2: Essays on Witchcraft and Crooked Path Sorcery*. Three Hands Press.

Harte, Jeremy (2001) *The Green Man*. Pitkus Guides.

Hasenfrantz, Professor Hans-Peter (2011) *Barbarian Rites: The Spiritual World of the Vikings and Germanic Tribes*. Inner Traditions.

Jackson, Nigel Aldcroft (1994) *The Call of the Horned Piper*. Capall Bann.

Jones, Evan John with Valiente, Doreen (1990) *Witchcraft – A Tradition Renewed*. Robert Hale.

Jones, Evan John and Cochrane, Robert. Edited and introduced by Howard, Michael (2001) *The Roebuck in the Thicket: An Anthology of the Robert Cochrane Witchcraft Tradition*. Capall Bann.

Letch, Yuri (2007) *Gwyn: Ancient God of Glastonbury*. The Temple Publications.

Lucas, Thresa A. (2011) *The Pale-Faced Goddess*, in *The Cauldron* No 141.

Matthews, John (2001) *The Quest for the Green Man*. Godsfield Press

Pocs, Dr Eva (1989) *Fairies and Witches in South-east and Central Europe*. Svomolalaven Tiedakaonia.

Rabinowitz, Jacob (1998) *The Rotting goddess: Origin of the Witch in Classical Antiquity*. Autonomedia.

Rhys, John (2002) *Glastonbury, Arthur and the Isles of the Dead*. Oakmagic Publications.

Schulke, Daniel A. (2005) *The Perfum'd Skull*, in *The Cauldron* No 116.

Wodening, Swein (2010) *Holda and the Cult of the Witches*, in *The Cauldron* No 128.

THE SETIAN WAY OF DEATH

BY MOGG MORGAN

> *"A new wave of archaeologists has termed the phenomenon of developing and interpreting ancient belief systems from material evidence as the pursuit of archaeological memory."*[156]

In our time the cult of the Egyptian god Seth has experienced a revival. It is represented in various sodalities and tendencies, the newest of which are the *'Companions of Seth'*, which is more of an ideology or *'cloud'* than a formal magical ordering. Companion of Seth is a translation of Middle Egyptian *'Smaut ne Set'* – sometimes rendered as *'Confederates'* or *'Conspirators'* which is pejorative and follows or takes sides with the Followers of Horus against the supposed *'murderers'* of Osiris. Even so, there were priests, priestesses, prophets and chantresses of the cult of Seth from virtually all periods of Egypt's long history. So it is possible to take a less loaded view and approach the mythology from the perspective of that priesthood.

Much has been made of the hieroglyphic pictogram of *'Smaut'* – which is said to be an image of the windpipe and lungs. The Smaut are literally conspirators – in the sense they are those who *'breathe'* together – which may well mean those who breathe together in a yogic sense of those who practice control of prana. Several contemporary Sethian groups have developed this connection.

The psycho-geographical centre of the *'Companions of Seth'* is a place called Ombos or Nubt. Ombos is very similar in name to the cult centre of Sobek the crocodile god, although these are quite distinct places.[157] The real Ombos was only discovered in 1895. Strolling in the desert Flinders Petrie, *"The father of Egyptian archaeology"*, discovered the remains of a very ancient town and nearby a vast necropolis, which he likened to the land of the dead, perhaps the origin of what is called the *'western lands'* of Egyptian mythology.[158]

---

156 Elizabeth Wickert, "Archaeological Memory the Leitmotifs of Ancient Egyptian Festival Tradition and Cultural Legacy in the Festival Tradition of Luxor: the mulid of Sidi Abu'l Hajjaj al-Uqsori and the Ancient 'Feast of Opet'" JARCE 45, 2009.

157 A recent part work called "The Glory of Ancient Egypt" included models of all the Egyptian gods, although Set was represented by Sobek. And I guess one might expect the crocodile to be a "typhonian" animal.

158 Petrie, W M Flinders & J E Quibell (1896a) Nagada & Ballas, London

Each grave is close by another in what to some might seem a communal mash-up. Moreover this necropolis seems to be an integral part of the nearby settlement of the living inhabitants. One might say that at Ombos there is no impermeable barrier between the living and the dead.

The pagan theologian Iamblichus wrote that religion in ancient Egypt was focused on two things:

The cult of the sun, and the continuation of the sun's course

Protecting the mysteries of Abydos – the cult shrine of the god Osiris[159]

This is considered a reasonably accurate view, both of the ancient magical religion and its reflection in, for example, the *'recon'* or revived version as found in sodalities such as the Hermetic Order of the Golden Dawn.

The Mysteries of Abydos contain the archetypal secret of the ancient Egyptian magical religion. It is probably also the *"secret capable of realizing the world-old dream of the Brotherhood of Man"* i.e. that supposedly possessed by many secret societies, such as the Freemasons and the Ordo Templi Orientis.

In later times, Seth was considered bad precisely because he threatened to reveal the ultimate secret of death. To the modern mind, revealing secrets, especially the archetypal ones, is where we are at. Sethian or not, secrets are there to be revealed. So in several important senses, the spirit of the modern age is Sethian.

It was once thought that the elaborate burial practices of high Egyptian culture developed from the archaic burial of the pre-dynastic times. For example natural mummification led to its simulated form in the practice of embalming. Recent research has tended to show that archaic and pharaonic methods represent two different and conflicting traditions (see the work of biomedical Egyptologist Vicky Gash.)[160]

When it comes to exploring so-called *'archaic'* attitudes to death and burial, there is no better place to start than the pre-dynastic city of Ombos. Petrie's early excavation at Ombos revealed many startling differences between the Sethian and Osirian way of death. Indeed the differences were so extreme that Petrie mistakenly thought he had discovered a *'new race'*. The differences are elaborated at some length in my book *The Bull of Ombos*.

My intention here is to extend some of those insights and show their continuing relevance. The original *primitive faith* of the Sethians was unlike the Osirian in that it may have focussed on good rebirth rather than physical resurrection!

---

159 (See Iamblicus De mysteriis VI, 7, 282, see discussion of this in Assmann, Lecture at the Ritual Dynamics and the Science of Ritual Conference, Heidelberg Sept-Oct 2008)

160 Gashe, Vicky, "Investigating Early Mummification" Ancient Egyptian Magazine Feb/Mar 2010

Whether the ancient Egyptians actually believed in reincarnation can be contentious. The ancients certainly thought so although modern scholars such as Henry Breasted thought that Greek writers such as Herodotus were mistaken.[161] Personally I find fairly convincing evidence of a popular belief in reincarnation in the *Tale of Two Brothers*.

The *Tale of Two Brothers* is an extremely interesting story that dates from the reign of Seti II, a New Kingdom king who ruled from 1200 to 1194 BCE. The *Tale of Two Brothers* can be viewed as an alternative version of the classic monomyth in which Seth murders his brother Osiris. The *Tale of Two Brothers* seems to tell the story from the Sethian point of view and perhaps reflects the views of the worshippers of Seth and of an ancient cattle cult. The story comes from a time under the Ramesside Kings when the cult of Seth experienced a revival. Evidence for such a revival comes from the great number of votive images that feature the god Seth.

The two brothers of the tale are Anpu (Anubis) and his younger brother Bata. Bata is another name for Seth. So already we are in unfamiliar territory, as in the *'official'* version of the myth Anubis is the son of Osiris, conceived in a clandestine union with Seth's wife Nephthys. This *liaison dangereuse* leads to much enmity between the partners and is sometimes said to be the motive for Seth's anger toward his brother Osiris.

However in the *Tale of Two Brothers* the roles are different. This time Anubis and Seth are brothers. They are farmers. Bata (Seth) spends much of the day with his beloved cattle in the fields. Anpu's wife has amorous desires for Bata, who she likens to the *'leopard of the south'*. When he rejects her she falsely accuses him of rape. Incidentally if you recognise some of these motifs from elsewhere, for instance the tale of Joseph and his Brothers, that is probably no coincidence.

Furious, Anubis tries to kill Seth. But the cattle warn him of the danger and he flees to the *'valley of the acacias'* (acacias are the sacred tree of Osiris). Bata emasculates himself and tells his brother that from thenceforth he will by magick cause his heart to live in the acacia blossom. If the tree is cut down, the heart will fall to the ground and Bata will die.

Meanwhile in his new home the nine gods take pity on Bata, fashioning for him a beautiful wife, whom the seven Hathors predict will die by the sword. In due course she is tempted away by the god of the Nile (Osiris), and marries the King. Bata is betrayed and his sacred acacia chopped down.

When Anpu's beer froths and wine becomes cloudy he knows his brother is dead. Anpu searches for the heart that has become a seed. When placed in water it revives and returns to Bata's corpse that at

---

161 James H. Breasted, Development of Religion and Thought in Ancient Egypt (London: Hodder and Stoughton, 1912), p. 277.

dawn is a great bull, a white triangle on his forehead, a mark like a vulture on his back, the likeness of a scarab on his tongue.

But again Bata's former wife betrays him. The bull is slaughtered that she may eat the liver. When from the blood a persimmon tree grows, this too she has hewn down to make a box. When a splinter enters her mouth she becomes pregnant with a child who becomes the next king. But remembering his previous life this prince Kaoushou has her judged and executed as the seven Hathors had predicted.

Apart from the many subtle differences in this narrative, it is also a very early example of a belief in the doctrine of reincarnation. It is usual to ascribe the origin of the doctrine to South Asia from whence it found its way into classical Greek sources. But the above and several other stories show its manifestation in ancient Egyptian society at a much earlier date. And that, if you don't mind me saying, is truly remarkable.

Examples such as the above lead me to surmise that ancient Egyptian culture is a lot more diverse than one is sometimes led to believe. For me the sign of a healthy culture would be some manifestation of scepticism and plurality. There is to the modern mind something unsavoury about a culture that appears one-dimensional.

Happily, despite the great distance in time, examples of Ancient Egyptian scepticism have survived. It's perhaps no surprise that Egyptian scepticism centres on the whole notion of bodily resurrection of a kind so well known from the cult of Osiris. The dialogue between a man weary of life with his own 'soul' (Ba) is an example of Egyptian wisdom literature. Sir Alan Gardiner says this is a product of the uncertain times at the close of the sixth dynasty, when various catastrophes were overwhelming Egypt. This is 2200 BCE but already 500 years, perhaps more, after the construction of the Great Pyramid.[162]

"Those who built in granite, who erect halls in tombs of excellent construction, from a time when the builders have become gods, their offering stones are desolate as if they had died [alone] on the riverbank for lack of a surviving relative [to do the honours]." - Dialogue of a man with his soul

I've amended this translation to bring out the sense. The *"builders who have become gods"* is almost certainly a reference to the architect of the pyramids Imhotep who was in later times venerated as a god. This verse therefore tells us of the fate of the pyramids, whose occupants have fared no better than those who died a natural death at the river's edge.

This text has been translated many times since the damaged papyrus was bought from the well-known dealer Anastasi (1780-

---

162 Gardiner (1927) pp. 24.

1857), famous as the source for the *Greek Magical Papyri*.[163] It is therefore quite possible that the above text was once a part of the Theban magician's library.

Several dozen translations have appeared based on Faulkner's hieroglyphic text.[164] Many occultists know this text through Bika Reed's translation *Rebel In the Soul*.[165] Bika Reed was a pupil of the alchemist/philosopher Schwaller de Lubicz, whose Sangraal Foundation continues its' work on Egyptian mysteries.

This highly evocative title stems from Reed's controversial translation of line 43. Faulkner has this line as *"I will ...."* saying in a footnote that he doesn't know the meaning of the word *'niAi'*. Miriam Lichthiem's celebrated anthology of ancient Egyptian literature has this as *"I shall make a [shelter]"*.[166]

These are all quite different to Bika Reed who has the rather startling, *"I am the progeny of the great Ass Iai"*, identifying Iai as the minor deity that appears in the ninth hour of the *Book of Gates* - deriding the evil serpent Apep/Apophis.

Professor James P Allen, who has just published his own extended study of this text, says that *"Bika Reed's translation is graphically and grammatically impossible. The text is jw.j r jrt njAj 'I am to make a njAj.' Although we do not know for certain what a njAj is, its determinative associates it with a shade, and it can be grammatically only the object of jrt 'make.' Reed's works are idiosyncratic and are not accepted as useful by any Egyptologist I know."*[167]

I mention all this as it shows how we occultists often taken a piece of misinformation and run with it. I'm told that Bika Reed's *Rebel in the Soul* was one of William Burroughs favourite books and hugely influential on works such as *'Seven Souls'*. This kind of Surrealist mis-hearing has been very creative within occult circles and maybe we have to accept it as part of the way creativity works for us.

The idea that the rebellious part of our psyche would be somehow related to the god Seth just seems too good an insight to lose. The god Iai[168] is a genuine if fairly obscure deity with clear Setian tendencies. That the scepticism of a kind clearly evident in *"Dialogue of a man with his soul"* would be a Sethian trait seems reasonable.

---

163 Betz, H D (1986) Greek Magical Papyri In Translation. Introduction.

164 Faulkner, R A (1956) JEA 42 pp21-40. De Lubizc (1997)

165 Translation Reed 1987.

166 Translation in Lichtheim, M (1980) Ancient Egyptian Literature, Vol 1.

167 Personal communication. Allen, J P, (2011) Dialogue between a man and his soul is published by E J Brill.

168   See Piankoff, A & N Rambova (1954) Ancient Egyptian Religious Texts & Rpresentations Vol III Book of Gates 9th hour from tomb of Ramses iv. IAii - "The Old One", plural iwyw for group with iAi moving against Apep. This scene and the famous one in the upper register where entity double headed as Horus-Seth stand against Apep. All this suggests a Setian connection with the diety iAi.

This is borne out by the mythology of the God Seth, who often threatens sacrilege by revealing the best kept secrets of gods – the inner mysteries of the cult of Osiris at Abydos.

Every year at Abydos in the month of Khoiak (October/November) the cult image of Osiris was taken out of its inner sanctum on a special ritual boat and carried by priests to a spot in the desert thought to be the last resting place of the god. Everyone got to see the procession but what happened at the tomb in the desert was mysterious and secret. There is the origin of the notion of the magical secret. It probably involved the whole process by which Osiris was killed, something never depicted in any surviving images or mythological narrative. Not surprisingly Seth threatens to reveal all. This secret is complex and there are no doubt many different interpretations. No doubt it has something to do with death, perhaps something within the process of mummification although it must also be something more than the already well-known facts.

Whatever the secret, it was something known to Seth and his companions, for how else could he threaten to reveal it – you cannot reveal something of which you have no knowledge. It is probably also true that the followers of Osiris find something about this hidden knowledge taboo and therefore disturbing. It was this line of reasoning that led me to the ideas that the complex mortuary temple of Seti I at Abydos may show this mystery in plain sight and that it must be somehow connected with the Osirieon, a secret chamber once connected to the main temple by tunnels. At the risk of letting my imagination run away with me in *'Dynasty'* fashion, perhaps Seth threatens to reveal that he is in fact the father of Horus!

To consider what might have happened in the Osirieon, it helps to consider more closely the Sethian way of death. I feel it is possible to discern an alternative within Egyptian magical religion. And this alternative is as relevant today as it was right at the beginning of Egyptian civilization circa six thousand years ago. Indeed there are aspects of the Sethian *'Plan B'* that seem more viable than the Osirian way of mummification and elaborate burial.

The Sethian two stage burial

The high profile necropolises of the Valley of the Kings or Queens grab our attention. But no less important historically are the ancient and often enormous archaic cemeteries that have their own tale to tell. Flinders Petrie discovered the lost citadel of Seth, ancient Nubt situated near modern day Nagada in Upper Egypt. Cheek by jowl with this urban settlement were the burials of the ancient inhabitants. The relationship between the living and the dead was very intimate in ancient Nubt. Petrie tells us that the necropolis was used over a long period of time and some burials are intrusive on others (i.e. the graves spaces were reused.) Many tombs were very close indeed to the houses, so close that sometimes well shafts and water courses pass through them. As is common in archaic settlements, children were sometimes buried under the floors of the houses. It is difficult to avoid some sort of symbolic meaning here, as if those who died in childhood were keep especially close so that they might in some way return. I'm reminded that when the Irish occultist and Golden Dawn initiate Maud Gonne lost her first (illegitimate) child to perinatal death, she was advised by fellow occultists to conceive again over the child's grave in order to channel her back.

Objects in these tombs show a marked degree of cardinality – i.e. they are placed at one of the four major directions. It is usually said that the principles of cardinality are bequeathed to us by the ancient Egyptians. North/South is the direction of the Milky Way. East/West is the path of the sun from dawn to dusk. The Egyptian word for left is same as East, i.e. it is predicated on one facing South, the direction of the Nile. Most graves at Nubt are oriented North -South whereas Osirians favoured an East/West.

The most common position for laying out a corpse was the foetal crouch, the knees drawn up to the chest, head to the north, facing east. (Figs 1-3, see photos). Very significantly, many of the graves, including at least a dozen that were undisturbed since the inhumation, show evidence of post mortem dismemberment, the bones rearranged, the feet or hands removed and often the skull inverted and placed nearby. It was this feature that led Petrie to say initially that these burials could not be Egyptian and the origin of his belief that he had found a new race. It's a bit of a digression but in 2011 London's Petrie museum organised an exhibit of the influence of Victorian racial and eugenicist theories on Egyptian archaeology.[169] It is an aspect of Victorian archaeology one has to negotiate when re-analysing the material.

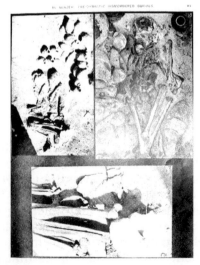

Pre-dynastic dismembered burials at El Gerzeh.

---

169   "Typecast: Flinder Petrie & Francis Galton", Exhibit 29th March – 22nd December 2011

No subsequent research has doubted what Petrie found. Excavations at another predynastic site at Gerzeh in the Feyyum provide published photographs of skeletons from the dozen undisturbed graves. Careful inspection confirms the tampering (see photos and captions).[170] At Nagada Tomb 5 from supposed high status cemetery T, provides clearest evidence (see sketch). Of this Petrie writes:

"[T5] This grave is one of the largest, but has every appearance of having never been opened. The valuable polished stone vases stood in perfect order, upright on the floor, the stone beads remained; etc ... Six skulls lay in the grave and a large quantity of bones, but not a single bone lay in connection with its fellow, The skulls lay on the floor, some close to the upright stone jars on either side of them. A mass of bones, many broken at the ends, and some split, lay together on the floor in a heap about two feet across and several inches high. Etc ..."[171]

Post-mortem decapitation is pregnant with symbolism and resonates throughout the Egyptian mythology. Petrie and his colleagues, notably Gerald Averay Wainwright and Margaret Murray, looked to what was then the lively disciple of European folklore for points of comparison. Could this, so they reasoned, be an indication that the people of Nubt thought the dead were somehow a danger to the living? Or perhaps this headless state had some other significance? Spell 43 in the *Book of Coming Forth by Day* (otherwise known as the *Book of the Dead,*) is a protection against decapitation:

"I am a Great one, the son of a Great One, I am a flame, the son of a flame, to whom was given his head, after it had been cut off. The head of Osiris shall not be taken from him and my head shall not be taken from me. I am knit together, just and young, for I indeed am Osiris, the Lord of Eternity."[172]

The *Pyramid Texts* are well known as the oldest of all religious scripture. Some of these texts reflect burial practices that are even older, in for example earthen graves beneath tombs built of mud brick.[173] The *Pyramid Texts* occasionally say that the body is placed in a sack or shroud, a practice older than the use of wooden and stone coffins.[174] Victorian commentators such as Gerald Wainwright think that the numerous references to decapitation, etc. are more than metaphors but are directly linked to pre-dynastic burial

170 Petrie, Flinders, G A Wainwright & E Mackey (1912) The Labyrinth Gerzeh and Mazguneh, BSA

171 Petrie, Flinders, Ballas & Nagada pp. 32

172 "Chapter for preventing a man's decapitation in the God's Domain" Raymond Faulkner Trans (1990) The Ancient Egyptian Book of the Dead.

173 Allen, James P (2005) The Ancient Egyptian Pyramid Texts, Society of Biblical Literature 2005:4.

174 Allen, James P (2005) Recitation 152 in long litany in Unas Pyramid.

practice.[175] Many aspects of the layout of the pyramid tombs and their texts are mysterious.[176]

Or what are we to make of *"Oh Teti! Your head has been tied to your bones for you, your bones have been tied to your head for you."*[177]? Wainwright gathered together various other examples from the *Pyramid Texts* that seem to require dismemberment.[178] Consider the celebrated *"Cannibal Hymn"* from the Pyramid of Unas:

"The King is one who eats men and lives on the Gods. . .

The King eats their magick, swallows their spirits."

(PT 273-74)[179]

More cautious modern commentators tend to favour metaphorical interpretations rather than the more sensational views such as Wainwright's. In Ancient Egypt decapitation was a common method of dispatch for human enemies, criminals & animals. So the argument goes, decapitation becomes symbolic of all kinds of death and therefore reverse decapitation as in *"your head is tied to your bones"* merely symbolises resurrection.[180]

Our instincts may revolt at the idea of dismemberment or ritual cannibalism, it may seem primitive and not how we want to view the high religion of Ancient Egypt. When in doubt call it a metaphor. But are we just being uptight?

I say there is nothing disrespectful about the Sethian way – after all when one learns the details of Osirian mummification, the process is hardly less intrusive and is tantamount to dismemberment followed by an elaborate reassembly. I say it's all relative. The Sethian way is simpler and perhaps, because of this, arguably more respectful and less alienating.

I was reminded by my friend Jack Daw that dismemberment is fairly common in Neolithic and indeed even Iron Age burials and in his opinion is more respectful than forms of mummification. After all, mummification constructs a fetish object to which a soul is bound, perhaps for a very long time. Dismemberment releases the spirit,

---

175 Wainwright wrote a famous chapter on dismemberment in Petrie, Flinders, G. A. Wainwright & E Mackey (1912) The Labyrinth Gerzeh and Mazguneh, BSA. Some of the evidence evaporates in more modern translations viz: "May Unas be dismembered as you [gods} are dismembered." Becomes "May Unas be furious as you gods are furious" in James P Allen's up-to-date translation. Allen (2005) Recitation 154.

176 The dual axis, Why does the ascension run west east then veer off to the other axis which is south north. (See Allen (2005) Introduction.

177 Wainwright, G.A. in Petrie et al (1912) quoted in Chapter V "The Ritual of Dismemberment" pp. 11. Translation here by Allen (2005) Recitation 144 in Teti's Pyramid

178 Allen, James, P "The Pyramid Texts verse 144, pp. 72. Wainwright quotes this as pp. 104 in the Maspero, Inscrps des Pyramids de Saqqarah.

179 Allen, James P (2005)

180 Eyre, Christopher (2002) The Cannibal Hymn, Liverpool

allowing them to return to the elements and perhaps therefore be reborn.[181]

But, if you'll forgive the pun, it was an obvious bone of contention amongst the cult followers of Osiris who may indeed have had a horror of the earlier, Sethian way of death that possibly involved dismemberment and, as some archaeological evidence indicates, decapitation.

What would be the modern equivalent? Perhaps organ donation is a form of post mortem dismemberment. I predict that organ donation will become more common amongst contemporary Sethians as a result. (My grandmother donated her husband's body for dissection; it was her fourth so perhaps she had become unsentimental!)

In modern times burial in the necropolis is once again the prerogative of the relatively wealthy. Many choose cremation for reasons of economy. But then again cremation would also qualify as Sethian practice. The burning of a corpse is anathema to the true Osirian, see for example the following Spell:

"I will neither be burnt not scorched, for I am Babai, the eldest son of Osiris for whom all the gods have assembled within his Eye in Heliopolis; I am the trusted heir when the Great one is inert my name will be strong for me, and assuredly you will live daily through me."[182]

Or consider natural burial, which could also be viewed as a modern version of the Sethian death rites. One of the pre-requisites for the kind of natural burial I personally favour is that the body is not embalmed with noxious chemicals that are the modern equivalent of the natron used by the ancient Egyptians. There is no legal requirement for embalming, in which the blood is drained and replaced by the embalming fluid, a blend of formaldehyde, methanol and ethanol. America uses 20 million litres of embalming fluid every year.

If after washing and plugging various orifices with cotton wool the un-embalmed cadaver is kept in a cool, unheated room it remains largely stable until the funeral, which can be within a week to ten days. A longer interval makes it easier for our modern far-flung families to come together although too long and it can become an emotional burden. Or the cadaver could be stored in a mortuary and come home for the night before interment or cremation. The laying out room needs to be kept cool but otherwise people can visit to pay last respects, undertake death rites, burn incense etc. My personal preference is to avoid those awful services in churches or funeral homes. Meet at the graveside with an awning if needed to keep off the inclement weather.

Returning to the topic of the archaic Sethian burials found at Nagada. The headless state brings to mind the lines from a later

---

181 Private conversation.

182 Spell 63a "Chapter for drinking after and not being burnt by fire" Raymond Faulkner Trans (1990) The Ancient Egyptian Book of the Dead.

invocation of Seth discovered amongst the *Greek Magical Papyri*, known in contemporary magick as *Liber Samekh.*

I've argued in several places that this is an exorcism rite that draws upon the power of several deities but principally the god Seth. Certainly from the time of the Hyksos in Egypt's 2nd Intermediate Period (c. 1500 BCE) and arguable even before, Seth was called upon to counter several life threatening disease entities personified as demons. It's as well to keep in mind the fact that in Ancient Egyptian magical-religion there was no impermeable line drawn between gods and demons. All the gods of the pantheon are capable of *'demonic'* behaviour, perhaps none more so than Seth.

So for example in the *Pyramid Texts* one reads the following banishing rite:

"May Osiris not come with his evil coming. Do not open your arms to him ..."[183]

From the time of the *Pyramid Texts* one could invoke the strength of Seth as protector. He was a powerful storm god who literally *raves* against dangerous spirits. At the climax of the ritual of Jeu the Hieroglyphist, the magician assumes the form of the God and says, amongst other things, *'I am the headless demon with my sight in my feet'.*[184] This latter is perhaps another reference to the tampering of head and feet observed in pre-dynastic *'Sethian'* burials.

A small group of Companions of Sethians have been working with this ritual material and have found that it leads to an unexpected meditation on death. Our Companions of Seth egregore distinguishes us from existing Sethian groupings such as The Temple of Set. This is not to pass an opinion one way or another on these groups, it's just that we are different, and perhaps grounded in the UK's distinct traditions of libertarianism. *'Companions of Seth'* is a possible reading of the Ancient Egyptian *'Smaiut en Seth'*, although this often appears in the Egyptological literature as the pejorative *'Confederates of Seth'.* The hieroglyph *'smaiut'* depicts a windpipe and lungs. [See image]. It therefore has connotes two or more people are of one mind in the sense that they are breathing together or sharing a breath, literally to con-spire.

To our post modern sensibility sharing breath is far from negative. It evokes ideas from Yoga and Taoism. And indeed this interpretation isn't really foreign to Egyptian iconography. Normative images of Horus and Seth show them intertwined by the emblematic plants, the blue lily for the southland, the papyrus for the North. Both gods rest their feet upon the smauit hieroglyph, indicating that they are of one breath, and one mind. [See image]

It is a notable fact that Yogic approaches to Egyptian magical-religion have emerged over the course of time, and the material

---

183 Pyramid Texts, § 1267, utterance 534.

184 Betz (1986: 103 [PGM V 145]) reproduced with some extra material in Morgan (2010) Wheel of the Year in Ancient Egypt.

seems to drawn one in such a direction. See for example the trajectory of adepts such as Nicholas Shreck and Zeena La Vey.[185]

Currently we begin our rite with the opening based on the ancient Egyptian Heptagram[186] or seven vowel opening, followed by the formal ritual based on the *"Liber Samekh/Rite of Jeu the Painter of Hieroglyphs"*. We supplement this with music based on material from the Egyptian-Arabic Zar exorcism cult.[187] When we are suitably tranced out we settle back into the death posture, cover ourselves with shrouds and mentally go down into the earth, envisioning ourselves at the point of death.

One of the first things to emerge was the importance of the line *"My name is a heart girt with a serpent"*. In ancient Egyptian *'anthropology'* the heart is the important seat of consciousness, perhaps also the soul, here represented as the Ba bird which is often represented as hovering over the heart. It's notable that in ancient rites of mummification the heart was left in situ. The serpent as a protective entity is a well known aspect of the Egyptian magical religion. There are many examples of its use to protect the heart.

The technique of *'encircling'* is an ubiquitous bit of Egyptian magical *'mechanics'* still widely used by all styles of practitioner. Consider the hieroglyphic image of the cartouche in which the name of the famous person is encircled by a rope. This is more than stylistic but is an ancient act of encircling magick whereby the encircling of the name protects its owner.

In our group, as we went deeper into the trance we found ourselves rehearsing our own death. This is a quintessentially Egyptian attitude. Contemporary occult doctrine would no doubt concur that psychological preparedness for death is somehow better than denial.

To do this safely one needs to feel protected. The phrase *'Empty spirit'* in *'Liber Samekh'* is almost certainly an ancient magical technical term. It tells us that such magical operations are to be approached with an *'empty spirit'*. There are several different interpretations of what this might mean. For us it seemed to go hand in hand with the assumption of the posture of death. It is during those moments of emptying out when one can also feel vulnerable to psychic attack. The ubiquitous demons of the Egyptian world are waiting to fill the vacuum. At this key moment we all felt that Lord Seth really was there to see us through. Very many ancient Egyptian texts testify to this healing and prophylactic role of Lord Seth, especially in the direst circumstances when noxious demons attack.

---

185 Demons of the Flesh: The Complete Guide to Left Hand Path Sex Magic, (2002) Zeena & Nikolas Schreck

186 See also Flowers, Stephen, Hermetic Magick: Weiser for another version of this rite.

187 See for example Lewis, I Ecstatic Religion, Penguin but also search for MAKAN online.

He has power over all the *'demons'* that manifest at such moments. To have such a strong ally really is a boon.

This leads me to thoughts of whether the Ancient Egyptian magical-religion really is all about death or as I suspect, that the dead are used for the benefit of the living? Archaeological memory and textual analysis provides countless examples of this. I suppose a controversial example of archaeological memory would be the revelation of tomb robbery. Many fine elaborate funeral assembles were, as is well known, robbed in antiquity by the locals. This speaks volumes for how the ordinary Egyptians viewed the funeral process. In my book on supernatural assault traditions I draw attention to the first things that the ancient tomb robbers took from King Tut's - the *'booze'*; many gallons of alcohol blended with the much valued narcotic blue lily. [188] Use of the dead? Perhaps?

Another more fruitful example would be the age-old Egyptian practice of writing to the dead. This was common. Many examples of such letters exist showing the continued Egyptian belief in the presence of the ancestors waiting to receive the letters. To me, writing to the recently deceased has great cathartic value. It is interesting that these letters, often written on domestic objects such as small bowls, are the first recorded messages of Egyptian women. The Egyptians went beyond mere pleasantries to enlisting their dead ancestors as allies in the otherworld, giving them specific tasks:

"Behold, this vessel was brought, because of this your mother shall decide. It would be pleasant if you agreed with her. Moreover, cause that one will bear a healthy male for me, as you are the excellent transfigured one (Akh). Furthermore behold these two servant girls who cause Seni to be unhappy, (namely) Nefer-Tentet and Itai - drop them.

Keep away from me all afflictions directed at my wife, for you know I have a need for this. May you live for me in order for the Great One to praise you. May the face of the great god be joyous because of you, so that he will give you pure bread with both his hands."[189]

It also strikes me that the dead literally are intermediaries between the world of the gods and our own.

To finish I'd like to again focus on the ancient necropolis at Nagada and to observe the most obvious way one might use the dead. Earlier we learnt of the possible dismemberment, arrangement and with all respect partial eating of the corpse.[190]

---

188 Morgan, 2010, Supernatural Assault in Ancient Egypt, Mandrake

189   Vessel   Chicago,   Chicago-Haskell   Oriental   Mus.   13945
First Intermediate Period

190 Petrie (1897:32).

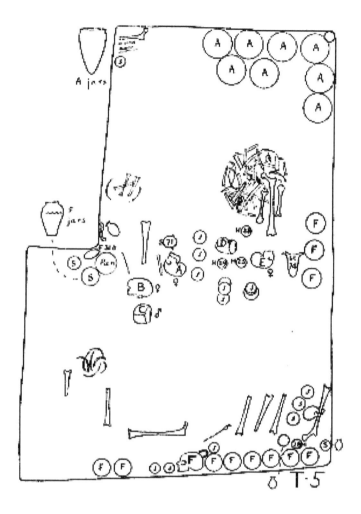

T.5 grave at Nagada.

The eminent pre-historian of Ancient Egypt, the late Michael Hoffman doubted the ritual cannibalism thesis because the bones, so he says, show no evidence of charring which is elsewhere characteristic of cannibalism and enables marrow extraction. Actually Petrie says that three human finger bones were found in a trench full of ashes, two of them burnt.[191] The report also describes how the marrow has been scooped out of some of the long rib bones in tomb T5 and there are signs of gnawing which cannot be attributed to animal disturbance.[192]

Hoffman does however confirm the unusual nature of grave T5, found whole and undisturbed, with piles of human remains piled

191 Petrie et al (1912) op cit, pp. 9.
192 Petrie et al (1912) op cit.

along the walls indicating secondary burial. Hoffman thought this all pointed not to cannibalism but human sacrifice, perhaps of low status *'retainers'.*[193]   However, later commentators point out that there is no evidence that any of these five individuals suffered violent deaths and that some unusual cut marks on the bodies could be posthumous. So the controversy continues.

James Cole is a researcher at Southampton University into archaeology and human remains. James has published a useful checklist for: *"any claim that cannibalism took place."* These signatures are:

- Lack of a cranial base (to get to the brain) on otherwise complete or near complete skeletons.

- The virtual absence of vertebrae (due to crushing or boiling to get at marrow and grease).

- Cut and chopmarks: result of striking the bone surface with a sharp stone tool leaving a deep, wide V-shaped scar (related to cutting strong muscle attachments or dismembering).

- Cutmark arrangement: position, number and placement on element (whether on muscle/ligament attachments etc).

- Long bone breakage (to get at the bone marrow).

- Anvil abrasions left where a bone has rested on a stone anvil whilst it is broken with a hammer stone.

- Comparable butchering techniques in human and animal remains: incidence, position and type of cut and chopmarks on human and animal/food bones should be directly comparable (although allowance should be made for anatomical differences between humans and animals).

- Post processing discard: have the bones been treated in the same way as the faunal remains? Indicating that hominins and animals were treated the same way in terms of food preparation and discard.

- Evidence of cooking in the form of burnt bone. If present this evidence would seem to suggest the comparable treatment of human and animal remains.

- Peeling: a roughened bone surface with parallel grooves or fibrous texture is produced when fresh bone is fractured and peeled apart.

- Percussion pits: the point of impact where a stone or any solid matter struck the bone cortex and scarred the surface.

- Scraping marks: the result of periosteal and muscle removal by scraping the bone surface and identified by a concentrated

---

193 Hoffman, M (1984) Egypt Before the Pharaohs, Arkana pp. 116.

series of parallel and superficial striations on a broad area of bone.[194]

The idea that the Sethians of Nagada had some tradition of ritual cannibalism is corroborated by other sources, notably the mythology. Perhaps cemetery T et al were remote in order to facilitate the practice? I can hear you thinking, ritual cannibalism seems hardly more savoury than ritual human sacrifice. But I'd argue that the memory of human sacrifice is preserved in most if not all of the world's religions as an enduring symbol. In some cases this is includes a continuing physical practice in, for example, male circumcision.

I'd also say ritual cannibalism fits with the desire for good rebirth. It is part of what "...*some archaeologists think is this process involving the breaking down of individual personalities, individual people, as they crossed over to the spirit world and entered the community of ancestors.*"[195]

Perhaps we could link this with the slightly more general idea of 'eating magick'. 'Eating magick' was another core technique of Ancient Egyptian magick. Robert Ritner's ground-breaking study of the same[196] tells us that the precedent for this style of magick is the so-called *Cannibal Hymn* from the *Pyramid Texts* quoted earlier. Eating magick is well represented in contemporary practice under the terms Eucharist magic, well known in Christian liturgy, or famously in *'Sabbatic'* Craft which is characterised by its increased emphasis on the Sabbatic feast and wine, etc. In most cases these can be viewed as symbolic cannibalism. Let me remind you that the bread symbolises the divine flesh and wine the blood.

Beyond that it becomes more controversial although I'd still say explicit cannibalism is there in normative magical practice. It may be controversial, but a great number of magical groups use blood in their rites although following the clarifications offered by Aleister Crowley, I am of course talking about menstrual blood and semen – despite the reframing this is still human flesh. This was consumed in his Gnostic Mass in a special prepared *'cake of light'*.

The use of bread in ritual has a very old pedigree. For instance the *'Myth of the Divine Cow'* stems from the time of oft-called *'Neolithic revolution'*, eight millennia in the past, when bread was substituted from human flesh and ochre flavoured beer for blood, all to placate the raging goddess Hathor.[197] Ancient Egypt developed the

---

194 Consuming Passions: Reviewing the Evidence for Cannibalism within the Prehistoric Archaeological Record (2006) James Cole by James Cole "It is evident that it is insufficient to assign the general term 'cannibalism' to a single 'signature' left on a hominid skeletal assemblage. Rather, by combining the signatures it is possible to identify, in certain circumstances, the specific type of cannibalism practiced."

195 Wallis (2004)

196 Ritner, Robert (1993) The Mechanic of Ancient Egyptian Magical Practice, Chicago.

197 Morgan (2009) "Seth: Demonic Initiator" in Rogers, The Blood Sacrifice, Mandrake.

ritual mechanics of this to a high degree, with special kinds of bread baked for ritual use. Pesen bread is a bit like our own *'Pitta'* or pocket bread. They also utilised miniature loafs in offerings, very like contemporary bread sticks or Italian *grissini*.

Classical sources give an example of the use of a special consecrated round bread loaf stamped with the image of a bound Ass. *"In Busiris and Lycopolis ... they make round cakes in the festival of the months Payni (Apr-May) and Phaophi (Aug-Sep), as an insult they stamp on them an image of the bound Ass."*[198]

The god Seth is often depicted as a bound Ass, certainly in Egypt as ruled by the Greeks and even before. Very old ritual dramas discovered in Egypt in both papyrus and inscribed on the walls of the temple of Horus at Edfu flesh out these rites. They were probably public mystery plays performed at specific festivals. Act III of the reconstructed play requires a cake stamped with an image of the Hippopotamus, (a more common avatar of Seth in the Middle Kingdom and earlier):[199]

"[Stage Direction.] Bringing in the hippopotamus in the form of a cake before Him-With-The-Uplifted-Arm. Dismembering by the Butcher. Recital of the Book Against Him by the Chief Lector on the twenty-first day of the second months of Proyet [Winter Solstice]."

...

[Isis] *"The foes bow down and are destroyed forever, O thou Avenger of thy Father. Come that I may instruct thee. Consign his foreleg to the House of the Prince, for thy father Osiris, while his shank remained in Dep for thy great father. Let his shoulder be taken to Hermopolis for Thoth, the great one in the valley. Give his ribs to Great-of Strength and his breast to Wnwt. Give the great meat-portion of him to Khnum in the Temple, his neck to Uto of the Two Uraeus-goddesses, for she is thy great mother. Give his thigh to Horus the Primordial One, the great god who first came into being. Give his liver to Sepa and his fat to the disease-demons of Dep. Give his bones to Hme-iyt, his heart to the Lower-Egyptian Songstress, Mine is his forepart, mine is his hinder part, for I am thy mother whom he oppressed. Give his tongue to the Yong Harpooner, the best of his inward parts to ... Take for thyself his head and so assume the White Crown and the office of thy father Osiris. What remaineth of him burn in that brazier of the Mistress of the Two lands. Ra hath given thee the strength of Mont, and for thee, O Horus, is the jubilations."*[200]

Modern commentators think the ancients used this talismanic cake in order to facilitate the act of public/symbolic derision of Seth.

---

198 Gwyn Griffiths, J (1970) trans of Plutarch's Isis & Osiris, Swansea. P 135. Verse 30 & commentary.

199 Blackman, A M & H W Fairman (1935/1944) "The Ritual Drama at Edfu" in Journal of Egyptian Archaeology Vol 21:26-36 (1935); Vol 28:32-38 (1942); Vol 29:2-36 (1943); Vol 30:5-22 (1944).

200 Blackman & Fairman op cit Act III scene iii

Although I feel sure that the use of bread also makes it easier for the celebrants to eat Seth. Eating is a well-attested method by which one absorbs the essence of an enemy and indeed a friend. Many contemporary pieces of Sethian liturgy use actions such as the above whose original intent is uncertain or ambiguous.

My thesis throughout the analysis of Egyptian mythology is that the texts themselves benefit from a little dismemberment or deconstruction. It seems to me that the triumphant faith of the Osirians often used liturgy whose origins are obscure and could possibly be derived from the cult that they are absorbing. In other words, it seems possible that the eating of the god can be a friendly or an unfriendly act depending upon one's point of view! Thus, as a contemporary Sethian I feel perfectly happy about reusing, reframing and reclaiming what ultimately was devised by the Sethians. In this we follow the common postmodern perspective, reclaiming pagan liturgy from *'survivals'* in the cults of their enemy.

Demeter's Wrath: How The Eleusinian Mysteries Attempted To Cheat Death

By Caroline Tully

Of all the ancient Mediterranean Mystery Religions, those concerning the grain goddess Demeter and her daughter Kore were the oldest and most famous. Celebrated for one thousand years at the Greek city of Eleusis and then suppressed during the Christian era, the Mysteries have again become the focus of Pagan attention. Beginning in Britain in 1888 with the Hermetic Order of the Golden Dawn, who incorporated titles of Eleusinian religious officials into their initiatory structure, attempted revivals of the Mysteries of Eleusis have been subsequently performed by many Pagan groups. Some of the more famous names include Aleister Crowley, whose *Rites of Eleusis* - a staple of the ritual calendar of the Ordo Templi Orientis - while valuable, have no real basis in the ancient Eleusinian mysteries. Other groups that have re-staged modern Eleusinian Mysteries are the US-based New Reformed Orthodox Order of the Golden Dawn and the Church of All Worlds, while author Jennifer Reif has published her reconstruction as *Mysteries of Demeter*. A perpetually fascinating subject to the modern Pagan, the secret rites of Demeter and Persephone at Eleusis are thoroughly deserving of study and attempted reconstruction. This article is my contribution so far to the contemporary Pagan discourse concerning these ancient Mysteries.

While we tend to think of the Eleusinian Mysteries as being centred on agriculture, in fact they were just as much, if not more, concerned with life after death. Chthonic deities such as Demeter, Persephone and Hades - the main gods of the Eleusinian Mysteries - were responsible not only for the crops in the ground, but for the human dead. The early Greek view of death and what lay beyond it was pessimistic to say the least. The dead were believed to go to the realm of Hades which was situated underneath the earth and characterized by gloom and darkness. This was the universal destination of the dead, a place that contained both aristocrats and common people. Only lucky heroes like Menelaus, who through his marriage to Helen daughter of Zeus, got to go to a pleasant destination such as *Elysion*. Everyone else, destined for the subterranean kingdom of Hades, could expect their souls to exist as insubstantial wisps, flitting about like bats in a cave. There were no redeeming features of the underworld where it seems that even great heroes led a glum existence. In the *Nekyia* (underworld scene) of Homer's *Odyssey*, Achilles tells Odysseus *"I would rather follow the plough as thrall to another/ man, one with no land allotted to him and not much to live on,/ than be king over all the perished dead."* It was no wonder, then, that the Greeks tried to make the most of life on earth by performing outstanding deeds in order to leave a lasting memory.[201]

During the Late Archaic period (800–500 BCE) however, attitudes began to change from a general acceptance of death to an outlook expressing greater anxiety about the afterlife and the possibility of post-mortem happiness. Alongside this change in attitude arose reassuring religious responses such as the Eleusinian Mysteries - first mentioned in the *Homeric Hymn to Demeter* composed around 650–550 BCE - which promised to modify the participant's lot in death.[202] The Eleusinian Mysteries were an optional activity within the wider sphere of Greek religion[203] and operated from the Archaic into the Late Imperial period, probably ceasing around 395 CE.[204] Dedicated to the goddess of the grain, Demeter and her daughter Persephone, entry into the Eleusinian Mysteries was via initiation. Unlike regular religion which was public, held in the day time and consisted primarily of animal sacrifice and sharing a feast with the gods, the content of the Mysteries was secret, rites were held at night and their content was privy only to those who had been initiated. Whereas regular religion was a way of maintaining right relations with the gods and essentially emphasized the vast chasm between mortals and immortals, the Eleusinian Mysteries on the other hand, involved direct experience of the divine and provided a much closer association with the two goddesses.[205]

The Eleusinian Mysteries may have started off as agriculturally-oriented rites, but by the 6th century BCE they had become mysteric. The benefits that the Mysteries offered initiates were success in life- probably of an agricultural nature- along with modification of their fate in death. Initiates did not expect to escape death,[206] but probably looked forward to a more pleasant experience in the underworld.[207] Held annually, the Eleusinian Mysteries consisted of two parts: the Lesser and Greater Mysteries. The Lesser Mysteries were founded in the 5th century BCE and held in Athens by the river Ilissos during the spring month of Anthesterion. They consisted of

---

201 Foley. Hymn to Demeter. 1994:85–86.

202 Sourvinou-Inwood. "Festivals and Mysteries." 2003:28.

203 Burkert. Ancient Mystery Cults. 1987:9.

204 Johnston. Religions. 2004:101.

205 Clay. Politics of Olympus. 1989:260.

206 Burkert. Greek Religion. 1985:289.

207 Aristophanes. Frogs. (101-164). "...you'll hear the sound of flute-playing and you'll come out into brilliant daylight, just like it is up here. Farther on you'll see plantations of myrtle, and happy bands of revelers, men and women, tripping around and clapping their hands...".

procession, sacrifice and purification and served as preparation for those intending to participate in the Greater Mysteries held six months later. The Greater Mysteries were celebrated in the autumn month of Boedromion at Eleusis, 22 kilometres north-west of Athens. While the sacred precinct at Eleusis dates to the Mycenaean period (15th century BCE), the first hall of initiation, the Telesterion, was not built until the 6th century BCE. There were two stages of initiation into the Greater Mysteries: the first and main one was the telete or myesis, and the second (which was optional) was the epopteia.[208] By the Classical period the Mysteries were open to everyone, slave or free, who spoke Greek and had not committed murder.

As mentioned above, the *Homeric Hymn to Demeter* is the first place we hear about the existence of the Eleusinian Mysteries. Composed by an unknown author, the Hymn was probably performed as a prelude to poetic performances at festivals of the gods and can be considered a type of aural votive offering.[209] While many modern Pagans would be aware of the various versions of the myth of Demeter, Persephone and Hades, it is the account as narrated in the Hymn that concerns us here. The *Homeric Hymn to Demeter* is etiological in that it informs the listener about the honours attributed to both Demeter and Persephone, as well as the founding of the Mysteries at Eleusis. The Hymn contains both a divine and mortal story. The divine story concerns the abduction of Demeter's daughter Kore, or Persephone, by Hades, lord of the underworld, with the permission of Zeus but with neither the knowledge nor consent of Demeter herself. After searching frantically for her daughter, Demeter withdraws in anger from the divine sphere and institutes a famine on earth. This eventually makes Zeus yield and permit a partial return of her daughter, however because Persephone has eaten a pomegranate seed whilst in the underworld she must return there for a third of each year, while spending the other two-thirds on Olympus. The mortal section of the story involves the female members of the family of Keleos, a king of Eleusis, whom Demeter visits disguised as an old woman during her stay on earth. While there she attempts to immortalize the infant Demophoon, son of Metaneira and Keleos, by anointing him with ambrosia and burying him in the hearth fire. After her plan is thwarted because she is interrupted by the child's mother, the men of Eleusis are instructed to build a temple in her honour. There Demeter remains until her famine succeeds in its purpose. At the close of the hymn Demeter bestows her Mysteries on the kings of Eleusis.

It is likely that the mortal participant in the Eleusinian Mysteries was identified with the mythical child Demophoon from the Hymn through ritual processes thought to mimic, echo or refer to Demeter's treatment of him and this process, while not able to cheat death,

---

208 Mylonas. Eleusis. 1961:239.

209 Graf. Greek Mythology. 1983:119.

nevertheless modified the initiate's experience of death. I think that the initiates were identified with Demophoon via ritual treatment with fire and to prove this I seek to link the Hymn with Eleusinian ritual. Despite romantic *'myth and ritual'* theories beloved of Classicists of the late 19th century such as Jane Ellen Harrison and subsequently many modern Pagans who read their works, in Greek religion ritual is not necessarily connected to myth. According to Versnel *"there are many more rites without myths and myths without rites than there are related rites and myths"*.[210] However, many contemporary scholars believe that Hymn to Demeter was an aition for the Eleusinian cult,[211] whether it was structured to explain the initial founding of the Mysteries as Foley believes[212] or had a more *'close and basic'* association with the rites as Parker suggests.[213] Either way, we need not necessarily expect a perfect match between what is described in the Hymn and what went on at Eleusis, especially as the Hymn was performed in public while the content of the Mysteries was secret.[214] According to Graf, an etiological myth need not correspond in every respect with a ritual, they may share only one feature, the myth may enlarge upon what is only suggested in ritual or elaborate upon a general feeling or mood.[215] There are at least two features of the Hymn that are generally accepted as being specifically linked to the Eleusinian cult: the search for Persephone by Demeter, and the entrance of the goddess to Metaneira's house. So where might these have occurred within the Mysteries? The Eleusinian ritual is believed to have consisted of three components: dromena: an enactment; deiknymena: sacred objects that were shown; and legomena: words that were spoken.[216] While there is disagreement on the value of reports regarding the content of the *legomena* and *deiknymena*, it is generally agreed that the *dromena* involved the enactment of Demeter's search for Persephone by the initiates. The scene in Metaneira's house where Demeter sits on a fleece-covered stool, refuses nourishment, and eventually drinks the *kykeon*, a mixture of barley, water and pennyroyal, is thought to refer to a preliminary part of the rites.

If indeed the Hymn contained material pertinent to the cult, while not exposing the secrets of the cult, there is probably at least a suggestion in there as to how the Mysteries worked in their capacity as a modifier of death for the initiate. I believe it is to do with the

---

210 Versnel. "Greek Myth and Ritual." 1988:121.

211 Mylonas. Eleusis. 1961:258–267; Richardson. Homeric Hymn. 1974:236; Parker. "Hymn to Demeter." 1991:4.; Foley. Hymn. 1994:65; Sourvinou-Inwood. 2003:29. Although Clinton. Myth and Cult. 1992:29, believes the Hymn to be an aition, not of the Mysteries but of the Thesmophoria. His arguments seem feasible and I think it could be related to both rites.

212 Foley. Hymn. 1994:84.

213 Parker. Hymn. 1991:4.

214 Johnston. Religions. 2004:99.

215 Graf. Greek Mythology. 1983:114.

216 Mylonas. Eleusis. 1961:261.

Demophoon episode. Although Demeter's motivation for attempting to immortalize Demophoon is not actually stated in the Hymn, one interpretation of her actions is that it was a way of gaining revenge on Hades and Zeus for the abduction of Persephone. Just as Hades withholds Persephone from her mother and the upper world, so Demeter attempts to withhold Demophoon from the lower world by making him *'deathless'*. Had she been successful in this initial experiment, she may have gone on to immortalize all humans thus depriving Hades of his rightful honours and seriously disturbing the order of the universe as ordained by Zeus. Demophoon—while not able to be saved from death because immortalization of mortals is impossible[217] and because it is not Demeter's *'department'* (her realm is agriculture, not the underworld)—is nevertheless now especially dear to Demeter and is to receive *"unfailing honour"* subsequently modifying his life and death, in lieu of prolonging his existence indefinitely. Demeter's relationship to Demophoon in the Hymn may be the mythical version of her relationship with mortals who undergo her Mysteries, which, as we know, modify the mortal experience of death. According to Clay, *"If Demeter had succeeded in making Demophoon a god, there would be no need for initiation...the fate of Demophoon forms a precondition to the possibility and desirability of initiation."*[218] It is likely that the Demophoon episode played a pertinent role during the rites, linking the initiates intimately with Demeter.[219] As Parker says *"one is reluctant to give the [Demophoon] incident, the centrepiece of the Hymn, no other function than to provide an aition for rites of secondary importance"*[220] i.e. the preliminaries, as Foley suggests.[221]

In the Hymn fire and ambrosia are the means by which Demeter attempts to bestow immortality upon Demophoon.[222] According to Price and Kearns *'ambrosia'* literally means *'immortality'*[223] so Demeter is directly bestowing immortality upon Demophoon whilst burning away his mortal parts in the fire.[224] In Greek myth fire can purge away mortality. The hero Heracles, after being immolated in his funeral pyre on Mt Oeta in which his mortal parts were burned away, was taken up to Olympus and made immortal;[225] the goddess Thetis attempted to immortalize her son Achilles in fire[226] and on a

---

217 Perhaps symbolized in the Hymn by Metaneira's interruption of Demeter's attempted immortalisation of Demophoon in the fire (Hymn 243–47).

218 Clay. Politics. 1989:244.

219 Richardson. Hymn. 1974:236, also links Demophoon episode with the central significance of Mysteries, not only the preliminary rites.

220 Parker. Hymn. 1991:9.

221 Foley. Hymn. 1994:114.

222 Mackie. "Achilles." 1998:8.

223 Price and Kearns Dictionary. 2003:22.

224 Might this have caused his earthly 'death' as part of his 'immortalisation'? In other versions of the myth Demophoon does die.

225 March. Dictionary 1998:386.

226 Mackie. "Achilles." 1998:1.

cista from Praeneste, Athena holds the infant Ares over flames.[227] Funerary rituals in Homer's *Iliad* utilize cremation to prepare the bodies of Patroklos and Hektor for their transition to the underworld. In Greek religion fire acts as a medium for relations between the human and divine worlds, transforming animal sacrifice into pleasant smoke for the gods and a feast for mortals.[228] According to Iamblichus, *"Fire destroys the material part of sacrifices, it purifies all things that are brought near it releasing them from the bonds of matter and, in virtue of the purity of its nature, making them meet for communion with the gods."*[229]

Fire was utilized during the Lesser Mysteries, along with fasting, washing and pig sacrifice, in order to purify initiates. Much Eleusinian sculptural and painted imagery includes depictions of fire in the form of torches. Torches were associated with Mysteries because they were performed at night, but in the case of Eleusis, they may also signify fire itself and refer to Demophoon encounter with immortality. Although torches are not the same as a hearth, they are both fire and as we have seen above, we need not expect an exact replication of the contents of the Hymn in the ritual. The second most important of the sacred officials in the Mysteries was the *Daidouchos* or torch-bearer which seems to imply a role for fire beyond that of merely lighting the space. We also know that the rites took place in darkness and that the culmination of the *telete* occurred amidst a bright light produced by a fire on the top of the *Anaktoron*, the central holy-of-holies within the *Telesterion*. Although we do not know exactly what was illuminated, it seems that fire was used in several dramatic ways in the rites. One of its applications may have been to identify the initiates with Demophoon.

If there was an enactment during the Mysteries, of Demeter's search for Persephone, and the actions of the goddess when she first arrives at Metaneira's house were also included, then there is no reason why the Demophoon episode might not also be performed, or at least alluded to, during the rites. Mortal initiates into the Mysteries may have been symbolically associated with Demophoon through ritual procedures such as the use of torches evoking Demeter's hiding of Demophoon in the fire, through narrative, or by watching some sort of enactment involving the *'Child of the Hearth'*, the only child initiate allowed to participate in the Mysteries. We know there was a *threptos* or nursling involved in the cult, that the goddesses may have *'adopted'* the initiates and that they *'nursed the rites'* at Eleusis. The sequence where, after failing to immortalize Demophoon, Demeter laid him on the ground may refer to the ritual of the *amphidromia*: the acceptance of a new baby into its family.

---

227 Richardson. Hymn. 1974:238.

228 Furley. Use of Fire. 1981:i.

229 Mackie. "Achilles." 1998:9, n 32.

An image of Herakles- who was supposed to have been initiated into the Mysteries before he went down to Hades to steal Cerberus[230] - on an object known as the Torre Nova sarcophagus may depict what the mortal initiate underwent in their identification with Demophoon.[231] In this image we see a veiled Heracles sitting on a low stool spread with a ram's fleece, evocative of the episode in the Hymn where Demeter enters Metaneira's house and sits on a fleece-covered stool. Behind him is a female figure, who may be a priestess, holding downward-pointing torches as if in the process of moving them around Herakles, literally surrounding him with fire as Demeter did with Demophoon.[232] In another image on the Lovatelli Urn we have almost the exact same configuration but whereas on the sarcophagus Herakles is being *'treated'* with flame, on the urn the priestess figure holds a *liknon*, or winnowing fan, above his head. Kerenyi claims that infants were sometimes placed in such baskets, which may link the image with Demophoon, however another interpretation is that the winnowing fan symbolized spiritual *'refinement'*. Just as it was used in the processing of grain to separate the rough outer husk, which was blown away in the wind, from the *'pure'* grain within, so might it have symbolized the removal of Herakles/the initiate's mortal *'husk'* during initiation in a similar way to fire. The fact that it was Herakles in particular who was depicted thus—the hero who achieved apotheosis after removal of his mortal frame by fire—may have been considered a symbol of great hope to potential Eleusinian initiates, even if they could not expect to replicate his immortality. If, as mentioned above, we need not expect an exact correlation between myth and ritual, then the Demophoon episode as translated into Mystery ritual need not look exactly the way it does in the Hymn and may have been simply alluded to rather than literally copied.

When trying to understand the Eleusinian Mysteries, or indeed any aspect of ancient Greek religion, we need to remember that the Greek gods were not overly concerned with the activities or individual fates of mortals. While it might seem appealing to believe that Demeter founded the Mysteries as a favour to humankind, I would suggest another interpretation of her actions. As I see it, the Eleusinian Mysteries were a type of earthly continuation of what began as the divine tug-of-war between Demeter (life) and Hades (death) over Persephone-Demophoon. The perpetuation of the Mystery rites functioned as a way for Demeter to impose upon the

---

230 Clark. Catabasis. 1979:90–92. Demeter is said to have founded the Lesser Mysteries especially on Herakles' behalf because he was ineligible for the Greater Mysteries, either because he was a foreigner or because he was tainted by blood guilt from slaying the centaurs, and needed to be purified. Other sources assume that he was initiated straight into the Greater Mysteries. Xenophon, according to Mylonas. Eleusis. 1961:240, n 85.

231 There is debate as to whether this depicts a separate ritual concerning the removal of blood guilt from Herakles, the Lesser Eleusinia, or some aspect of the Greater Mysteries. Mylonas. Eleusis. 1961:242.

232 Kerenyi. Eleusis. 1967:57.

underworld through the modification of mortals' plight in death, just as Hades intruded on her world when he abducted Persephone. In that way, the Mysteries were a type of revenge for Demeter, motivated by the seizure of Persephone. While Demeter may have had some empathy for the mortal condition because she had, to an extent, experienced it herself, Eleusinian initiates were really pawns in her battle with her brothers, Hades and Zeus: the good results the Mysteries provided for mortals were simply by-products of this.

Demeter did not succeed in depriving Hades of human victims, or in obtaining the unconditional return of her daughter. The Mysteries mirror this situation; they did not immortalize humans and cheat Hades of his due, however they did modify death, impose upon it, and it is likely that this was achieved by the ritual identification of the initiate with the child Demophoon. As we have seen, this may have been achieved by various ritual methods such as hearing a narrative, watching or participating in an enactment, the dramatic use of fire at critical stages in the rites, and through individual *'treatment'* by cult officials involving the application of torches. Fire's particular associations, related to ideas of purification, refinement and immortality, would have been pertinent to its employment in rites which promised to affect the post-mortem state of the Eleusinian participant. While not able to avoid death, at least the mortal initiate, by undergoing a ritual identification with the mortal nursling of Demeter, could look forward to an improvement in their experience of the underworld.

Bibliography

Aristophanes & Barrett, David (trans) (1964) *The Frogs*. London: Penguin.

Bremmer, J. (1987) *Interpretations of Greek Mythology*. London: Croom Helm.

Burkert, W. (1985) *Greek Religion*. Oxford: Blackwell.

Burkert, W. (1987 *Ancient Mystery Cults*. Cambridge: Harvard university press.

Clark, R.J. (1979) *Catabasis Virgil and the Wisdom Tradition*. Amsterdam: B.R. Gruner.

Clay, J.S. (1989) *The Politics of Olympus: Form and Meaning in the Homeric Hymns*. Princeton: Princeton University Press.

Clinton, K. (1992) *Myth and Cult: The Iconography of the Eleusinian Mysteries*. Uppsala: Svenska Institutet I Athen.

Cosmopolous, M.B. (ed) (2003) *Greek Mysteries: The Archaeology and Ritual of Ancient Greek Secret Cults*. London: Routledge.

Foley, H.P. (ed) (1994) *The Homeric Hymn to Demeter: Translation, Commentary and Interpretive Essays*. Princeton: Princeton University Press.

Furley, W.D. (1981) *Studies in the Use of Fire in Ancient Greek Religion*. Salem: Ayer company.

Graf, F. (1983) *Greek Mythology*. Baltimore: Johns Hopkins University Press.

Johnston, S.I. (ed) (2004) *Religions of the Ancient World*. Cambridge: Belknap Press.

Kerenyi, C. (1967) *Eleusis: Archetypal Image of Mother and Daughter*. Princeton: Princeton University Press.

Mackie, C.J. (1998) *Achilles in Fire*, in *Classical Quarterly* 48.2:1-10.

March, J. (1998) *Cassell's Dictionary of Classical Mythology*. London: Cassell.

Mylonas, G.E. (1961) *Eleusis and the Eleusinian Mysteries*. Princeton: Princeton University Press. Princeton.

Parker, R. (1991) *The Hymn to Demeter and the Homeric Hymns*, in *Greece & Rome*. Vol. 38.1:1-17.

Price, S. & Kearns, E. (eds) (2003) *The Oxford Dictionary of Classical Myth and Religion*. Oxford: Oxford University Press.

Richardson, N.J. (1974) *The Homeric Hymn to Demeter*. Oxford: Clarendon Press.

Dogs And Death
– Guardians, Omens And Psychopomps

BY IVY KERRIGAN

I had come there to die. Numb with drink I lay back on the grass and let the night take me. A warm blackness enveloped me and I let my mind sink deeper and deeper into the darkness. There was no pain, just warmth and support. I could feel others around me encompassing me with sweet whispers and feelings of affection. I let go of pain, of hurt, of life – nothing mattered there in that infinite night. The feeling of release of freedom was amazing and my mind frayed like a ball of tangled wool – strands slipping out of the whole searching out other thoughts floating in the warm night. My mind unravelled seeking the others in the darkness – meeting and melding with them into one big whole.

What's going on? My younger brother has died, I've broken up with another abusive boyfriend, I have no job, I'm going through a court case and I've had a fight with my mother and whichever stepfather it was at that particular time. A few months ago I'd had a similar experience at a party where a fight with said boyfriend led me outside to cool down. Drunk and wearing only a slip dress I lay on the frosty ground to look at stars. All I remember is being warm and safe and then very, very cold, lots of noise and being wrapped in tin foil.

It occurred to me this was a good way to die. I thought about such things a lot back then. I had worked as a pharmacy technician so I knew overdose was a bad way to go, especially with the painkillers most people used – slow and ever so painful. I'd experimented with self harming and craved the release it gave me but couldn't bring myself to cut deep enough to make it matter. So I continued numbing myself with drink and men until I came across what I thought would be the answer. Normally when I was in this sort of state I'd visit Daniel's grave and the horror and selfishness of my actions would be bought back to me in a rush with the pain and suffering his death had wrought, normally that snapped me out of these moods but not this time. I'd hit rock bottom and I led down on his grave to die.

As I was floating in the gentle currents, becoming one with all that was around me, she came. She wasn't quiet or friendly, gentle or noble: she was an immense wave of spitting, snarling blackness. On some level I recognised her; dogs had been coming to me for a while but like everyone else I'd been pushing them away. I knew she was there to take me back and I didn't want to go. I ran blindly, stumbling and crying in my haste but still she caught me. Her teeth sank into my skin pulling, hauling me back towards the light, towards the pain. Snapping and growling she pushed me back towards my body but I was too far gone. My mind, my thoughts, my personality had started to unravel, returning to wherever it came from. She howled, calling the pack and they came. They herded the strands of me, collecting them, forming my substance into a ball. She took this ball and grabbing me by the scruff of the neck like a puppy shoved it back into my skull. The pain was immense and my world was forever changed. In doing this, in saving me, we, the dog and I, became inexorably linked, some of her mingling with some of me so now I am her and she is me, with Ivy being both of us.

This had a profound effect on me. I wasn't me anymore, I was more and together we could do anything. I started taking responsibility for my actions, paid off my debts, stopped drinking and many other nasty things. This was my chance to throw off the masks to stop trying to fit in where I didn't belong, to stop insisting I was normal and instead to be me and with her help I could do it. The next week I signed up for a local course in Wicca, found I liked raw steak and started exhibiting a few doggy behaviours but was better for it all and I have never looked back. In the otherworld I have a pack, this group of beings has grown over the years and no longer just includes Ivy's pack of hounds; they are all sorts of beings with one thing in common: they have my back. They look out for me and advise me, they make life both better and easier. I've tried to replicate that in this world by building my own pack, a group of people who are all warriors in their own way. People who take responsibility and fight for what they believe in, people who I care for, people I would stand and fight with and people I would protect with my last breath. This is living; this is what life is about.

On Dogs

Let's start from the beginning. There is a lot of guesswork and theories concerning when, how and why dogs became dogs. I don't really want to get bogged down in that minefield so the short version is: *Canis lupus familiaris* was probably domesticated from the grey wolf (*Canis lupus*) somewhere between 30,000-7,000 BCE and is the earliest domesticated animal. This is quite an achievement for early man and gives us an inkling of the powerful species that we will become. That these people could take a wolf, the epitome of wildness, and through kindness or cunning persuade it to throw in its lot with mankind is a huge accolade.

Unlike their closest relatives the wolves, jackals and coyotes, these animals chose to give up their freedom and co-exist with mankind. I suspect our complementary behaviours and social groupings made this easier. These proto-dogs recognised their own traits in mankind and it made the transition from wild creature to *'pet'* much easier. I suspect these same shared traits give rise to werewolf mythology, making the man and the wolf so much easier to meld into one, but that's another story. Over the years we evolved together helping and supporting one another and I wonder if either of our species would be where they are today without the other. Such trite terms as *"Man's best friend"* reflect the long term symbiosis between our two species. Dogs help us with all aspects of our life: hunting, herding, pulling loads, protection, war, law enforcement, alerting us to danger, giving warmth, guidance, caring for the sick, companionship, food, fur – the list is practically endless.

I work in a shamanic way and as a child I was scared of dogs but - as is often the case when we are scared of things - I needed the dog, and since then she has become my most constant companion. Recently my gods and spirits have also introduced me to spiders, and while I appreciate all this help to grow as a person I just hope they do not go as far as rats! Anyway I was told long ago at the start of my journey that dogs could not be power animals as domesticated animals have no power – it has been stolen by man. I didn't like this so, as is my want, I ignored them and set about doing it my way. I found out that although dogs are a lot less fashionable than wolves or coyotes or stags or many other wild creatures, they do have a place in mythology and a powerful one at that. When I Googled the dog as a *'power animal'* I came up with the following traits: fellowship, healing, loyalty, friendship, unconditional love, reliability, nobleness, trustworthiness, fierce energy of protection and service.

I found that dogs continue to love, even when badly abused and it was this trait that I first saw as their curse. I rejected them as weak, stupid and pathetic but as so often happens it turned out to be a blessing and is in fact their real strength. It takes a lot to make a dog go bad; they take anything that we can chuck at them. Neglect and abuse just washes over them, harming the body but not touching the spirit within, and this is why so many are able to be re-habilitated through rescue centres. It seems that they have faith in humankind's goodness even if we have lost sight of it.

It is my opinion that as dogs accompanied us in life, making themselves indispensable to their masters, so they began to accompany us in death, guarding that ultimate frontier. Men took these valued guides and protectors and trusted them to do the same on the other side of the veil to lead them in the ultimate unknown. Quite a lot of faith to put in something don't you think? I believe this is where our mythology of canine companions for death gods and psychopomps comes from.

But there is another side to dogs, they have a dual nature. Gods of healing can bring sickness and gods of death are gods of life. In the same way protectors can be hunters, the tame can be untamed and love can turn to hate. Just under the surface of the dog, when the veneer of civilization is ripped away, a snarling, snapping and above all wild animal is found. These animals evolved to hunt, to kill and if pushed as large carnivores they can do so again. It's like woman's eternal attraction to the Byronic male. Under that layer of sophisticated polish is something that's still mad, bad and dangerous to know. We are attracted to that enlightened exterior but also to the untamed wildness that lies beneath while simultaneously being repelled by it (well, I never said we were sensible, as Voltaire says: *"All women are crazy!"*)[233] I think this illustrates the love/hate relationship we have with dogs, shown through our mythology of dogs as death omens and bringers of death but also as guardians and helpers.

In Judaism and Islam dogs are seen as unclean scavengers. In fact in Islamic mythology it is said that angels will not enter a house where a dog lives. In Christianity they have come to represent faithfulness and healing as shown in the stories of St. Lazarus (see image, above) whose wounds were licked by dogs, St. Roch or Rocco who was saved from the plague by the kindness of a dog or Tobit's son who is accompanied by a dog on his travels in the *Book of Tobit.* In a roundabout way it was actually the deutero-canonical *Book of Tobit* that led me to study dogs and death. The book is a central theme in another book by Sally Vickers called *Miss Garnet's Angel,* and when I was in Venice I even made a pilgrimage to the church mentioned in the book.

In Asian countries dogs are kind protectors, such as the Xiezhi in China/Korea. This fire-eating dog guards its owner against disasters and prejudice. In Nepal dogs are honoured on Kukur Puja on the second day of the five-day festival of Tihar. The relationship between dog and man is honoured and dogs are given gifts of garlands and food. Among Native Americans the dog is seen as a fierce protector leading to several warrior societies variously called Dog Men, Dog Soldiers, Crazy Dogs or Foolish Dogs. Tradition states that these aggressive and highly effective fighters would pin themselves to a chosen piece of ground in battle and on that place they would either stand or fall. I've always had a soft spot for these societies (possibly bought on by the film *"Last of the Dogmen"*) who were crucial in Native American resistance to European invasion. Perhaps one of the most famous doggie tales told in Europe, and one of my favourites, is the Irish legend of Cú Chulainn. Originally called Sétanta, he killed the guard dog of Culann. As reparation he offered to guard the house until a replacement was found. From this moment on he was known as Cú Chulainn, the hound of Culann. After many dazzling exploits the hero then died after breaking a *geasa* forbidding him to eat dog meat.

I'm going to make special mention of Zoroastrianism. In Sally Vickers' book mention of the rite described below started me on this thread of research. Followers of this religion believe that dogs are

---

233 Voltaire, "All Women are Crazy" from the album, "Hate Lives in a Small Town", 2010.

highly beneficial animals whose gaze can purify by driving off evil spirits. Particularly useful is the four-eyed dog or a dog with spots above his eyes. The *Vendîdâd*, part of the holy book the *Zend Avesta*, describes in *Fargard 13, 14*, and *15* the types of dogs, their uses and how they should be treated:

"Whosoever shall smite either a shepherd's dog, or a house dog, or a Vohunazga dog, or a trained dog, his soul when passing to the other world, shall fly amid louder howling and fiercer pursuing than the sheep does when the wolf rushes upon it in the lofty forest.

'No soul will come and meet his departing soul and help it through the howls and pursuit in the other world; nor will the dogs that keep the Kinvad bridge help his departing soul through the howls and pursuit in the other world."[234]

The dog also forms a vital part of a funeral rite called Sagdid where the dog is led along the route travelled by the corpse in an effort to chase off evil spirits and purify it for normal usage. This is described in *Fargard VIII*:

"You shall therefore cause the yellow dog with four eyes, or the white dog with yellow ears, to go three times through that way. When the dog is brought there, then the Drug Nasu flies away to the regions of the north, in the shape of a raging fly, with knees and tail sticking out, all stained with stains, and like unto the foulest Khrafstras."[235]

In modern western life we have become somewhat divorced from this mythological view of dogs as heroes, protectors and warriors. Dogs are now seen by most people as just dumb companions. I believe this is due in some part to the dog's success in diversifying into so such a large number of breeds. This is their triumph and has enabled them to access every level of our society but it also enables us to compartmentalize them. The large number of canine shapes and sizes allows us to separate the dogs of death, war and protection from our cuddly pets and from their mythology and their power – maybe this is why abuse cases are becoming more and more common? The dogs associated with death, war and even protection tend to be large and black – proper hellhounds such as Dobermans, Rottweilers and Alsatians while our cuddly pets are small and cute like poodles or spaniels. Of course we forgot that even these pretty dogs were once working dogs.

I cannot go onto the next section without mentioning another doggie something that has had a profound effect on my life – depression. Like death, depression crosses borders and pays no heed to social standing, picking its victims indiscriminately and with inescapable inevitability. And like death it is also linked with the black dog archetype maybe because phantom dogs are said to spread madness in their wake. The term *"the black dog"* was bought into common usage by Sir Winston Churchill. I love and use this

---

234 From Fargard XIII (translated by James Darmesteter), 2010.

235 From Fargad VIII, trans. Darmesteter, 2010.

metaphor for my own bouts of melancholy. The term conveys the familiarity with which I greet him each time he comes and my attempts to become his friend or master so as to better deal with his visits. What we now know as depression, from the Latin verb *'to press down'* (how apt this is), was first described by Hippocrates as *melancholia* (one of my favourite words), and since the time of Aristotle depression has been linked with humankind's most brilliant and influential people, both intellectuals and people who have changed the world such as Buzz Aldrin, Abraham Lincoln, Martin Luther, Michelangelo, Mozart and Sir Isaac Newton. So you see I don't hate my depressive nature. In some ways I am grateful for it as it brings me closer to some of my great heroes such as Agatha Christie, Thomas Huxley, Spike Milligan and Friedrich Nietzsche. I almost feel sorry for those who haven't been admitted to this illustrious society.

On Death

I've always had a morbid streak: I put it down to seeing my granddad die of a heart attack when I was just three years old and we were picking raspberries. Since then the Grim Reaper and I have had an uneasy relationship, with him claiming a cousin, a grandma, a younger brother, another granddad, friends and several more acquaintances. I don't know if it's just me but this seems like a lot of death for so short a life – I wouldn't say I handle it well but it is a familiar blanket. Not good or bad in itself – just there, and in some ways he's comforting. He is the one who is always there and will never leave me. He can't be tricked or turned from his mission; there is no one more honest or more reliable. Here is one of my favourite quotes about death from *Elegies* by Propertius, capturing him in all his unswerving glory:

"Hither all shall come, hither the highest and the lowest class: evil it is, but it is a path that all must tread; all must assuage the three heads of the barking guard-dog and embark on the grisly greybeard's boat that no one misses."

I trust him with my life and when it's my time I will go into his comforting arms – maybe not without sorrow, fear or regret but I will go – the next step on a great adventure. I'm a firm believer in life after death – I'm not sure what it is, whether its reincarnation or heaven or hell or even if it's the same for everyone but there is something. Almost all my spirits are chthonic, underworld deities mingled with demons and the dead, and I love nothing more than playing in the dirt and the rain, the sand and the sea, in the dark and the pale light of the moon.

Most of my young life was spent in rural surroundings with plenty of pets and plants. I didn't have a great childhood and this prompted me to spend as much time out of doors as possible. I was lucky in that both sets of grandparents had small holdings with chickens and vegetables. I would think nothing of going to select the bird for Sunday lunch, but it did upset me when the fox killed the lot and didn't even eat them. I think this early introduction into the circle of life has helped me understand death better than some others. I don't like it, I grieve like any other but I see it as a necessary part of life. The words of Barney Bardsley in the book *A Handful of Earth* sum it up perfectly:

"Perhaps the most useful thing a garden can do is the least obvious, and certainly the least glamourous. It teaches us about loss... Nature will win. Death happens. Yet the brightness of new life, of fresh possibility, is already germinating underneath."

In modern society we are divorced from death; many people don't experience it until early adulthood. Even then it rarely touches us and when it does it is from a distance. Our move from the countryside with its knowledge of exactly where our food comes from, of life and of death, to the barren urban centres has hastened this gap. People in our lives no longer die, they just disappear without a trace. A friend recently had her dog put down. The deed was done at home and the vet suggested that they lay the body in its basket and let the new puppy sniff the corpse before it was buried. This apparently makes it much easier for the living to process. If this isn't done then to the other members of the pack that dog is just missing – not dead and they need to be found. I can relate to this as I was not allowed to see my brother's body and unconsciously spent many years looking for him. Our ancestors knew about death, they lived with it day in and day out. As we've lost our familiarity so we have gained a deep fear.

Guardians of the underworld and companions of death gods

If someone says dogs and mythology in the same sentence then Kerberos is often the first thing that springs to mind. But Hades' mighty watchdog is only one of many dogs entrusted with the task of guarding the gates of death. Over the years as death became a dirty word and the pagan underworlds or places of the dead became associated with the infernal, these dogs became monsters who guard the gates of hell itself in service of the devil.

Wikipedia, that great god of (mis)information, gives the meaning of the word guardian as *'One who guards, preserves, or secures; one to whom any person or thing is committed for protection, security, or preservation from injury; a warden.'*

Guardianship of our dead is a big job. The dogs linked with death are often seen as huge monstrous beings with fangs dripping poison and any other nasty thing you can think of. Would you entrust your beloved granny to such a being? I think it's likely that early man gave this job to dogs because he had observed in life how dogs could guard the homestead against wild animals or other men while he was out hunting. He trusted the dog to do the same with the realm of the dead to keep death at bay, to stop an incursion of the dead into the land of the living. I believe it was only as time wore on and the dead became more and more vilified in our society that their guardians became more and more beastly in response.

Now I will take you on a tour of various underworlds and their canine inhabitants starting with my favourite. The Ancient Greeks were my first love but not for me the shining heights of Olympus: I was fascinated by the gloomy depths of Hades peopled by shades and monsters and guarded by Kerberos. He is the son of Typhoeus the storm giant and Ekhidna who was a monstrous mix of serpent and woman.[236] An enormous black hound, he has three heads (although Hesiod gives him fifty!)[237] a mane of snakes, the claws of a lion and a serpent as a tail. His insatiable appetite for living flesh prevents the living entering Hades and stops shades leaving to return to the land of the living. Before being named by Hesiod he was known simply as the Hound of Hades. However, this mighty watch dog was not infallible, and he has weaknesses just like the rest of us, such as a very feminine fondness for cake, and myth gives us instances when Kerberos was outwitted or beaten. The cake incidents I think are best described by Virgil when the Sibyl and Aeneas (the mortal son of Aphrodite) drug him in the *Aeneid*:

"Huge Cerberus, monstrously couched in a cave confronting them, made the whole region echo with this three-throated barking. The Sibyl, seeing the snakes bristling upon his neck now, threw him for bait a cake for honey and wheat infused with sedative drugs. The creature, crazy with hunger, opened its three mouths, gobbled the bait; then its huge body relaxed and lay, sprawled out on the ground, the whole length of its cave kennel. Aeneas, passing its entrance, the watch-dog neutralized, strode rapidly from the bank of that river of no return."[238]

And by Apuleius when Psykhe tempts him with barley cakes in *The Golden Ass*:

"But you are not permitted to touch that either, for all these and many other distractions are part of the ambush which Venus will set to induce you to release one of the cakes from your hands. Do not imagine that the loss of a mere barley cake is a trivial matter, for if you relinquish either of them, the daylight of this world above will be totally denied you. Posted there is a massive hound with a huge, triple-formed head. This monstrous, fearsome brute confronts the dead with thunderous barking, though his menaces are futile since he can do them no harm. He keeps constant guard before the very threshold and the dark hall of Proserpina, protecting that deserted abode of Dis. You must disarm him by offering him a cake as his spoils. Then you can easily pass him, and gain immediate access to Proserpina herself. . . When you have obtained what she gives you, you must make your

---

236 Hesiod, Theogony, 310 (2009).
237 Ibid (2009).
238 Virgil, Aeneid 6.417ff (2010).

way back, using the remaining cake to neutralize the dog's savagery."[239]

Described by Virgil in his *Georgics*, when Orpheus went to the underworld to rescue his beloved Eurydike, he lulled the huge hound with sweet music:

"Stirred by his song, up from the lowest realms of Erebeus came the unsubstantial shades . . . Still more: the very house of Death and deepest abysses of Tartarus were spellbound, and the Eumenides with livid snakes entwined in their hair; Cerberus stood agape and his triple jaws forgot to bark."[240]

I know of only once that Kerberos has been beaten without trickery and that is by Herakles as part of his twelfth and final labour. His task was to capture Kerberos alive without the use of weapons. A fearsome task as shown in this quote from Homer's *Odyssey*:

"He once sent me even here to fetch away the hound of Hades, for he thought no task could be more fearsome for me than that. But I brought the hound out of Hades' house and up to earth, because Hermes helped me on my way, and gleaming-eyed Athene." [241]

I have always hated Herakles with a fiery passion and I hope from this next passage, also describing his twelfth labour, you will see why. Written by Seneca and taken from *Hercules Furens*, it is narrated by the goddess Hera:

"Nor is earth vast enough for him; behold, he has broken down the doors of infernal Jove, and brings back to the upper world the spoils of a conquered king. I myself saw, yes, saw him, the shadows of nether night dispersed and Dis overthrown, proudly displaying to his father a brother's spoils. Why does he not drag forth, bound and loaded down with fetters, Pluto himself, who drew a lot equal to Jove's? Why does he not lord it over conquered Erebus and lay bare the Styx? It is not enough merely to return; the law of the shades has been annulled, a way back has been opened from the lowest ghosts, and the mysteries of dread Death lie bared. But he, exultant at having burst the prison of the shades, triumphs over me, and with arrogant hand leads through the cities of Greece that dusky hound. I saw the daylight shrink at sight of Cerberus, and the sun pale with fear; upon me, too, terror came, and as I gazed upon the three necks of the conquered monster I trembled at my own command."[242]

It's good to know that even the mighty Olympians with all their bright arrogance are fearful of death's mighty watch dog!

Here we leave Kerberos and make a quick detour to another Greek hellhound. Kyon Orthros is not a guardian of the dead as such

---

239 Apuleius, The Golden Ass 6.19 ff (1999).

240 Virgil, Georgics 4.471 (2009).

241 Homer, Odyssey 11.623 ff (2010).

242 Seneca, Hercules Furens 46ff (1917).

but I think he deserves a mention as brother of Kerberos and as further illustration of my hatred of Herakles who destroyed this whole family. Orthros was the mate of Khimaira and the sire of both the Sphinx and the Nemean lion (also killed by Herakles as his first labour). The hound Orthros was owned by the giant Geryon. Along with Eurytion the herdsman, he protected and cared for Geryon's famous red-skinned cattle on the isle of Erytheia. Herakles was tasked with getting these cattle as part of his tenth labour, killing poor Orthros, Eurytion and Geryon in the process as immortalised by Pseudo-Apollodorus in *Bibliotheca 2*:

"When he reached Erytheia he camped on Mount Abas. The dog smelled him there and went after him, but he struck at it with his club, and when the cowherd Eurytion came to help the dog, he slew him as well."[243]

That's just plain nasty! From Ancient Greece we voyage to Wales and meet the Cŵn Annwn or Hound's of Annwn. These ghostly dogs reside in and protect Annwn the otherworld of Welsh mythology and actually fit into all three of the categories that I'll be mentioning. Originally they are the companions of Arawn a lord of Annwn but later they become a version of the wild hunt under psychopomp Gwynn ap Nudd and are also known as a portent of death. At this early stage Annwn is an otherworldly paradise, essentially a place of immortality where disease has no foothold and tables overflow with food and riches. Later it becomes a realm of death with Arawn at its head.

In the *Mabinogion* translated by Lady Charlotte Guest the story of Pwyll Prince of Dyfed tells us of Pwyll's encounter with the hounds while out hunting:

"Of all the hounds that he had seen in the world, he had never seen any that were like unto these. For their hair was of a brilliant shining white, and their ears were red; and as the whiteness of their bodies shone, so did the redness of their ears glisten."[244]

The hounds had taken down a stag which Pwyll himself had been hunting so fearlessly. He chased off these foreign dogs and let his own feed upon the corpse when an unknown hunter appeared and identified himself as owner of the hounds and:

"'Arawn, a King of Annwn, am I.' 'Lord,' said he, 'how may I gain thy friendship?' 'After this manner mayest thou,' he said. 'There is a man whose dominions are opposite to mine, who is ever warring against me, and he is Havgan, a King of Annwn, and by ridding me of this oppression, which thou canst easily do, shalt thou gain my friendship.'"[245]

This passage suggests that there are many (or at least two) kings in Annwn at this time even though Arawn is often cited as the only

---

243 Pseudo-Apollodorus, Bibliotheca 2. 1975:106-108

244 Guest, trans. The Mabinogion, 1877:339-340.

245 Guest, Lady Charlotte, trans. The Mabinogion, 1877:340.

king. By taking his place as King of Annwn for a year and vanquishing Havgan, Pwyll makes up for his bad behaviour and gains Arawn's friendship. Later Gwyn ap Nudd will usurp Arawn's place as King of Annwn, claim the Cŵn Annwn as his own and become the Welsh lord of the dead.

From Wales we head north to Scandinavia and the realm of the goddess Hel where Garm resides. He is described as a bloodstained watchdog that guards Hel's gate and it is said his baying will mark the start of Ragnarok. Garm is mentioned in his capacity of the guardian of Hel in the *Poetic Edda* called *Baldrs Draumar* (translated by Henry Adams Bellows) although he is not mentioned by name:

> *2. Then Othin rose, | the enchanter old,*
> *And the saddle he laid | on Sleipnir's back;*
> *Thence rode he down | to Niflhel deep,*
> *And the hound he met | that came from hell.*
> *3. Bloody he was | on his breast before,*
> *At the father of magic | he howled from afar;*
> *Forward rode Othin, | the earth resounded*
> *Till the house so high | of Hel he reached.*[246]

His role in the coming of Ragnarok is described in *Teutonic Myth and Legend* by Donald A. Mackenzie:

"To guard the island of the Gulf of Black Grief the gods bound there, nigh to Loki's monster son, the great watchdog Garm, which is greater than Hate-Managarm, the moon devourer, so that it might bark with loud alarm if Fenrer broke free. There, too, beside the fettered wolf, was Loki bound in after days."[247]

I find it interesting that Garm the watchdog who will warn us about the coming battle then chooses to fight on the *'wrong'* side, but my husband maintains that he is just following his nature. Again from *Teutonic Myth and Legend*:

"The Ship of Death is sailing over the sea. On board are the sons of Muspel, who were bound; the stricken Jotuns, freed from bonds; Garm, the watch-dog; and the unfettered wolf Fenrer. Monsters gaunt and grim are in the ship, and Hel is there also. Loki is the pilot and holds the rudder."[248]

I've always had a soft spot for the tricky Loki, so I suppose I cannot complain.

Finally we depart the snow covered wastes of the north and journey to the lands of the Hindus where we meet Yama the god of death. Dogs wander Yama's country as his messengers and two four-eyed brindled dogs guard the gates to his realm. These dogs are said to be children of Sarama who in Hindu myth is referred to as the mother of all dogs and also the bitch of the gods. The *Rig Veda*, Book

---

246 Bellows, trans. Poetic Edda, 1936:195.
247 Mackenzie, Teutonic Myth and Legend, 1912:95.
248 Mackenzie, Teutonic Myth and Legend, 1912:180.

10 has three hymns addressed to Yama but for our purposes we are only interested in Hymn 14 which says:

> *"10 Run and outspeed the two dogs, Saramā's offspring,*
> *brindled, four-eyed, upon thy happy pathway.*
> *Draw nigh then to the gracious-minded Fathers where they*
> *rejoice in company with Yama.*
> *11 And those two dogs of thine, Yama, the watchers, four-*
> *eyed, who look on men and guard the pathway,—*
> *Entrust this man, O King, to their protection, and with*
> *prosperity and health endow him.*
> *12 Dark-hued, insatiate, with distended nostrils, Yama's two*
> *envoys roam among the People;*
> *May they restore to us a fair existence here and to-day, that*
> *we may see the sunlight."*[249]

Here we leave the dark gloom of the underworld realms and move onto our next theme.

Dogs as Omens of death

Phantom black dogs or Hellhounds are especially popular in northern European myth and are most often seen as harbingers of death, pestilence, madness and storms.

Wikipedia gives the meaning of the word omen as *"An omen (also called portent or presage) is a phenomenon that is believed to foretell the future, often signifying the advent of change. Though the word "omen" is usually devoid of reference to the change's nature, hence being possibly either "good" or "bad", the term is more often used in a foreboding sense, as with the word "ominous"."*

Phantom dogs are usually either the spirits of the wronged, of unbaptised children or agents of the devil. They are said to haunt places of execution, graveyards, crossroads, bodies of water, ancient pathways and dark forests: all *'pagan'* places of power. So the souls of the dead, of our ancestors and the places where we might once have gone to talk to them have been demonised. Both dealt with in one foul swoop – how efficient! These sacred spaces are all liminal places where one can move between worlds so perhaps it should be no surprise that travellers are particularly vulnerable to Hellhounds when moving through that uncertain world between the real worlds of their departure and their destination.

Ghostly dogs vary in size from that of a large dog to the size of a horse. They most often have glowing, even flaming red, eyes, shaggy black fur, super strength, great speed, ghostly characteristics and leave a sulphuric smell. Another interesting point about black dogs is they are often able to shape-shift, particularly taking the guise of horses, dark skinned people or witches. In fact they are particularly associated with magic users, such as *'Padfoot'* in the Harry Potter series by J. K. Rowling; this may spring from the use of dogs as

---

249 Griffith, trans. The Rig Veda, Book 10, Hymn XIV, 10-12 (1896).

tutelary spirits or familiars. Shamans of many cultures take animals as tutelary spirits or are born with a particular animal helper as their *'fetch'*. In Native American tribes a youth coming of age might kill an animal that he dreams of in his initiation and put parts of the animal into a bag to become his medicine or power. In West Africa during the same rite of passage the spirit and person create a blood bond, a link so close that if one dies the other follows. In Melanesia there is a belief in an animal counterpart to a person that shares the same soul as in Philip Pullman's *His Dark Materials* trilogy.

From the continent we have stories of the Gaueko, described as a great black wolfhound that can walk upright and devours shepherds and their flocks in the Basque region. The Dip from Catalonia is an evil emissary of the devil and sucks victims' blood, and also from Catalan myth is the Pesanta who enters houses at night and sits on the chests of sleeping people making it hard to breath and causing nightmares. From Flanders we have a cannibalistic shapeshifter called Oude Rode Ogen and later De Nekker. The legend goes that in the 17th century a man was linked with the disappearances of several children; he was seen running away and when shot at turned into a dog. Later, people caught and skinned a black man, burying the skin at St Rumbold's cathedral in Mechelen. From then on a 7ft tall man who changes into a dog with fiery red eyes can be seen wandering Mechelen: he is said to be hunting his skin so that he can become whole again.

Great Britain appears to have the greatest concentration of these spectres, with legends ranging from the Mauthe Doog in the Isle of Man, to the Freybug in Norfolk, the Yeth Hound in Devon, the Gwyllgi in Wales and the Barghest in Yorkshire. One of the most notable is the Gytrash from Northern England. Made famous in the book *Jane Eyre* by Charlotte Brontë this hound is said to haunt lonely roads in the shape of a horse, dog or mule:

"I remembered certain of Bessie's tales, wherein figured a North-of-England spirit called a 'Gytrash', which, in the form of horse, mule, or large dog, haunted solitary ways, and sometimes came upon belated travellers, as this horse was now coming upon me. It was very near, but not yet in sight; when, in addition to the tramp, tramp, I heard a rush under the hedge, and close down by the hazel stems glided a great dog, whose black and white colour made him a distinct object against the trees. It was exactly one form of Bessie's Gytrash--a lion-like creature with long hair and a huge Head."[250]

There is of course also the Black Shuck native to Norfolk, Essex and Suffolk; this black dog is said to have a pedigree dating back to before the Vikings. His claims to fame are sightings in Bungay and Blythburgh on the very same day in August 1577 during a monumental storm. The Blythburgh sighting is described by one of my favourite songs, *Black Shuck* by the Darkness:

---

250 Brontë, Charlotte, Jane Eyre, chapter XII, 2009.

"A nimbus of blue light surrounds a crimson paw
As he takes another fatal swipe
At the Blytheburgh Church Door."[251]

The Black Shuck is said to have flung open the church doors, terrifying a large congregation and killing a man and boy; as he left the church he scorched the north door, the marks of which can still be seen and are often called the devil's fingerprints!

My personal favourites are the two Celtic fae dogs, the Cù Sìth and the Púca. The Cù Sìth is said to haunt Scottish highlands with dark green, shaggy fur and a long braided tail but in Ireland he appears black with flaming eyes. When roaming he would bark a warning to farmers to lock up their womenfolk lest he steal them away to the realm of the Fae. The Púca is another Celtic hound with the ability to shift in to the forms of a horse, rabbit, goat or goblin type figure. The interesting things about the Púca are that he can speak; he is a trickster rather than a killer and when courted kindly can even be very helpful to humans. Other benevolent black dogs include the Gurt Dog from Somerset who is said to accompany lone travellers and the Church Grim from English and Scandinavian folklore. These are the guardian spirits of churches and can appear as dark skinned men who love to ring the bells loudly. The Swedish version the Kyrkogrim is said to be the spirit of a completely black dog which, when a new church was built, was buried alive on north side. The Christians believed the resulting spirit would defend against the devil.

A similar sort of legend and one that I couldn't bear to leave out due to its gruesomeness is that of the Inugami of Japan. The Japanese believe that you can create an Inugami by burying a dog up to its neck. You should surround the dog with food that it cannot reach and then every day until it dies you should visit it and tell it over and over that the pain it feels is nothing compared to your own. When it finally dies the resulting spirit is an Inugami which will do your bidding and wreak revenge on your enemies. The spirit is obviously very angry and very, very hungry so the food is given to appease it. Caution is advised, though, as always when dealing with such a nasty spirit, as when the dog's corpse finally rots away the Inugami cannot return to it and so is free to turn on the sick person that created it.

Finally, in this section we come to the phantom dogs of the wild hunt. This is maybe the most famous, widespread and enduring myth of spectral hounds. The wild hunt traditionally rides between Samhain and Beltane and is associated with the coming of stormy weather. The time of year around Samhain when the storms roll in, nights draw closer and a frosty nip rides the air is my absolute favourite, and I've often felt a deep kinship with the hunt. Standing on or running along a cliff top feeling the full force of the wind and watching the storm whip the sea into a frenzy of crashing, smashing

---

251 The Darkness, Permission to Land, 2003.

waves is my favourite pastime at this time. Despite looking for it often I've never seen the hunt streak across the sky, which may be for the best as witnessing it is thought to be a very bad omen bringing death, plague, war or just bad luck as told in *The Hosting of the Sidhe* by William Butler Yeats:

> *"And if any gaze on our rushing band,*
> *We come between him and the deed of his hand,*
> *We come between him and the hope of his heart."* [252]

Our myths give us various names, hunters and reasons for the hunt but the myths themselves are pretty much the same. The hounds are variously known as Yeth Hounds, Wisht Hounds, The Devil and his Dandy Dogs, Cŵn Annwn, Gabriel's Hounds or Retchet Hounds. Whatever they are called they fit the descriptions of our other phantom black dogs. I love this excerpt from the Wordsworth poem *"Though narrow be that old man's cares"*:

> *"He oftentimes will start,*
> *For overhead are sweeping Gabriel's Hounds,*
> *Doomed, with their impious lord, the flying hart*
> *To chase for ever through aerial grounds."* [253]

And here soaring high above the world chasing their streaking prey we leave the phantom dogs to their hunt and to carry on with our quest.

Psychopomps

In keeping with their dual nature dogs are associated with many spirits who have power over liminal places such as the Vodou loa called Papa Legba. These gods are gatekeepers; they often have aspects of home protection via the threshold and can help facilitate travel between the worlds by opening the ways. Psychopomps are such beings who have these powers but use them especially to open the gates of death and guide the newly dead through. Why dogs are so able to slip between the worlds is not explained but maybe it is due to the way they have one foot in the untamed wilderness and one in the home or maybe just because their colour (usually black) associates them with the underworld.

Wikipedia gives the meaning of the word Psychopomp as *"Psychopomps are creatures, spirits, angels, or deities in many religions whose responsibility is to escort newly deceased souls to the afterlife. Their role is not to judge the deceased, but simply provide safe passage."*

Psychopomps are often associated with horses, ravens, dogs, crows, owls and water. I think it's very interesting that most of our

---

252 Online at http://www.online-literature.com/yeats/784/ Accessed November 4th, 2011.

253 Online at http://www.poemhunter.com/poem/though-narrow-be-that-old-man-s-cares/. Accessed November 4th, 2011.

underworld myths involve travelling over or under the water. People often think of the underworld as an earthly realm but water plays a part as does fire if you believe in a more infernal mythos. In fact I find the element I have the most trouble connecting with is air, the one least often associated with my chthonic ways. According to Jung the psychopomp is the messenger between our unconscious and conscious. While I appreciate Jung's work I do find the whole idea that magic, demons and gods are all in our head doesn't cut it for me. My gods are real, and if that makes me mad then that's ok with me! In many places the shaman takes the role of the psychopomp and it's interesting to note that psychopomps play as much of a role in birth as they do in death.

In Mesoamerican myth the dog itself fulfils the role of a psychopomp by carrying the dead to the afterlife across a body of water. Since the pre-classical times in this area dogs have been buried with the dead. These frequent finds strongly suggest that the dog as an underworld guide or protector was prevalent throughout Mesoamerican history (dog burials are also frequent in Celtic Britain, Ancient Egypt and other cultures). In art the dog is sometimes shown as carrying a torch, and this may be a reference to the fact that dogs were said to give fire to the Mayans, but I think it's likely to have something to do with their guiding role as many psychopomps carry torches to light the way into the unknown.

Xolotl is an Aztec god that shows the link between dogs and psychopomps. He is depicted as a monstrous dog and while not described as a psychopomp, he aided the dead's passage to Mictlan in some myths. He also guarded the sun each night on its perilous underworld journey. I like the following legend as it shows the life-giving qualities of a psychopomp. It is said that after the destruction of the fourth sun Xolotl journeyed to the underworld and stole from Mictlantecuhtil, the Lord of the Dead, all of the bones of the people from the previous suns. He then pierced his penis and gave life to the bones with the blood from the wound. Therefore he resurrected all these people in the new fifth sun.

The leaders of the Wild Hunt and the hunt itself are often seen as psychopomps as one of the legendary functions of the hunt is to collect dead souls and take them on to the otherworld. There are many tens if not hundreds of names connected to the hunter who is variously dead, a lost soul, a cursed immortal, one of the fae or a deity. The most famous leaders are probably Gwynn ap Nudd, King Arthur, Woden, the Devil or Old Nick, Herne the Hunter, Holda and Odin. The wild hunt like many of the black dog myths we've looked at, became more and more diabolical as we became more and more Christian but it has had something of a revival after medieval times with romantic writers turning it into a host of the fae. We should remember that myth isn't dead, it evolves and changes and we should make an effort to interact with it in our own time as well as with the dusty stories of old. Some of my favourite depictions of the wild hunt are in modern fantasy fiction with C. E. Murphy's *Walker*

Papers who gives Cernunnos or Herne as the hunter, Laurell K Hamilton's *Merry Gentry* series which links the hunt to the Irish legend of the Sluagh, and Jim Butcher's *Dresden Files* where the hunt is led by the Erlking.

We come again to Gwyn ap Nudd who in later myth replaced Arawn as Annwn's king. Gwyn was a mighty warrior whose prowess is commended in the *Poem referring to Gwyddno and Gwynn ap Nudd* from the *Black Book of Carmarthen* (translated by William F. Skene). The poem ends:

> *"XX. I have been where the soldiers of Prydain were slain,*
> *From the East to the North;*
> *I am alive, they in their graves!*
> *XXI. I have been where the soldiers of Prydain were slain,*
> *From the East to the South*
> *I am alive, they in death!"*[254]

His role as a psychopomp may grow out of his familiarity with battlefields and as leader of the hunt he can gather up the fallen souls and help them pass over just like the Norse myth of the Valkyries.

My favourite of the various huntsmen is also my second favourite angel (after Lucifer). The archangel Gabriel appears in a Christianised version of the Wild Hunt where he leads the Gabriel hounds in the search for human souls. His hounds glow either green or white but have the usual flaming red eyes. I have to wonder if he became associated with the hunt due to his Christian role as the angel of resurrection? It is said he will blow the horn that will bring about the last judgment. I think this quote from *Mother Shipton's Prophecies* is excellent:

> *"For storms will rage and oceans roar, when Gabriel stands on sea and shore, and as he blows his wondrous horn, old worlds die and new be born."*

Now from Christian Britain we travel full circle and leave off where we began in Ancient Greece and two of my favourite spirits.

Hekate's origins are a dark and murky mystery, no one can say for certain where she originated from or her original attributes. For our purposes she has come to be associated with liminal places such as city gates and doorways where images called Hekataions were erected to her. She is also linked to dogs such as the black bitch called Hekabe - once a Trojan queen, she committed murder, was transformed into a black dog and claimed as Hekate's familiar. Hekate is also associated with poisonous plants, and she is said to have a garden in Colchis consisting mainly of poisonous plants where she trains witches like Kirke and Medea in the use of herbs (it is my ambition to have one of these myself one day!); and necromantic sorcery, all kinds of ghosts, infernal spirits and the dead answer to her as shown in Ovid's *Metamorphoses*:

---

254 Skene, trans. The Four Ancient Books of Wales, 1868:293.

"Out of Erebos and Chaos she called Nox and the Di Nocti and poured a prayer with long-drawn wailing cries to Hecate ... a groan came from the ground, the bushes blanched, the spattered sward was soaked with gouts of blood, stones brayed and bellowed, dogs began to bark, black snakes swarmed on the soil and ghostly shapes of silent spirits floated through the air."[255]

She is a chthonic deity residing in the underworld with Hades, Persephone and Hermes Khthonios. Among her many symbols are the torch, the key, the serpent and of course black dogs as this excerpt from Apollonius Rhodius' *Argonautica* tells:

"Hekate Brimo ... hearing his words from the abyss, came up ... She was garlanded by fearsome snakes that coiled themselves round twigs of oak; the twinkle of a thousand torches lit the scene; and hounds of the underworld barked shrilly all around her."[256]

Early representations of Hekate are single faced (this is how I see her) but later she appears with three heads, sometimes animal heads. These are most usually the dog, serpent and horse. This triple form is particularly associated with crossroads and crossroads are very important to the goddess as offerings of meat and/or garlic are left at them. She is also the main deity of the border between life and death with many necromantic rites calling on her before Hades or Persephone to open the ways, much like Papa Legba is called on in Haitian Vodou. This quote from Apollonius *Rhodius' Argonautica* is excellent:

"Medea forced herself to speak to him. 'Hear me now,' she said. 'These are my plans for you. When you have met my father and has given you the deadly teeth from the serpent's jaws, wait for the moment of midnight and after bathing in an ever-running river, go out alone in sombre clothes and dig a round pit in the earth. There, kill a ewe and after heaping up a pure over the pit, sacrifice it whole, with a libation of honey from the hive and prayers to Hekate, Perses' only daughter. Then, when you have invoked the goddess duly, withdraw from the pyre. And to not be tempted to look behind you as you go, either by footfalls or the baying of hounds, or you may ruin everything and never reach your friends alive."

I have to include one last quote before we leave Hekate as I adore it and think it's so evocative of the rites practiced to her. I also find it interesting that she is cited as coming at dawn a liminal time. This is from Virgil's *Aeneid*:

"The Sibyl first lined up four black-skinned bullocks, poured a libation wine upon their foreheads, and then, plucking the topmost hairs from between their brows, she placed these on the altar fires as an initial offering, calling aloud upon Hecate, powerful in heaven and hell. While other laid their knives to these victim's throats, and caught the fresh warm blood in bowls, Aeneas sacrifices a black-fleeced lamb

---

255 Ovid, Metamorphoses, 10.403. (2009)

256 Apollonius Rhodius, Argonautica 3.1194. (1959).

to Nox, the mother of the Furiae, and her great sister, Terra, and a barren heifer to Proserpine. Then he set up altars by night to the god of the Underworld, laying upon the flames whole carcases of bulls and pouring out rich oil over the burning entrails. But listen! - at the very first crack of dawn, the ground underfoot began to mutter, the woody ridges to quake, and a baying of hounds was heard through the half-light: the goddess was coming, Hecate."

Hekate then leads Aeneid down into Hades and this is where we leave them to move onto our next psychopomp.

Hermes is a very popular god with a variety of functions; guard dogs are particularly sacred to him due to his roles as the god of flocks and as a protector of the home. The *Homeric Hymn 4 to Hermes* states:

"And from heaven father Zeus himself gave confirmation to his words, and commanded that glorious Hermes should be lord over all birds of omen and grim-eyed lions, and boars with gleaming tusks, and over dogs and all flocks that the wide earth nourishes, and over all sheep; also that he only should be the appointed messenger to Hades, who, though he takes no gift, shall give him no mean prize."[257]

Also in this vein phallic stones called Herma were erected to him in doorways and on roads to claim his protection.

Many of us will know Hermes as Zeus' messenger boy but he is a powerful god in his own right and the only member of the Olympians that I have much time for. He is a trickster type character with many shamanistic attributes such as powers over divination, initiation, magic and contact between the worlds. In his aspect as a messenger between gods and man he evokes images of the Christian angels but he is also a contact between the gods of the upper and lower worlds. Hermes is one of the only gods who can freely enter and leave the realm of death and this serves him extremely well in his role of psychopomp. Later depictions of Hermes show him with winged hat and sandals but I've read sources that have said these are later additions and my Hermes certainly does not like them.

I find it interesting that among his other attributes he is listed as a god of dreams, omens and of sleep. This is probably connected to his psychopomp ability as he can awaken people from that final sleep and lead them into death as in Homer's *Odyssey*:

"Hermes Kyllenios began to summon the suitors' ghosts; he held in his hand the golden rod that he uses to lull men's eyes asleep when he so wills, or again to wake others from their slumber; with this he roused them and led them on, and they followed him, thinly gibbering. As in a recess of some eerie cave a chain of bats may be hanging downwards from the rock, but one of them drops from the clinging cluster and then all the rest flit squeaking round, so did these ghosts travel on together squeaking, while easeful Hermes led them down through the ways of dankness. They passed the streams of Okeanos,

---

257 Evelyn-White (trans.) The Homeric Hymns, IV. To Hermes, 568a-573. 1914

the White Rock, the Gates of the Sun and the Land of Dreams, and soon they came to the Field of Asphodel where the souls, the phantoms of the dead have their habitation"[258]

His main association that we are interested in is the protection of travellers both on mundane journeys and the ultimate journey into death. I think my boss was slightly taken aback one day when we were flying (something I hate to do and avoid at all costs) over Geneva and a storm hit. I was sat next to him clutching a piece of rainbow fluorite, a plastic representation of Squirt from *Finding Nemo* (Hermes likes tortoises and turtles) and muttering hymns to Hermes. One of my favourite invocations to him, one that shows him in his darker aspect and explains where he got his psychopomp powers from, is the *Orphic Hymn to Chthonian Hermes*:

"To Hermes Khthonios, Fumigation from Storax. Hermes, I call, whom fate decrees to dwell near to Kokytos, the famed stream of Hades, and in necessity's dread path, whose bourn to none that reach it ever permits return. O Bakkheios Hermes, progeny divine of Dionysos, parent of the vine, and of celestial Aphrodite, Paphian queen, dark-eyelashed Goddess, of a lovely mien: who constant wanderest through the sacred seats where Hades' dread empress, Persephone, retreats; to wretched souls the leader of the way, when fate decrees, to regions void of day. Thine is the wand which causes sleep to fly, or lulls to slumberous rest the weary eye; for Persephone, through Tartaros dark and wide, gave thee for ever flowing souls to guide. Come, blessed power, the sacrifice attend, and grant thy mystics' works a happy end. "[259]

Now it is time to finish and I have barely even scratched the surface of this amazing thread of mythology. I will finish with one final quote from Tryphiodorus' *The Taking of Ilias* as I urge you to go out and start your own explorations of the shady realms of dogs and death:

"And Hades shuddered and looked forth from his seat under earth, afraid lest the great anger of Zeus Hermes, conductor of souls, should bring down all the race of men."[260]

So even the most mighty lord of death is sometimes sickened by it all. It is here in Hades among the shades of our ancestors that I will leave you....

---

258 Homer, Odyssey 24. 1 & 99 ff. (2010)

259 Taylor, trans. The Hymns of Orpheus, 1792:188-9.

260 Tryphiodorus, The Taking of Ilias, 568 ff. Online at www.theoi.com/Text/Tryphiodorus.html, accessed 4 November 2011.

Bibliography

Apollodorus, & Aldrich, Keith (trans.) (1975) *Library of Greek Mythology (Bibliotheca 2)*. Coronado Press

Apollonius of Rhodes, & Rieu, E.V. (trans.) (1959) *The Voyage of Argo: The Argonautica*. Penguin Classics.

Apuleius, & Kenney, E.J. (trans.) (1999) *The Golden Ass*. Penguin Classics.

Bardsley, Barney (2008) *A Handful of Earth*. Hodder PB.

Bellows, Henry Adam, (trans.) (1936) *Poetic Edda*. Princeton University Press.

Brontë, Charlotte (2009) *Jane Eyre*. Readable Classics.

Darmesteter, James (trans.) (2010) *The Zend-Avest, Part 1: The Vendidad*. Nabu Press.

Evelyn-White, Hugh G. (trans.) (1914) *The Homeric Hymns*.

Griffith, Ralph T. (trans.) (1896) *The Rig Veda*.

Guest, Lady Charlotte (trans.) (1877) *The Mabinogion*. Bernard Quaritch.

Hesiod, & West, M.L. (trans.) (2009) *Theogony and Works and Days*. Oxford University Press.

Homer, & Rieu, E.V. (trans) (2010) *The Odyssey*. Penguin Classics.

Mackenzie, Donald A. (1912) *Teutonic Myth and Legend*. Gresham Publications.

Mair, A. W. (trans.) (1928) *Oppian, Colluthus, Tryphiodorus*. Loeb Classical Library.

Ovid, & Melville, A.D. (trans.) (2009) *Metamorphoses*. Oxford University Press.

Propertius, Sextus, & Gantillon, Peter John Francis (trans.) (2010) *Elegies*. Nabu Press.

Seneca, & Miller, Frank Justus (trans.) (1917) *Tragedies, Volume 1: Hercules Furens, Troades, Medea, Hippolytus or Phaedra, Oedipus*. Loeb Classical Library.

Shipton, Mother (1998) *The Prophecies of Mother Shipton*, facsimile of 1870 edition. Pryor Publications.

Skene, William F. (trans.) (1868) *Four Ancient Books of Wales*. Edmonston and Douglas.

Taylor, Thomas, (trans.) (1792) *The Hymns of Orpheus*.

Vickers, Sally (2001) *Miss Garnet's Angel*. Harper Perennial.

Virgil, & Fagles, Robert (trans.) (2010) *The Aeneid*. Penguin Classics.

Virgil, & Fallon, Peter (trans.) (2009) *Georgics*. Oxford University Press.

Discography

The Darkness. *Permission to Land*. Atlantic, 2003.

Voltaire. *Hate Lives in a Small Town*. CDBY, 2010.

Tomb-Cults, Caves, Stars & Blessed Isles: Heroic Interactions With The Otherworld & Life After Death

By Karen F. Pierce

"...heroes were a subset of ancestors and shared in the nature and prerogatives of the dead. Not all had actually experienced death; some had merely disappeared..."[261]

The hero, due to his very nature, achieves great deeds, often living a short but glorious life; he then leaves this mortal coil, though is not forgotten. This paper will look at mythical heroes and where they go when they have passed over from this life; more specifically we shall look at the mythical heroes of two societies, that of the Classical World, and that of the British/Celtic world. The heroes we will discuss may once have been real men, although in many ways that is not important, their mythical lives are the ones that live on in our memories, stories and poems; and as each has a life that is remembered as heroic, what happens to them once this life is ended at times is equally important. For just as we want our heroes to live on in our memories, so too we don't quite want them to just die and be buried. We want their life to carry on after death, to demonstrate that they are more than just mere mortals. Some of the heroes we will look at also interact with the Otherworld while they are still living, passing between the boundaries of worlds for a variety of reasons. Although most do not quite become gods, occasionally some do become deified. So what does happen to a hero when he dies?

1. Blessed Islands and Elysian Fields

"The terms 'Elysian field' and 'Isle of the Blest,' denoted a place of spontaneous cultivation, far removed from ordinary life and completely unconnected with any known city or land, where special souls could dwell undisturbed with the gods."[262]

---

261 Antonaccio, Carla M. An archaeology of ancestors, 1995:1.

262 Cole, S, G. 'Landscapes of Dionysos and Elysian Fields' In, M. B. Cosmopoulos (ed.) Greek mysteries: the archaeology and ritual of Ancient Greek secret cults, 2003:212.

Along with many other societies the two we are looking at, although separated by time, distance and geography, both believed in some form of an afterlife, as evidenced by grave goods in burials that included food and drink and possessions that might be needed in the next world. In Greek myth the main construct of the afterlife was the underworld of Hades, which although not on a par with the Christian Hell, was a grey place, without joy. It was situated underground, although to approach it one had to go to the ends of the known world. A body of water needed to be crossed, although sources differ from whether this was the great river Oceanus, or the rivers Acheron or Styx; a boatman (usually named as Charon) would ferry the dead across for a small charge, which we see later reflected in Hellenistic burial practice when a coin was left in the mouth of the deceased. A more extreme realm of the dead was Tartarus where punishments were meted out, so for example it is here that we find Sisyphus forever rolling his rock uphill, and Tityus stretched on the ground having his liver torn out. However, in contrast to both these places the Greeks also had the Elysian Fields and the Isles of the Blessed which were two paradise-like dwelling places for immortalised human beings. Similar in description, it is difficult to tell what difference, if any, lay between them. [263] They are first mentioned in Homer and Hesiod, but as will become apparent the variations in myth demonstrate that there were different beliefs about what happened to heroes when they died. In Homer we find the heroes of the Trojan War have ended up in Hades after their deaths, along with everyone else. This is most obviously demonstrated when Odysseus makes the journey to the Underworld to converse with Tiresias: whilst there he sees many of his fallen comrades.[264] Even Achilles is found to be dwelling in Hades and wishing he was elsewhere, rather a slave on earth than a ruler of the dead. The one exception to this rule is Menelaus who is told by the sea god Proteus that he will be sent to the Elysian plain because he is married to Helen and is therefore a son-in-law of Zeus.[265] Homer describes the Elysian Fields in Proteus' prophecy to Menelaus thus:

...but to the Elysian Plain and the ends of the earth will the immortals convey you, where dwells fair-haired Rhadamanthus, and where life is easiest for men. No snow is there, nor heavy storm, nor

---

263 See Davies, 'Description by negation: history of a thought-pattern in ancient accounts of blissful life' Prometheus 13:265-84, who looks at the descriptions of places of 'paradise', and notes that in general they are described using negative features, i.e. no snow, no rain, no storms, etc. See also Sourvinou-Inwood, 'Reading' Greek death: to the end of the Classical period, 1995:17-55, for an elaboration of the underworld.

264 We have here an early example of necromancy; for it is Circe who provides Odysseus with detailed directions on how to get to the Underworld, and who also gives him instructions on how to call up the ghosts of the dead and control them once he is there.

265 Homer, Odyssey. 4.561-69.

ever rain, but always Ocean sends up blasts of the shrill blowing West Wind that they may give cooling to men.[266]

However, when Hesiod comes to describe the Isles of the Blessed, he is informing us about the resting place of some of the heroes from the Trojan War:

There some of them were engulfed by the consummation of death, but to some Zeus the father, son of Kronos, granted a life and home apart from men, and settled them at the ends of the earth. These dwell with carefree heart in the Isles of the Blessed Ones, beside deep-swirling Oceanus. Fortunate Heroes for whom the grain-giving soil bears its honey-sweet fruits thrice a year.[267]

Thus even at an early date there is some discrepancy about the eligibility of entry to these Islands. Pindar goes even further in his description, and in the entry requirements, extending it to non-heroes, men who are good, just and noble (but not actual *'heroes'*):[268]

> But those with the courage to have lived
> three times in either realm, while keeping their souls
> free from all unjust deeds, travel the road of Zeus
> to the tower of Kronos, where ocean breezes blow round
> the Isle of the Blessed, and flowers of gold are ablaze,
> Some from radiant trees on land, while the water
> nurtures others; with these they weave
> garlands for their hands and crowns for their heads,
> in obedience to the just counsels of Rhadamanthus,
> whom the great father [Kronos] keeps ever seated at his side,
> the husband of Rhea, she who has
> the highest throne of all.[269]

Plato (*Gorgias* 523A-E) also offers an account of those who are eligible to go to the Isles of the Blessed, a pleasurable, gentle place where life (after death) continues in an easy manner. Rhadamanthus rules over the Elysian Fields, and Kronos, or Rhadamanthys again, rules over the Isles of the Blessed. It is difficult to tell whether these two places were in fact the same place, or whether, firmly distinct originally, their similarities have helped to merge them in the minds of the poets. It appears that later writers often described Elysium as a section of Hades separated from the area where the ordinary dead resided; whilst the Isles of the Blessed were occasionally seen to be located in the Ocean to the far West.

Menelaus may be the only hero in Homer to escape the fate of Hades, but his place in an immortal afterlife appears to be assured due to his relationship with Helen which is reinforced in later sources. Euripides' *Helen* (1676-7) has him given a home in the Isles of the Blessed; whilst Apollodorus (*Epitome* 6.30) also places the

---

266 Homer, Odyssey 4.563-568.

267 Hesiod, Works and Days 167-173.

268 See also Pindar Dirges 129-130 (95).

269 Pindar, Olympian Ode 2.68-77.

couple in the Elysian Fields (following on from Proteus' prophecy). After undergoing all the trials and tribulations of war, once Menelaus has reclaimed his wife, he is apparently rewarded with immortality. That Helen goes to the Elysian Fields seems to be perfectly understandable, she is a daughter of Zeus, and thus her place should not be in the Underworld. If the poets believe that she and Menelaus are supposed to be together, then for this to be possible he has to be immortalised too. In some ways this bears similarities to Helen's brothers, the Dioscuri, where only Polydeuces was the actual son of Zeus, and therefore immortal. When Castor is killed his brother begs for him to be immortalised so that they should not be separated in death.[270] Their lives are thus spent alternating between one day on Olympus and the next in the underworld (or between 'heavenly sky' and earth).[271]

While Menelaus appears to be singled out for special treatment, so too is Achilles, post-Homer, who is ascribed an island of his own – Leuke (the White Island). According to Pausanias (3.19.11-13) the people of Croton and Himera held the belief that Helen, rather than spending eternity with Menelaus on the Elysian Plain/Isles of Blessed, was actually married to Achilles and living with him on an island sacred to him.[272] This 'White Island' appears to be somewhat akin to the Isles of the Blessed in concept, as the other inhabitants consisted of Trojan War heroes, including the son of Ajax Oileus, the son of Ajax Telamon, Patroclus and Antilochus. They were seen by Leonymus, a general of Croton, after he was sent to the island by the Delphic Pythian priestess to be cured of a wound.

In Proclus' *Aethiopis* Achilles' body is snatched from his funeral pyre by his mother, the goddess Thetis, along with the Muses and her sisters, and he is taken to the White Island. It is inferred that Thetis would have revived him on the Island, and made him immortal. Pindar (*Olympians* 2.79ff) has Thetis take him instead to the Isles of the Blessed, whereas Ibycus, Simonides, and Apollodorus all place him with Medea either in Elysium or on the Isles of the Blessed.[273]

What's good enough for epic heroes subsequently becomes good enough for ordinary men as we have seen in Pindar, and is reiterated in Plato's *Gorgias* (523 A-E):

"Now in the time of Cronos there was a law concerning mankind, and it holds to his very day amongst the gods, that every man who

---

270 See Pierce (2011). Pindar, Nemean Ode 10.49-91.

271 Cf. Heracles in the Odyssey (11.601-4) whose phantom is in the underworld while he dwells with the gods).

272 Aethiopis (Proclus Chrestomathy lines 20-22 PEG), cf. Pindar Olympian Ode 2.79ff and Nemean Ode 4.49-50. Cf. Edwards (1985) for a discussion of the apparent contradictory elements of Achilles' death and afterlife.

273 Apollodorus Epitome 5.5. A scholiast on Apollonius Rhodes 4.814-15 notes that both Ibycus and Simonides place Achilles and Medea together in Elysium, (Ibycus fr. 291 PMG).

has passed a just and holy life departs after his decease to the Isles of the Blest, and dwells in all happiness apart from ill; but whoever has lived unjustly and impiously goes to the dungeon of unrequital and penance which, you know, they call Tartarus.[274]

He goes on to say that men were traditionally judged as to which category they fell into, however over time this system became unreliable (for example, those who dressed well were viewed in a more positive light); changes were made, including ensuring men were stripped naked before being judged, and three judges were appointed – Minos, Rhadamanthus and Aeacus. Mankind was judged in the meadow at the dividing road, and if successful would go on to the Isles of the Blessed.

As we will go on to see in other mythical traditions, the concept of the afterlife, whether in the underworld or on a sacred island, appears to frequently involve the crossing or traversing of a body of water. In Greek myth the great river Oceanus is crossed by Odysseus to reach Hades, and the river Styx is first mentioned in the *Iliad*, plus there is also the river Acheron. As Trubshaw notes: *"...earlier people regarded water as a boundary between the mundane world and the otherworlds".*[275] We should also not forget the importance of water in general, as essential for life. In Iron Age Britain the respect due to water, and the belief in it as an otherworldly threshold, can be evidenced by the many votive deposits that have been discovered in bogs, lakes and rivers; whilst the idea of having to cross water to reach the Otherworld/afterlife is found in cultures other than the Classical and Celtic worlds.[276]

2. The Celtic Otherworld(s) – Annwn, Magh Meall, Tir na Nog and Avalon

In a discussion about the *'Celtic otherworld'* we need to be aware that we are actually talking about several slightly differing traditions which fall within the broad *'Celtic'* umbrella, including those focused on here of Wales and Ireland. Green notes that the Irish otherworld *"...is basically a happy one, free from care, disease, old age and ugliness. Abundance, magic, music and birdsong dominate the scene."*[277] However, despite the appearance that it is a place that all seem welcome to, and despite grave goods found in Iron age burials attesting to the implication of the belief in an afterlife which reflected the life lived (aristocratic graves often include horse drawn four-wheeled vehicles, as well as fine weapons), there is little literary evidence that the Otherworlds described were places for the dead, rather they are for the *'ever-living ones'* and are only visited by select

---

274 Plato, Gorgias, 523 A-B.

275 Trubshaw, Sacred places: prehistory and popular imagination, 2005:27.

276 See for example the Babylonian Epic of Gilgamesh, and also Egyptian and Mexican mythology.

277 Green, The gods of the Celts, 1986:122.

(heroic) mortals; [278] and there seems to be only one instance where these heroic mortals return to the Otherworld after death. This was the case of Connla, Laegaire mac Crimthann and Nera, three sons of King Lugaid Menn who had married three fairy women, the daughters of Midir. It is only because of their *'divine'* marriages that they were granted permission to live on in the sidhe of the Tuatha de Danaan – much as Menelaus could live on in Elysium because of his marriage to Helen, daughter of Zeus. We do find however, some form of a *'land of the dead'* which is presided over by the god Donn, and which seems more akin to the Greek Hades than to the Isles of the Blessed.[279]

Annwn

"...the ancient Welsh conceived of Annwn, abode of the former divinities, as a palace which appeared and then disappeared in a familiar landscape setting, or as a delightful subterranean region, or as an Elysian isle."[280]

In Welsh mythology Annwn was the Otherworld, it was ruled by Arawn, and later by Gwyn ap Nudd. Although the *'Otherworld'* was normally perceived as being an island, or across a body of water, the first mention of Annwn in the first branch of the *Mabinogi* locates it in Dyfed. The myth of Pwyll, the Prince of Dyfed, tells how he offends Arawn by letting his dogs claim a stag that Arawn's hounds had brought down. To make penance he agrees to exchange places with Arawn for one year. Arawn was involved in a conflict with Hafgan, and was losing, so had come to the mortal realms to find an ally. Pwyll and Arawn swapped places (and likenesses) and each ruled in the other's place. Pwyll defeats Hafgan, and during his yearlong rule in Annwn, refrains from sleeping with Arawn's wife. From this time on Pwyll and Arawn are firm friends, and Pwyll earns the title Pen Annwn (Head of Annwn).

The myth gives us a mortal prince who is also a ruler of the Otherworld, and may be a story constructed to explain how Pwyll could be known as both. That the Otherworld is located in Dyfed at this point may be due to that location being wild and unknown to those from across the border. Even in the 14th century the Welsh poet Darydd ab Gwilym referred to Dyfed as *'Land of illusion'* and *'Realm of glamour'*. As we will see below, many key places in Arthurian legend can also be located in Wales.

Later tradition moves Annwn from Dyfed and places it across the sea, as the Preiddeu Abbwfn, in the *Book of Taliesin*, describes. King Arthur leads a voyage to a variety of Otherworld locations in order to retrieve the cauldron of the Head of Annwn. Various names and

---

278 See Loomis, Wales and the Arthurian legend, 1956:141ff, for a more detailed discussion of this point.

279 See the Irish Otherworld island of Tech Duinn.

280 Loomis, Wales and the Arthurian legend, 1956:141.

descriptions are given of places either within Annwn, or nearby: Caer Sidi,[281] Caer Pedryvan, Caer Vedwyd, The Isle of the Strong door, Caer Rigor, Caer Wydyr, Caer Golud, Caer Vandwy and Caer Ochren. Within this story, although three boatloads of men went with Arthur, only seven men returned from the journey, indicating that the mission and voyage were highly treacherous.

Tir na Nog

Tir na Nog was an Otherworld realm of Irish mythology where people were forever young, and as such is sometimes known as *'The land of youth'*. Located in the far west, and over the ocean, this Otherworld is not known to be a realm of the dead, or a place where heroes went after death. Instead it was visited by heroes and sailors during their lifetimes, but it took a long voyage to reach there (accounts of visits to Tir na Nog were told in the Irish *echtrae* (adventure) and *immram* (voyage) tales). However, it was also known through the story of Oisin and Niamh. Oisin was one of the Fianna, a follower of Fionn; as a group they were out hunting one day near Lake Killarney when they were approached by Niamh, a woman of incredible beauty (indeed a goddess). She told them she was the daughter of the Son of the Sea (Manannan Mac Lir) and she chose Oisin to be her lover. He joined her on her fairy horse and they rode across the land and sea until they came to Tir na Nog. Here they lived for 300 years, though as this was a fairy land it did not seem that long to Oisin. After a while he grew homesick and wished to visit his own country and people; Niamh gave him a fairy horse for the journey but warned him not to get off or let his feet touch the ground. As is to be expected, despite Oisin's good intentions, he does indeed end up touching the ground when he stops to help some men lift a marble slab, because the girth of the saddle broke. Once he has touched the earth, he turned from a young heroic man to an old withered one, as all the years he had been absent in Tir na Nog caught up with him. Some traditions have him die straight away, others have him struggling to survive until St Patrick takes him in and tries to convert him to Christianity. There are many ballads which feature dialogues between Oisin and Patrick, and some even have Patrick succeeding in converting the pagan. In many ways Tir na Nog is typical of the Celtic or fairy Otherworlds, where humans can spend what seems to them a brief amount of time, but on return to their own land find many years or even centuries have passed. Oisin found that when he asked after Fionn and the Fianna he was told they were names of people who had lived long ago, and whom stories were written about in old books. Although heroes may visit this land, it is however, as stated above, a realm for the living rather

---

281 Although translated as the 'revolving' castle, it is highly possible that this name comes from the Irish tradition, and Sidi is sidhe – the Irish fairy mounds and their inhabitants. See Sims-Williams (1991:57).

than the dead; however, one does gain some form of immortality by living there (as long as one doesn't return to the mortal world).

Oisin's story however is just one of many where a mortal man is enticed to an Otherworldly realm by a goddess, occasionally this role is fulfilled by a god, as in the Welsh tale of Pwyll and Arawn, but more normally supernatural women are the protagonists. For instance, Finn is lured to the Otherworld by a goddess in the guise of a fawn, from the *sidhe* of Donn mac Midir; the goddess Cliodna has a liaison with the hero Tadg; and the voyage of Bran is a classic story of enticement. Bran is lulled into a magical sleep, and he sees a vision of a beautiful woman who sings to him of her enchanted otherworld, a paradise of islands. The next day Bran, his three foster-brothers, and twenty-seven warriors set sail to try and find these islands. They discovered the Land of Women, and spent a year there. After this Bran's companions begged to return home, the goddess warned that disaster would strike if they set foot in Ireland, (just as with Oisin and Niamh). And just like Oisin they discovered that three hundred years had passed in the mortal world; whilst one man flung himself into the sea and was overcome with old age, the others continued to wander across the oceans. These stories clearly share a lot of features. Green suggests that:

"The apparent need of humans by these goddesses may even reflect a kind of reverse sacral kingship, whereby Otherworld power was increased by the union of deities with mortals. The two worlds seem to have enjoyed a mutual dependence, a symbiotic relationship: the crossing of the boundary between them, whichever way it occurred, enhanced the potency and authority of both."[282]

Magh Meall

Far more akin to the Greek Elysium Fields is the Irish Magh Meall (or Mag Mell) – *'The plain of happiness'*. When the Irish gods, the people of Danu, were defeated by men, many went west across the sea and one of the places they ultimately ended up in was Magh Meall. Mankind at that time was believed to have been descended from the god of death, even Caesar tells us in *De Bello Gallico* (VI, 18) that the Gauls believed themselves to be descendants of Dis Pater or Pluto the god of the Underworld (thus the idea of men defeating gods was not as strange as if first sounds, as men were essentially of divine descent too). Those gods that remained in Ireland ended up residing in barrows or hillocks, known as *sidhe*, which were also doorways to an Otherworld. These gods became known as the *'people of the hills'* (*Aes Sidhe* which became shortened to just *sidhe*). These fairy hills are the prehistoric barrows and burial mounds constructed by the people who inhabited Ireland before the arrival of the *'Celts'*. Probably the most famous today are Newgrange, Knowth and Dowth,

---

282 Green, Celtic goddesses: warriors, virgins and mothers, pp. 88.

which are situated in a grand complex comprising fourteen other barrows near the river Boyne.

Avalon

"...it was Margan a Goddess of Annwfyn [Annwn] that had hidden him [Arthur] in Ynys Afallach to heal him of his wounds."[283]

Avalon, the well-known resting place of Arthur and mysterious Otherworld; to what extent did this realm belong purely to Arthur? In many respects it was in fact the realm of Morgan.[284] As has previously been noted,[285] the quote above appears to imply that Avalon (Ynys Afallach) and Annwn are either the same place, or that one is located in the other. This would tie Avalon into the wider mythology of Otherworldly realms, and despite its later embellishments, would root it in earlier traditions. In Geoffrey of Monmouth's *Vita Merlini* he describes the Insula Pomorum (an attempted translation of Ynys Avallach), where nature provides abundantly (much like the classical Isles of the Blessed), and where nine sisters dwell, the most important being Morgen who has healing skills, and who can also shape-shift and fly through the air. Arthur is brought here after the battle of Camlan for Morgen to attend to. The concept of nine supernatural maidens living on a (Celtic) sacred island is attested to elsewhere, as Pomponius Mela (c. 45 CE) describes the island of Sena, off the coast of Brittany, where nine virginal priestesses of a Gaulish deity reside.[286] It is also believed that Geoffrey's concept of Avalon owes much to the description of the Fortunate Isles described by Isidore of Seville.[287]

Glastonbury has long claimed Avalon as its very own Isle of Apples as demonstrated by Giraldus Cambrensis in his *De Principis Instructione*. However, although the most common assumption is that Geoffrey of Monmouth's *Insula Avallonis* derives from the Welsh apple – *'afal'* or apple-tree *'afallen'* it could also be an individual called Afallach. William of Malmesbury in his c.1125 work *De Antiquitate Glastoniensis Ecclesiae* suggests that it could be named after *'a certain Avalloc who is said to have lived there with his daughters on account of its being a solitary place'*. This suggestion is also backed up by Giraldus Cambrensis who suggests *'Avallonia is so*

---

283 Giraldus Cambrensis Speculum Ecclesiae.

284 Morgan – there are many versions of her name, and indeed of who she was. Morgan, Morgen, Morgan le Fay, Morgaine – she is a supernatural female, sometimes the healer of Arthur, sometimes his half-sister, and Avalon appears to be her realm. She also has a Welsh counterpart in the form of Modron, who was the daughter of Avallach.

285 See Loomis, Wales and the Arthurian legend, 1956:155, and Blake & Lloyd The keys to Avalon: the true location of Arthur's kingdom revealed, 2000:140.

286 We should also not forget that the magical cauldron in the Preddeu Annwn, that Arthur sought to steal from the Lord of the Underworld, could only be brought to the boil if heated by the breath of nine virgins.

287 Etymologiae: XIV.6.8 Fortunatae Insulae. These islands are thought to be the Canaries.

called either from British aval which means apple, because that place abounded with apples, or from a certain Avallo, lord of that land.' Even Ashe suggests *"Quite likely the modern philologists are right, and Avalon was the realm of Avallach, a lord of the dead."*[288] Looking at the Welsh form of Avalon, Ynys Afallach, Blake & Lloyd (2000) also highlight that *'ynys'* not only means *'island,'* but also *'a kingdom or realm'* thus giving us the *'realm of Afallach.'* Thus we have the possibility that rather than Arthur being taken to the Isle of Apples, he is taken to the Realm of Afallach.[289] Taking their research further, Blake & Lloyd track their way through a variety of texts and early Welsh genealogies to identify the Lord Afallach and his realm within Gwynedd in North Wales.[290] They indicate that their conclusions are confirmed by the *Vera Historia de Morte Arthur* a medieval text that was only published in full with an English translation in the later part of the 20th century, which states:

"At length the king slightly restored by an improvement in his condition, gives orders to be taken to Venedocia [Gwynedd] since he had decided to sojourn in the delightful Isle of Avalon because of the beauty of the place (and for the sake of peace as well as for the easing the pain of his wounds)"

If Avalon, or the Realm of Afallach, was located in a physical landscape, or the gateway to this Otherworld was located here, then the area of Gwynedd indicated is indeed a strong contender, containing (as Blake & Lloyd note)[291] 547 Bronze Age barrows, as well as burials from other periods. The most visible of these is the Gop, a giant cairn 14 metres high, and 100 metres across, with Neolithic burials in caves at its base. This is truly a Land of the Dead.

3. Heroes as Stars

"Is it not true, then, what people say, that we become stars when we die?"[292]

The stars appear nightly, twinkling in the sky above, moving to their own merry dance; where better for heroes to ascend, to stride across an indigo velvet land, watching over us? The constellations of the Western world have been with us almost unchanged since the time of the Ancient Greeks. Many of the images and myths attached to the constellations can be found to have origins in the star pictures

---

288 Ashe, King Arthur's Avalon: the story of Glastonbury, 1957:19.

289 Avalon as the Isle of Apples may also correspond to a similar realm in Irish mythology, where the sea god Manannan is ruler of an Otherworld known as Emhain Abhlach - Island of the Apple Trees (sometimes identified as the Isle of Arran, or the Isle of Man).

290 Blake & Lloyd, The keys to Avalon: the true location of Arthur's kingdom revealed, 2000:124-130.

291 Blake & Lloyd, The keys to Avalon: the true location of Arthur's kingdom revealed, 2000:142-143.

292 Aristophanes Peace 832-33.

of the Egyptians and Babylonians, but given their own Greek mythological perspective.

The first references to constellations that we find in the Greek literature occur in Homer and Hesiod. In Homer's *Iliad* the description of Achilles' shield included four constellations:

> *"And on it all the constellations that festoon the heavens,*
> *The Pleiades and the Hyades and the strength of Orion*
> *And the Bear, whom men give also the name of the Wagon,*
> *Who turns about it a fixed place and looks at Orion*
> *And she alone is never plunged in the wash of the Ocean"*[293]

Hesiod's *Works and Days* also mentions the same four, in the context of using them as signals when to undertake specific tasks, such as harvesting, ploughing or sailing. Apart from naming them, neither Homer nor Hesiod ascribe any mythical tales to these constellations.

From the Hellenistic era collections of thematically related literature and knowledge gained in popularity and it is from this period that we have Ps Eratosthenes' *The Constellations*[294] and Hyginus' *Poetic Astronomy* giving us myths and stories attached to the stars and constellations, but it is not clear how all these myths evolved into their celestial connections.

When we consider the number of Greek heroes celebrated by epic poetry, there are relatively few that we actually find *'in the sky'*; these are Heracles, Perseus, Orion, Castor, Polydeuces and Asclepius – although other Greek characters and animals also feature. From this list two examples stand out for different reasons. Firstly, the Dioscuri (Castor and Polydeuces), as I have discussed elsewhere (and indeed other divine twins) are celestial in nature and have several links to stars, constellations, and the sky.[295] Castor and Polydeuces became associated with the constellation known as Gemini (from the Latin for twins). According to Ps.Eratosthenes this was because Zeus wished to commemorate their comradeship (*The Constellations* 10) because they *'surpassed all others in their brotherly devotion to one another'*. Similarly, Hyginus notes (*Poetic Astronomy* 2.22) that they were the most loving of brothers, who never acted without mutual consent, and that Jupiter (Zeus) *'placed them among the most prominent stars on account of their dutifulness'*. Although the most common thought is to place Castor and Polydeuces as the twins in Gemini, the constellation itself has been associated with other characters in Greek literature, such as Heracles and Apollo, the Great Gods of Samothrace, and Phaon and Satyrus, for example.

---

293 Homer Iliad 18.509-12. See also Odyssey 5.269-75.

294 Emanating from Eratosthenes Catasterismi which was probably written in the last half of the 3rd century BC, this epitome of his work by an anonymous author dates to the 1st or 2nd century CE.

295 Pierce, 'Riders upon swift horses: the divine twins of Greek myth' In, Huggens, Kim (ed.) Vs: duality and conflict in magick, mythology and paganism, 2011:164-166.

If the figures in the sky all followed this pattern, then we could say that heroes were rewarded by a place in the stars, and that mankind could look up to those special individuals who achieved much in life. However, to be placed in the stars was not always a sign of heroism, or a special favour from the gods. Cassiopeia for example boasted that she excelled the Nereids in beauty, and as a punishment she was put among the stars, and according to Hyginus *'on account of her impiety, as the sky turns, she seems to be carried along lying on her back'.*[296]

One of the earliest constellations to accrue mythical connections, mentioned in both Homer and Hesiod, was that of Orion. His place among the stars is attributed to a variety of reason, but in general it was because he had angered one of the gods in some way;[297] either because he attempted to rape Artemis/Diana, or because he boasted about the prowess of his hunting skills.[298] So, unlike the Dioscuri, Orion does not become a constellation because he has achieved greatness, but generally out of dishonour. He is also associated with the Pleiades because he tried to attack/rape Pleione when she was travelling with her daughters: although she escaped, Orion tracked her for seven years, and Jupiter pitying them placed the women as stars. Thus we see (the constellation) Orion appearing to follow the (constellation) Pleiades.

As Condos notes, many of the stories connected with Orion are most probably astral myths, in other words they have arisen due to the position of constellations and their relation to one another and the horizon.[299] So, we have myths such as the Pleiades fleeing Orion, Orion's ability to walk on the sea, and his flight from the Scorpion.

From this brief look at the Western star myths, despite the often stated generalisation that the figures in the constellations were placed there by the gods to honour their lives or deaths,[300] there seems to be a variety of reasons why heroes and other figures are placed in the sky, and it is more likely that the stories that arose to explain the movement or pattern of the stars are attached at later dates to some figures. Although a nice idea that truly great heroes are turned into stars to watch over us, and for us to remember their great deeds, in actuality we are just as likely to be reminded to be aware of hubris and divine retribution.

---

296 Hyginus, Poetic Astronomy II.10.

297 Aratus (Phaenomena 635ff), Pseudo-Erat. (Catasterismi 7) and Hyginus (Fabulae CXCV and Poeticon Astronomicon II,34) speak of an insult to or attack on Diana; Pseudo-Erast. (Catasterismi 32), Hyginus (Poeticon Astronomicon II. 26 and 34), and Ovid (Fasti V.535-544) attribute his death to a boast leading to Earth's revenge. The alternate rising and setting of Orion and Scorpio are explained by these two stories.

298 Although an alternative version has Artemis nearly marrying Orion; this situation angers Apollo and he tricks Artemis into killing Orion. Mourning him greatly she puts him into the stars.

299 Condos, Star myths of the Greeks and Romans: a sourcebook, 1997:150.

300 See for example, Condos, Star myths of the Greeks and Romans: a sourcebook, 1997:84 and Grant, The myths of Hyginus, 1960:14.

4. Heroes, Tombs and Cults

In Greece, from the 8th century BCE onwards, there was a widespread propensity towards the phenomena of hero cults and tomb cults; what might generically be seen as cults of ancestors. The two terms have often been viewed as interchangeable, though there is difference in the practices they describe. A simplified view suggests that hero cults involve the construction and worship at a shrine dedicated to an individual, which may well be situated on a site of previous occupation; whereas tomb cult, as the name suggests, is based around tombs or graves, and can involve the veneration of ancestors, or could be at an *'anonymous'* tomb which has either been ascribed an individual (such as an epic hero) or remains anonymous (the *'hero'*), or a presumed or adopted ancestor.[301] It is thought that during the 8th century several factors combined to influence these cults. On the one hand there was the panhellenic circulation of the Homeric epics, and on the other society was emerging from the Dark ages and groups were struggling to stake an identity within the emerging polis. 8th century Greeks were partly in awe of the Mycenaean tombs that sat within their landscape, and were also seeking to claim, in some places, descent from heroes featured in the Homeric poems. If, as a people, they were looking into the past, consciously looking back to an heroic age since gone, by looking around their own landscape for traces of this heroic past, and having seen ruins on top of a hill, for instance, they might have surmised that this is where their heroes lived, or alternatively that this was *'politically'* an ideal location to visualise their community *'ancestors'*, and begin to venerate them. This would also enable the community to forge a shared identity.

Although the proposition of a conscious historicising is conjectural, like suggesting that activity took place on a site because of an inherent reverence, both viewpoints are based on the belief that the past is important, and a geographical location that is strongly linked to the past (via ruins etc.) holds a certain power within the minds of the populace. Politically, this power can be manipulated to act as a coalescing, or strengthening force within the community.

One good example of a hero cult that we have evidence for is the Menelaon at Therapne, near Sparta. Literary evidence notes that the shrine is dedicated to Helen, or Menelaus, or to both of them; and the site is named as the Menelaon in ancient times.[302] Archaeologists first paid attention to the site in the 1830's when Ludwig Ross

---

301 For more detailed discussions about tomb cults and hero cults see Antonaccio, *An archaeology of ancestors: tomb cult and hero cult in early Greece*, Boardman, *The archaeology of nostalgia: how the Greeks recreated their mythical past*, pp. 45-78, and Morris 'Tomb cult and the 'Greek renaissance': the past in the present in the 8th century BC.' *Antiquity* 62: 750-61.

302 Helen's shrine; Herodotus 6.61, Menelaus' shrine; Pausanias 3.19.9-13, shared shrine; Isocrates *Helen* 63, named as Menelaon; Polybius 5.18 & Livy 34.28.

identified it as the Menelaon; since then there have been many excavations at the site and surrounding area, most notably in the 1970's under the direction of Hector Catling. What archaeology has discovered is typical of hero cults. There is evidence of occupation on the site dating back to Mycenaean times, but not evidence of worship of Helen and Menelaus at that period. The shrine was constructed on a natural outcrop and enclosed by a platform, this location may have suggested that it was a burial place for heroes, but although seven skeletons have been found on site they are not 'royal burials', indeed three are believed to have died in the final destruction of the Mycenaean site (i.e. are not actual burials). What we do have, however, are large numbers of votive offerings, primarily large quantities of lead figurines in all kinds of shapes – warriors, winged goddesses, animals, and representations of textiles, and most significantly some inscribed objects dedicated to Helen and Menelaus, firmly identifying the shrine as theirs. Helen and Menelaus were local heroes to Sparta, and thus it is no surprise that they should be venerated here on a site of previous (Mycenaean) occupation. Was there a folk memory of the 'royals' who had lived there centuries ago, or did the ruins and natural outcropping just suggest an idealised setting? Whatever the reason, Helen and Menelaus came to be established there, and Helen was even said to have made an appearance at the shrine (Herodotus 6.61).

Ancient Greece is not the only society to look to its mythical heroes in order to legitimize contemporary beliefs. Within Britain the concept and image of Arthur has repeatedly been used. Culturally we are continually reinventing Arthur to suit the needs of the time we live in. Hutton[303] touches upon this theme while discussing the impact of Arthurian legends on twentieth century academics. He describes how in the 1960's Cadbury Castle in Somerset was excavated with a view to discovering whether it was in fact the legendary Camelot as local legend had it, and although the idea of Camelot was a 12th century invention, the dig did reveal that the site had potentially been constructed to house a British war band of considerable size. With books on the archaeology of the period being published in the early 1970's, the public and contemporary culture embraced a Celtic war-band Arthur with a television series, *Arthur of the Britons*. As Hutton points out, this portrayal of Arthur with long hair and moustache reflected the image of contemporary hippies, and could be embraced by the counter culture movement. By the time Richard Gere and Sean Connery were celebrating the Arthurian legend in *First Knight* we were back to a glamorous medieval portrayal, whilst Hutton[304] describes the knights in *Excalibur* as *"the chivalric equivalents of punk"* with their *"grotesque armour and brutal ways"* in stark contrast to the hippy sentiments of *Arthur of the Britons*.

---

303 Hutton, Witches, druids and King Arthur, 2003:49-54.

304 Hutton, Witches, druids and King Arthur, 2003:53.

Long before the twentieth century the image of Arthur was being manipulated. Back in the 12th century monks from Glastonbury abbey (apparently encouraged by Henry II, who, according to Giraldus Cambrensis was keen for the grave of Arthur to be found) excavated and found what they claimed was the grave of Arthur. They discovered a stone slab and lead cross inscribed with the words (as recorded by Giraldus Cambrensis) *"Hic iacet sepultus inclytus rex Arthurus cum Wenneveria uxore sua secunda in insula Avallonia"* (Here lies buried the famous King Arthur with Wenneveria his second wife in the isle of Avalonia).[305] Beneath the slab was a coffin made from a hollowed out oak tree, and within this was some bones, a damaged skull and some fair hair. The tomb remained (and was a tourist attraction) until the dissolution of the abbey in 1539 on the orders of Henry VIII.

It is now widely accepted that the finding of the grave and its contents were a medieval fraud. In 1184 a great fire had destroyed most of Glastonbury Abbey, and thus the monks were no doubt keen to exploit any avenue possible in bringing revenue and renown back to the Abbey. Following the fire, many saintly relics suddenly appeared at Glastonbury (even those known to be held elsewhere); the interest and subsequent propaganda surrounding the discovery of Arthur's grave helped to put Glastonbury firmly on the medieval tourist map as a centre of pilgrimage. The finding of the grave also intimated that Arthur truly was dead, and that there was no point in hoping that he was waiting to come to the aid of the Britons, which was also an astute piece of political manipulation for the time. It had commonly been believed that Arthur's grave either did not exist, or could not be found as expressed by William of Malmesbury in 1125:

> *"Arthur's tomb is nowhere to be found, for which reason*
> *ancient fables declare that he will return again."*

And as noted in the Welsh *Stanzas of the Graves*, within the *Black Book of Carmarthen*:

> *"A grave for March, a grave for Gwythur,*
> *A grave for Gwgan Bloody-sword*
> *An enigma for ever a grave for Arthur"* [anoeth y byd]

In Ireland, it is not the heroes who dwell in the mounds there, but the gods themselves. As mentioned above, the barrows called *sidhe* which gave their name to those who dwelt there contained the last of the gods who did not flee Ireland. As time has passed they became known as fairy mounds. Originally prehistoric burial mounds they would probably have contained brave warriors and heroes, and rich rulers. The Newgrange complex is especially interesting, containing seventeen mounds in close proximity. This indeed was a realm of the dead, which became a realm of the gods

---

305 Later chroniclers give the inscription as "Here lies the famous King Arthurus, buried in the isle of Avalon" and neglect to add that Guinevere was mentioned, or that she was called his second wife!

and a link to the Otherworld, as was The Realm of Afallach discussed above, located in Gwynedd.

5. Stones, caves and giants: the hero in the landscape

The hero Arthur is firmly embedded in the landscape of Britain, as a plethora of sites and place names attest to. Geoffrey Ashe (1980) produced a guidebook to many of these sites, and in 1993 John Godfrey Williams published a *'comprehensive'* list of prehistoric sites and place names connected to Arthur, which number almost three hundred, 124 of which are in Wales. These range from the obvious: Arthur's Quoit, Arthur's Table, Arthur's Stone etc, to the more tenuous: Penmyarth (the Fish stone near Crickhowell) which William's suggests is a possible corruption of Pen-y-arth (Head of the Bear). The name Arthur is generally believed to mean *'bear'* and Williams suggests that it derives from the Welsh words *'Arth'* and *'vawr'* (i.e. Great Bear). He also further postulates that these stones and sites are connected to the constellation Ursa Major which points to the Pole star and is a way of finding North. As we have seen above the Bear constellation is named in Homer, and is known as such in a variety of cultures.[306] Whether Williams' suggestion about the connection between *'Arthur'* places and the polestar and Ursa Major has any validity or not, and whether his, at times, tenuous suggestions regarding words with *'arth'* in them bear any truth, we cannot get away from the fact that there are still an awful lot of features, or sites, in the landscape that are firmly connected to Arthur. Some of which still have a *'story'* attached to them. For instance, at Llangadog is Coetan Arthur, a boulder that was supposedly thrown by King Arthur from Pen Arthur Issa, a farm a mile and a half away; Carreg Carn March Arthur (the stone of the mound of Arthur's warhorses), at Mold, Flintshire, which bears the mark of a large horse shoe; King Arthur's Round Table, a castle mound at Caerleon - connecting the round table myth with the idea that Caerleon was a base for Arthur. We have several Arthur's Seats or Chairs, ranging from Edinburgh, and a variety of other Scottish sites, to Haydon Bridge in Northumberland, and to Nevern in Pembrokeshire; at least four Round tables (Stirling, Penrith, Cadbury, and Caerleon) plus three other Tables, not specified as round, in Wales; and several claims to graves, from Glastonbury to Melrose, Roxburghshire and two in Pembrokeshire. If nothing else we can say that these illustrate to a certain extent which areas in Britain have the strongest claims on Arthur (Wales, Scotland, Northern England) perhaps retaining folk memories of the activities and battles of the Britons.

A couple of places have boulders that were thrown by King Arthur, of a size that would clearly be impossible for a man to do so,

---

306 As Halyes notes in the foreword to Williams work: "The Arabic names for two of its stars mean 'The Back of the Great Bear' (Thahr al Dubb Akbar) and 'The Loin of the Bear' (Al Marakk).

such as Coetan Arthur at Llangadog, and Coetan Arthur at Reynoldstone (Gower), where the capstone is said to be a pebble from the giant Arthur's shoe, thrown from Carmarthenshire when he was walking to Camlann. At this site Arthur's ghost is also said to walk down to the sea when the moon is full, dressed in glowing armour. In this respect, these *'stories'* are closely related to other giant stories. At Arthur's Stone, Dorstone (Herefordshire, 5 miles east of Hay on Wye) it is traditionally believed that King Arthur killed either a giant, or a king, and that the giant (or king, or even Arthur himself) is buried here. A nearby stone under a hedge called the Quoit Stone has hollows on it that are said to be either the marks of the giant's elbows, or Arthur's knees where he knelt to pray. Early stories about Arthur place him on a par with giants on a variety of occasions. Geoffrey of Monmouth has him defeat a giant on his way across to Europe, at Mont St. Michel, and he is one of the heroes involved in the killing of the giant Ysbaddadon, to enable the marriage of Culhwch and Olwen, in the Mabinogion.[307]

He is often described in larger than life terms, and in Giraldus Cambrensis' description of the grave discovered at Glastonbury in 1191, his bones are larger than a normal sized man:

> *"You must also know that the bones of Arthur thus discovered were so huge that the words of the poet seemed to be fulfilled:*
> *'And he shall marvel at huge bones in tombs his spade has riven'*
> *For his shank bone, when placed against that of the tallest man in the place and planted in the earth near his foot, reached (as the Abbott showed us) a good three inches above his knee. And the skull was so large and capacious as to be a portent or prodigy, for the eye socket was a good palm in width."*

Thus, even this forged medieval grave contains a giant of a man trying to lend credence to the idea that this was indeed Arthur. In the Welsh triads, we even have Guinevere as the daughter of a giant.

The three great queens of Arthur's court:

"Gwennhwyfar daughter of (Cywryd) Gwent

And Gwenyfar daughter of (Gwythyr) son of Griediawl

And Gwenyfar daughter of (G)organ the giant"[308]

Earlier implied evidence of Arthur's stature is found in Nennius, where his dog Cabal leaves a pawprint in a stone (while they were hunting the boar Twrch Trwyth), in the region of Buelt. The stone became the top of a carn (Carn Cabal), and if ever moved would magically reappear at the top of the carn the next day. Surely only a

---

307 He also defeats the giant Rhitta on Snowdon, the three sisters of the giant Cribwr of Glamorgan and the giant of Brent Knoll near Glastonbury.

308 Miller, 1970:111. Various stones and boulders in Yorkshire are said to have been dropped or thrown from Guinevere's apron, and at Sewingshields King Arthur is said to have stood on King's Crags throwing boulders at Guinevere on Queen's Crags.

giant of a dog could have done so (like master, like dog). Incidentally, the name Cabal could be derived from Caballus, which is the Latin for horse, giving the implication that his dog is perhaps as large as a horse. Additionally, in Nennius' description of the tomb of Anir, who he called Arthur's son, when men came to measure the length of the grave is was variously found to be 6 ft, 9ft, 12ft and even 15ft. Both these stories have a supernatural element about them, both imply large stature (like father, like son), and also interestingly, both give us features in the landscape which are already associated with Arthur in the early 9th century, and are still visible today. Williams suggests that the location of Carn Cabal could be within the parish of Penbuallt, Breconshire, where there is a line of four cairns, three of which are culled Tri Chrugiau, the location is to the south of Llanafan Fawr Cribarth or, Bear Ridge. So, the notion of Arthur as a giant, or a man of great stature, has lingered in the folk memory of the landscape.

The paw print on the stone is not the only association in the landscape with Cabal that we have, there are also some burial mounds/quoits that have names such as *'Gwal-y-filiast'* or *'Llech-y-filiast'* the stone or kennel of the greyhound bitch, such as the dolmen at St Lythans, in the Vale of Glamorgan, commonly known nowadays as Tinkinswood, or at Castell Carrell Carreg. These structures, no longer necessarily recognised as burial chambers, having lost their earth mounds, and possibly having been looted, were then given other attributes relating to Arthur, although it is also possible that they were in fact utilised as some form of dog kennels, or animal shelters, in the mundane world.

Further evidence of Arthurian sites becoming integral parts of the landscape (and indeed tourist attractions) comes in the early 12th century; Herman of Tournai (1146) visited England in 1113 as part of a group of monks attempting to raise funds for the rebuilding of the cathedral of Laon. Whilst on his trip he was shown Arthur's Chair and Arthur's Oven on the road between Bodmin and Exeter. He also notes that a fight broke out between a Cornishman and a Frenchman, when the Cornishman claimed that Arthur was still alive, and he compared this to the differences of opinion held between the Bretons and the French over Arthur. This passage is important in several respects. It demonstrates that prehistoric monuments were firmly associated with Arthur by the 12th century, and that they could be seen as tourist attractions (or places of interest to visit/see); it also demonstrates the long-seated tradition that many people believed Arthur to be still alive, which brings us round to Arthur's *'death'*.

"*Hic jacet Arthurus rex quondam rexque futures*" (Here lies Arthur, the once and future King) Malory *Le Morte D'Arthur*

According to the *Annales Cambriae* (c. 950) Arthur fell at the Battle of Camlann, along with Medraut (i.e. Mordred). Geoffrey of Monmouth in his *Historia Regum Britanniae* (1136) says that Arthur killed Mordred,[309] but was grievously wounded in the process, and thus goes to Avalon to have his wounds attended to. Giraldus Cambrensis (*De Principis Instructione*, c. 1195) is the source which describes the discovery and contents of the grave at Glastonbury and also notes that:

> *"...the body of King Arthur, which legend has feigned to have been transferred at his passing, as it were in ghostly form, by spirits to a distant place and to have been exempt from death..."*

Malory is the instigator of the story we are familiar with whereby, once Excalibur has been thrown into the lake, and claimed by the Lady of the Lake, a barge containing three queens arrives to take Arthur away to the Isle of Avalon. Because Sir Bedivere delayed in throwing the sword into the lake (pretending to have done so the first two times), he is lead to believe that by the time Arthur was taken away in the barge it was too late to save him, and that he was brought back to be buried during the night. However, there is doubt as to whether Arthur is buried, or is hidden away in another place, or Otherworld. As Layamon's Brut tells the story:

> *"The Britons believe yet that he is alive,*
> *And dwelleth in Avalon with the fairest of fays;*
> *And the Britons still look ever for Arthur to come*
>
> ...
>
> *But there was once a prophet, Merlin by name;*
> *He foretold in words – his saying were true, -*
> *That an Arthur must still come to help the Britons."*

As there has been constructed a veil over the death of Arthur there has been the opportunity to manipulate the idea further. With Arthur away in Avalon we have the construct of the Otherworld, where a hero lives in a paradisiacal setting, much like the Greek Isles of the Blessed, and other comparative Otherworlds. Although normally once one has reached such an Otherworld this is the permanent place of residence, there are instances where heroes (and heroines) appear to mortal men, usually acting in some kind of saviour role; thus Helen and the Dioscuri prevent an attack on Sparta their home town. Arthur may now dwell in Avalon, but there remains a hope that he may return at any point to save the Britons.

This idea of the potentially returning hero has also resulted in the *'sleeping hero'* legends that have sprung up around Arthur. In these he is not dwelling in Avalon, but sleeping in a cave, or underground within a Mountain or mound, along with his faithful knights, waiting for the time when he is needed. We know that he is doing so because the folk tales that relate these legends have someone entering the cave, usually for some kind of gain (riches, etc), and they accidentally waken the knights too early, and are often punished as a result. The sleeping hero legend is found all over Britain, in Gloucester, Sewingshields, Alderley Edge (Cheshire), Isle of Man, Isle of Skye,

---

309 Although that cannot be inferred from the Annales Cambriae, where they could just as easily have been allies.

Vale of Neath (Glamorgan), Ogof Arthur (Anglesey) and a version was also told by Iolo Morgannwg (Edwards Williams) where the mortal protagonists first meet on London Bridge.[310] Many of the references to these legends are predominantly found in 19th century literature and folk-lore collections,[311] however, Loomis [312] does relate some examples from the 13th century which have Arthur resting within Mount Etna.[313] Pennick[314] believes that this sleeping hero myth relates to that of a former god, who was exiled to an island in the west at the end of the golden age. He sleeps, waiting to be recalled. Legends of caves also relate to the Tuatha de Danaan who retreated underground. Craig-y-Ddinas, at the head of the Vale of Neath, as well as being associated with the sleeping hero of Arthur, is also said to be one of the last places in Wales where the *'little people'* lived. Caves are liminal spaces, entrances to Otherworlds, hiders of secrets and doorways, and as such often need to be guarded. Pennick[315] suggests that: *"In some places, legend particularizes the spirit guardian into an immortalised hero-figure."* As a figure who ventured into the Otherworld of Annwn in order to steal the magical cauldron, Arthur already has a connection to the Otherworld. He has been a mover between the worlds, and who better to guard an entrance to the Otherworld than one who can move between both, who belongs in both.

6. Wild hunt

Arthur also becomes linked to the Wild Hunt, a folkloric motif found throughout Northern Europe, and primarily in Germany, Britain and Scandinavia. The hunt, as would be expected, consists of a pack of hounds and hunters, led by a certain individual. Ghostly and wild, they pursue their quarry across the skies, and bring terror to those who see them; usually appearing around Yule time. The hunters are sometimes made up of those who have recently died; and if one gets in their way there is the risk of being whisked away to the realm of the dead. The animals of the hunt, the hounds and horses are usually black, white or grey; sometimes they have fiery eyes, or breathe fire. In the Welsh version, the Cwn Annwn (Hounds of Annwn), are white with red ears. There is a long list of individuals

---

310 A cave on Barra (Outer Hebrides) is the location for a similar sleeping hero legend, but this time the hero is Ossian, son of Fionn (Finn Mac Cool), he is believed to fulfil a similar role as Arthur, a protector of the land (Scotland) who will return when needed. See also Frederick Barbarossa who sleeps in the Kyffhauserberg, Germany.

311 See Loomis, Arthurian tradition and folklore.' Folklore 69:1-25 (1958), and Simpson, 'King Arthur's enchanted sleep: early nineteenth century legends.' Folklore 97:206-209 (1986) for references.

312 Loomis, 'Arthurian tradition and folklore.' Folklore 69:13-16 (1959).

313 Gervase of Tilbury Otia Imperialia, Caesarius of Heisterbach Dialogue Miraculorum, and [unknown author] Floriant and Florete. See also Williams, 'King Arthur in history and legend.' Folklore 73:85-86 (1962).

314 Pennick, Celtic sacred landscapes, 1996:101.

315 Pennick, Celtic sacred landscapes, 1996:100.

that are associated with leading the Hunt, ranging from Norse gods and supernatural beings, such as Odin, Wodan, Gwynn ap Nudd, and Herne, to more human kings (King Waldemar, Charlemagne, Herla), and even a Cornish lawyer (Jan Tregeagle). The Hunt itself comes under different names, depending on occasion as to who is leading it; hence Woden's Hunt, Herlathing, Cwn Annwn, Cain's Hunt, Gabriel's Hounds, Asgardreia and Mesnee d'Hellequin, for example.

"...being enlisted into the Hunt is a dubious sort of honour, for it is associated with penance and punishment as well as power. Such power, when present in the stories, comes in the form of Otherworldly status conveyed upon an earthly king or hero, a way of keeping their memory alive by placing them into the landscape, associating them with successive generations of traditional lore and ghostly heroes."[316]

By the late 12th century Arthur is thought to have become the leader of the Hunt as noted by Gervase of Tilbury, and he is later seen *'haunting'* places he has become associated with, for example being seen in the Hunt along King Arthur's Lane (a track leading down from the hill fort at Cadbury), and along a nearby causeway. As noted the Wild Hunt is a motif that becomes localized, and associations pertinent to the local population accrue to it. It is no surprise that Arthur becomes attached to this legend, and he is not the only British *'hero'* to do so. Similar stories are told about Edric the Wild, a Shropshire forester who refused to submit to the rule of William the Conqueror. Despite being a historical figure, his story attracts supernatural elements and he becomes associated with the fairy world, and also becomes a *'mine-spirit'* similar to the Cornish *'Knockers'*. His appearance usually heralds the outbreak of war. We even have Sir Francis Drake becoming the leader of the Hunt, again being seen at times where Britain is under threat.

Seeing the Hunt was not a good omen, and could precede death and violence; where the Master of the Hunt was a supernatural being the witness could well be in trouble; however where the Hunt has tended to acquire localized heroes as leader the danger indicated tends to be more for the country as a whole, rather than the individual. The Yuletide appearances of the Hunt generate from a time when there was a belief in the veil between the mortal world and the Otherworld being thin between Yule and Twelfth Night. According to Berk & Spytma Norwegian peasants would leave a sheaf of grain out during this season to feed the Huntsman's horses, and young men would enact the Wild Hunt at the winter solstice: *"Costumed and masked, they embodied the souls of their ancestors. Their task was to punish those who violated the rural traditions, usually by stealing beer and livestock."*

As with the idea of Arthur being a mover between worlds, and therefore an idealised figure to guard the cave entrances to the

---

316 Berk & Spytma, 'Penance, power, and pursuit: on the trail of the Wild Hunt', 5 (2002).

Otherworld, the figure of the leader of the Wild Hunt tended often to be someone who had ambiguous connections between life and death.

Conclusion

While the Greeks looked to the monuments and ruins of their ancestors and ascribed them to heroes, as their tombs or their dwelling places, venerating them as such, and utilising them as ancestral claims to the land and the landscape as their own domains, here in Britain a similar thing was being done with our own heroes, in particular with Arthur. People looked to the prehistoric monuments, the tombs, mounds, and stone as well as natural features and put a claim in for Arthur, in many respects attempting to indicate that *"Arthur was here"*. These are the stones he threw, this is where he hunted, this is where his round table was, this is where he was buried: claiming Arthur as their own, sometimes for potentially financial reasons (a good tourist draw, even in the 12th century). A warband leader of the Welsh (if he did indeed exist) whose fame spread throughout Europe, his story being embellished many times along the way. Here he fought giants, here he won battles. We have laid claim to Arthur continuously throughout our landscape, people turning monuments of the past that they didn't understand into a new reality, giving them to a hero they wanted to believe in.[317]

According to Blake & Lloyd (2000) Avalon was a real place in Gwynedd, North Wales, but the mythical tradition that grew up around Avalon and overshadowed the realm of Afallach has given us a rich poetic tradition of an Island of Apples, and mysterious figures guiding barges across the waters. That two mythical traditions so far apart geographically, and linearly (Greece & Britain) should ascribe to certain of their heroes a life beyond death in a realm across water, a mysterious Blessed Isle where all their earthly needs are met, is perhaps a coincidence, or it perhaps demonstrates a deep seated desire within our collective unconscious for our heroes to be more than we are, and to survive when we cannot. Whether they are placed in the stars looking down on us, or living on just out of our reach in a paradisiacal realm, or even sleeping beneath a hill, awaiting the time when they will be needed again.

In general, while the myths of the Greeks gave us heroes who departed to a better life after death on a paradise-like island, the British myths give us stories about heroes who visit the Otherworld while still living. However, there are occasional instances where the opposite occurs. Odysseus of course visits Hades, the land of

---

317 As Loomis, Wales and the Arthurian legend, 1956:72, notes: "The evidence we have culled from mainly twelfth-and early thirteenth-century sources establishes the fact that the Welsh and Bretons adapted their concept of the immortal Arthur to already familiar concepts of a supernatural king, He assumed the part of the Maimed King, the faery lord of Avalon, the leader of the Wild Hunt, the sleeping king in the hollow mountain."

Persephone, to find out how he can get home, and although he never truly enters this land fully, the ghosts and shades of departed comrades and acquaintances come to speak to him once he has made the blood sacrifice. Orpheus goes to the Underworld to find his wife Eurydice; and another myth has Theseus and Perithous enter Hades with the intention of kidnapping Persephone, a foolhardy idea from the start, and one that sees them punished. We do however perhaps see reflections of this mission appear in stories of the Celtic heroes who are either enticed to the Otherworld by a fairy woman/goddess, or who enter with the idea of kidnapping one.

Collectively we have placed our heroes, or reminders of our heroes, in the landscape all around us; whether some of these places contain folk memories of actual events remains to be seen. But the idea that there is a mythical landscape overlaying, or influencing the geographical landscape, means that our heroes can be found whenever we need them.

Bibliography

Antonaccio, Carla M. (1995) *An archaeology of ancestors: tomb cult and hero cult in early Greece.* London: Rowman & Littlefield.

Ashe, Geoffrey (1957) *King Arthur's Avalon: the story of Glastonbury.* London: Collins.

Ashe, Geoffrey (1980) *A guidebook to Arthurian Britain.* London: Longman.

Berk, Ari & Spytma, William. *Penance, power, and pursuit: on the trail of the Wild Hunt.* 2002. [Originally appeared in *Realms of Fantasy*; accessed online at: http://www.endicott-studio.com/rdrm/forhunt.html] on 19/10/2006

Blake, Steve & Lloyd, Scott (2000) *The keys to Avalon: the true location of Arthur's kingdom revealed.* Shaftesbury: Element.

Blake, Steve & Lloyd, Scott (2002) *Pendragon.* London: Rider. [republished in 2004 as *The lost legend of Arthur: the untold story of Britain's greatest warrior.*]

Boardman, J. (2002) *The archaeology of nostalgia: how the Greeks recreated their mythical past.* London: Thames & Hudson.

Bromwich, Rachel, Jarman, A.O.H. & Roberts, Brynley F. (eds.) (1991) *The Arthur of the Welsh: the Arthurian legend in medieval Welsh literature.* Cardiff: University of Wales Press.

Cohen, Ada (2007) *Mythic landscapes of Greece* in, Woodard, Roger D. (ed.) *The Cambridge companion to Greek mythology.* Cambridge: Cambridge University Press, pp.305-330.

Cole, S, G. (2003) *Landscapes of Dionysos and Elysian Fields,* in, M. B. Cosmopoulos (ed.) *Greek mysteries: the archaeology and ritual of Ancient Greek secret cults.* London/New York, pp.193-217.

Condos, Theony. *Star myths of the Greeks and Romans: a sourcebook (containing 'The constellations' of Pseudo- Erastosthenes and 'The poetic astronomy' of Hyginus).* Grand Rapids: Phanes Press, 1997.

Davies, M. (1987) *Description by negation: history of a thought-pattern in ancient accounts of blissful life,* in *Prometheus* 13:265-84.

Edwards, Anthony T. (1985) *Achilles in the Underworld: Iliad, Odyssey,* and *Aethiopis,* in *Greek, Roman & Byzantine Studies* 26:215-27.

Gantz, T. (1993) *Early Greek myth: a guide to literary and artistic sources.* Baltimore: Johns Hopkins University Press.

Grant, Mary ([trans. & ed) (1960) *The myths of Hyginus.* Lawrence: University of Kansas Publications.

Green, Miranda (1986) *The Gods of the Celts*. Stroud: Sutton Publishing.

Green, Miranda (1995) *Celtic goddesses: warriors, virgins and mothers*. London: British Museum Press.

Hutton, R. (2003) *Witches, druids and King Arthur*. London: Hambledon Continuum.

Kightly, Charles (1982) *Folk heroes of Britain*. London: Thames & Hudson.

Loomis, Roger Sherman (1956) *Wales and the Arthurian legend*. Cardiff: University of Wales Press.

Loomis, Roger Sherman (1958) *Arthurian tradition and folklore*, in *Folklore* 69:1-25.

Miller, Helen Hill (1970) *The Realms of Arthur*. London: Peter Davies.

Morris, Ian (1988) *Tomb cult and the 'Greek renaissance: the past in the present in the 8th century BC*, in *Antiquity* 62:750-61.

Pennick, Nigel (1996) *Celtic sacred landscapes*. London: Thames & Hudson.

Pierce, Karen F. (2011) *Riders upon swift horses: the divine twins of Greek myth*, in Huggens, Kim (ed.) *Vs: duality and conflict in magick, mythology and paganism*. London: Avalonia, pp.150-168.

Simpson, J. R. (1986) *King Arthur's enchanted sleep: early nineteenth century legends*, in *Folklore* 97:206-209.

Sims-Williams, Patrick (1991) *The early Welsh Arthurian poems*, in, Bromwich, Jarman & Roberts (eds.), pp.33-71.

Sourvinou-Inwood, C. (1995) *'Reading' Greek death: to the end of the Classical period*. Oxford: Clarendon Press.

[Squire, Charles] (1999) *Celtic mythology*. New Lanark: Geddes & Grosset.

Trubshaw, Bob (2005) *Sacred places: prehistory and popular imagination*. Loughborough: Heart of Albion Press.

Williams, Mary (1962) *King Arthur in history and legend*, in *Folklore* 73:73-88.

Williams, John Godfrey (1993) *Arthur: prehistoric sites & place names: a comprehensive list*. Hay-on-Wye: West House Books.

"Now I Am Harvested And I Die": The Theatre Of Sacrifice In The Book Of The Provider

By Peg Aloi

The Book of the Provider is a series of seven rituals based upon an agrarian calendar of planting and harvest, drawn from seasonal festivals performed in Europe and the United States. These rituals have been performed by a modern witch coven in the greater Boston area (and their sister covens throughout New England) for over thirty years. This chapter considers the implications of the performance of rituals enacting human sacrifice within the context of contemporary paganism. I will begin by offering a brief introduction to the ritual text and its historical and cultural context (and perhaps before I go any further I should add that I am both a researcher and a practitioner of pagan witchcraft, as well as a member of the Boston coven I have referred to, which has afforded me access to and long-term experience of the ritual text I am going to discuss). The Provider Cycle, as it is also known, was inspired in part by several contemporary literary works, including the novel *Harvest Home* by Tom Tryon, and Robert Duncan's poetry collection *The Opening of the Field*. The rituals are structured as modern mystery plays in that they are based upon a known mythological structure, with designated speaking roles for both singular and group parts. This is a fairly common format for contemporary ritual, and dates from Gerald Gardner's writings in the 1940s. Tanya Luhrmann's ethnographic study *Persuasions of the Witch's Craft* examines the myriad ways in which modern witchcraft practitioners express their spiritual beliefs through ritual performance:

"Magic is replete with psychologically-powerful images of death, fertility and regeneration, moulded in the symbolism of earlier cultures. The magician makes the ancient imagery personally relevant through meditation, story-telling, and theatrical enactment, and his involvement with the imagery seems to provide him with intense religious experience."[318]

In the case of the Provider Cycle, the imagery is that of a stylized act of human sacrifice, the slaying of the Harvest Lord, an act performed with the intention of propitiating the Mother or Earth Goddess, who serves as both consort and nurturing parent. This dyad of mother/son, creatrix/victim, is seen in many tales in world

---

318 T.M. Luhrmann, Persuasions of the Witch's Craft, Cambridge: MA, 1989:337.

mythology, from Isis/Osiris to Psyche/Eros, and is illustrated with numerous examples in Frazer's well-known (if conjectured and reductive) anthropological work, *The Golden Bough*.[319] As Tanya Krzyswinska states, the contemporary appeal of witchcraft and paganism *"lies in their functioning as modern mystery religions"*, and Frazer's view of the sacred *"was grounded in violence and sacrifice"*.[320]

The rites begin in spring with the *'Day of the Awakening'* (wherein the Corn Maiden and Harvest Lord meet for the first time), continue with the *'Rite of Sowing'*, the *'Rite of Seasoning'* (performed three times for each full moon in summer), *'The Coming of Autumn'*, and culminating in October with *'Harvest Home'* (when the Corn Maiden takes on the role of the Earth Mother and kills the Harvest Lord in an act of ritualized slaughter). Rituals observing this seasonal cycle of planting/seasoning/harvest, representing the universal cycle of birth, death and rebirth, are common among pagan witches, and even though this calendar is based on the climate and agriculture of feudal Britain, contemporary American witches appreciate that the old folk festivals are still alive in some areas – thereby enabling them to partake of an ancient and living tradition. The cycle is rooted in the Demeter/Persephone dyad and the Eleusinian mysteries, as well as other sacrificial and fertility rites described in *The Golden Bough*, and in anthropologist Margaret Murray's study of figures of male divinity in European witch cults, *The God of the Witches* (1931). Luhrmann, who worked with a number of pagan witch covens when researching her dissertation, describes the ways in which such mythological texts can have a contemporary resonance in the context of pagan magical practice:

"In magic, ancient images of Persephone, Ceridwen, Osiris and so forth directly confront powerful psychological issues – death, pain, maturation, a mother's grief at the loss of a daughter to marriage, a son's rebellion at a father's command. They cast individual traumas of death, separation and love into the dramatic themes of romantic fantasy. Through the practice, the magician loads these mythologically redolent images with personal relevance and feeling. Potent images like the sickle-wielding crone, the destiny-spinners, the elderly guide, mischievous youth, or virgin huntress come to represent attitudes and events; dragons, moons, sacred chalices and magical stones embody personal fantasy."[321]

The Provider Cycle's dramatic structure is certainly of the same primal bent described by Luhrmann above – its purpose is to encourage attunement with nature but also to further self-awareness through the exploration of mythic narratives. The cycle also borrows

---

319 The first volume of Sir James George Frazer's The Golden Bough was published in 1890, the twelfth and last volume in 1915. Aftermath, a supplement appeared in 1936.

320 Tanya Krzyswinska, A Skin for Dancing In, Trowbridge, 2000:73.

321 Luhrmann, Persuasions of the Witch's Craft, 1989:340.

structural elements (and prose excerpts) from Thomas Tryon's 1973 novel *Harvest Home*. The ritualized courtship and lovemaking of the dramatis personae is central to The Provider Cycle, and the poetic excerpts are intricately woven together, creating a bucolic and often erotic tension, reminiscent of the many odes and paeans to pagans deities (particularly the forest god Pan) penned by the English Romantic poets, who were themselves standard-bearers for the rebirth of paganism in the nineteenth century.

The thematic heart of this ritual cycle is threefold: the cosmological theme of birth, death and rebirth, often referred to as the Eternal Return; the anthropological or Frazerian theme of the youthful sacrificial king (also seen as a dying vegetation god); and the dramatic theme of romantic love and loss found in classical tragedy. DesRosiers creates a ritual structure that supports these three thematic elements by carefully establishing the dramatis personae and the central dramatic action with selected poetic and prose excerpts, as well as original passages of writing. The imagery that is central to the rituals, including fields, crops, orchards, the sun, the moon, young men planting or reaping, the sickle, pregnancy, birth, abundance, grain, flowers, fruit, rain, etc. are repeated and gather heightened emotional and dramatic effect as the cycle progresses. The development of the relationship between the two key players, the Harvest Lord and Corn Maiden, likewise intensifies, and identical passages of poetry may take on new meaning with repetition, as the players act out their meeting, flirtation, courtship, lovemaking, sacred vows, and, finally, slaughter and death.

The poetic passages chosen are thus rendered replete with complex meaning, and although many participants know what is coming, the cycle's climactic finale is no less affecting. The purpose of ritual is in part connected to self-actualization and self-awareness; in her essay *"Gleanings from the Field: Leftover Tales of Grief and Desire,"* in the collection *Researching Paganisms*, researcher Sarah Pike states that *"Neo-pagan rituals are not just about experience, but also about making meaning of experience through narrative."*322 In this way, the contemplation of mortality and the value of one's life and death is a natural outgrowth of the experience or performing the Provider Cycle, and its repetition every year allows participants to deeply consider their own attitudes about death and dying. Given that the cycle was in part inspired by two popular films (one of them adapted from a novel), it is not implausible to conclude that audiences who do not subscribe to neo-pagan beliefs might also have experienced such resonance in viewing or reading the source texts. I would like to now turn to a discussion of the source material for these rituals and the unique methodology employed in their creation.

---

322 Sarah M. Pike, "Gleanings from the Field: Leftover Tales of Grief and Desire," in Researching Paganisms (Blain and Ezzy, eds), Lanham, MD, 2004:109.

Aquarian Musings: The Birth of a Tradition at the Height of the Occult Revival

The method employed by the author of the rituals is unorthodox, to say the least. DesRosiers, known under the magical pseudonym *'Lucifer'*, founded the Coven of the Cthonioi in 1969, and was a Religious Studies major at Boston University. The coven soon spawned other groups who formed the Order of Ganymede. Because DesRosiers was a gay man and a number of the other coven members were also gay, the name chosen was a nod to the homoerotic subtexts in this name. Ganymede is the boyish youthful forester in Shakespeare's *As You Like It* (actually Rosalind in disguise), as well as the young cupbearer and lover of Zeus, a Trojan boy of extraordinary beauty. The name Ganymede also has astronomical significance: it is the largest moon in the solar system, one of the moons of Jupiter discovered by Galileo in 1610. The cupbearer motif is also related to the astrological period known as The Age of Aquarius, which was frequently referenced during the sixties as it was considered a potent period of transformation leading to a shift from the 2000-year long Age of Pisces (the fish, associated with Christ) and before that, the Age of Aries (the bull, and symbol of various Mithraic cults in the early modern age). That the personification of the magical order should be an androgynous godlike figure was important to its gay founder, but DesRosier's magical name *'Lucifer'* (God's fallen angel) also affirms Ganymede's commentary upon and rejection of the constructs of Christianity. In his essay *"The Homosexual Pastoral Tradition"* author Riktor Norton examines the evolution of homosexual themes in literature and imagines the conclusions drawn by medieval clerics:

"The scholarly monks poured (sic) over the antique manuscripts every morning - but each afternoon they recited pagan Latin epigrams with their young pupils, and in the evenings abbot and novice together learned the more subtle realities of brotherly love. In the shadow of the risen Christ the brotherhood glimpsed the risen Ganymede - were not both of them shepherds, and had not both ascended directly into heaven?"[323]

In addition, the creation of DesRosiers' unique body of ritual literature was unlike anything that had been done before, and has not been equalled since in terms of scope (rites encompassing Wicca, Hellenism and ceremonial contexts), quantity (rites for each seasonal festival, each moon phase, each planet, a collection of rituals for Isis, and various others) and quality (many guest participants comment on the highly literary quality of the rituals). In this way, DesRosiers' choice of a shepherd figure seems apt in that he was indeed creating a tradition and accompanying body of literature which served to gather together a large and disparate flock of seekers (many of them met at Boston University in the library or the Department of

---

[323] Rictor Norton, 'The Homosexual Pastoral Tradition: An Era of Idylls' http://www.infopt.demon.co.uk/pastor01.htm (1974, 1997)

Religion), and the legacy has been a not insignificant one: the Order of Ganymede is the longest-running pagan group of its kind (still containing original founding members) in the North-eastern United States.

After graduation DesRosiers worked in the university library until his death in 1997. With virtually unfettered access to most of the great poetic works of the English language, the author drew upon a diverse array of original source material, and filled out the borrowed passages with his own writing. This seems sloppy at best, plagiaristic at worst. But DesRosiers' obfuscation was deliberate. He believed that by deliberately using written elements whose copyrights may or may not have expired, this would prevent unauthorized duplication or distribution of the ritual material, which was, after all, intended only for the eyes of the initiated members of the coven.

The author has also stated that he saw no point in crafting rituals out of whole cloth when he could piece together 'new' liturgical works whose words were apt and memorable, and also believed that focusing upon authorship detracted from the magical purpose of the text. Luhrmann observes a similar sentiment in an interview with a coven high priest who intentionally 'buried' his authorship of rituals he wrote for his group: *"If you want the tradition to persist, you must deny your intervention. That's good magic."*[324] Quite literally, DesRosiers would open a book he might have been replacing in the library stacks, and happen upon a line of poetry that was either right for a ritual he was working on, or an entire poem that inspired a significant portion of the ritual's structure or thematic content (as with Longfellow's *'Song of Hiawatha'*, excerpted at length for the *'field blessing'* segment of the Rite of the Seasoning in the Provider Cycle). Given the influence of the film *The Wicker Man* upon the creation of this ritual cycle, it is interesting to note that this approach is markedly similar to the methodology followed by Anthony Shaffer, the film's scriptwriter: *"I was leafing through a book on related subjects, when I came across the well-known picture of the Druids' wicker colossus. It just leapt off the page at me."*[325]

Oddly enough, the primary method which has aided coven members in discovering the original source material of the ritual material is identical to this one: while reading poetry or prose for their own purposes, they found that lines would *'leap off the page'* or otherwise ring familiar, and realize they'd remembered them from rituals they'd done many times before. At a subsequent coven meeting the member would excitedly share the information that they'd uncovered *'one of Lucifer's sources'*. This sort of reverse reconstruction reinforces the idea that these words and ideas are part of a collective literary legacy pagans should be encouraged to use for spiritual enrichment.

---

324 Luhrmann, 1989:243.

325 Allan Brown, Inside The Wicker Man, London, 2000, 21.

For the purposes of my research and my efforts to deconstruct the Provider Cycle rituals and identify the source material they borrowed from (as DesRosier kept no records), even internet search engines had their limitations when trying to find the origin of individual lines, and I was grateful when my hopeful but arbitrary perusal of a particular poet's books yielded, if you will, fruit. Poring over poems of Marvell, Shelley, Keats, Yeats, Archibald Lampman, and a number of modern and contemporary poets allowed me to find not only excerpts that DesRosiers had chosen, but also to wonder at passages he did not use but easily might have. Tanya Luhrmann offers a sometimes harsh but ultimately generous assessment of this practice:

"The justification which allows them to borrow myths from others does so by arguing for the importance of personally evocative symbolism and the irrelevance of historical pertinence, and so they invent their myth and history from what historical material lies at hand, a sophisticated, self-conscious bricolage. This invented history makes excellent mythology in a skeptical modernity, for even when explicitly called myth, the invented history contains the aura of genuine history, meaningful within the authoritative canon of apparently objective science."[326]

Later, she summarizes bluntly: *"They poach from the past in the interests of the present and plunder the world's mythology for their symbolic goods."*[327] In the occult-obsessed society of the 1960s, the *'interests of the present'* comprised the maelstrom of cultural upheaval and change which gave birth in part to the modern witchcraft movement in America, after it had spread throughout Great Britain a few years earlier. The Provider Cycle rituals provide modern practitioners with a performative experience that conjures a connection to archetypal human emotions and a search for meaning in uncertain times. Shifting attitudes about sexuality, women's rights, secularism, spirituality and politics inform these rights, and certainly the omnipresent spectre of the Vietnam war was a potent parallel to the image of the youthful male sacrifice and the mother and who mourns him. I would now like to explore the various thematic elements of the rituals that provide a powerful and poetic literature for the modern pagan expression of the meaning of life and death.

Sex, Death and the Eternal Return

The dramatic structure of the Provider Cycle culminates in the demise of the Harvest Lord, but before that he is the Corn Maiden's lover. The association of the ritual sacrifice with a ritual act of sex permeates every ritual in the cycle, from the more innocent language of courtship to the pantomimed and etheric performance of ritualized

---

326 Luhrmann, Persuasions of the Witch's Craft, 1989:244.

327 Luhrmann, Persuasions of the Witch's Craft, 1989:244.

intercourse, as a sympathetic enactment of the sowing of seed in the fields. The language of the rituals is richly evocative and often encodes erotic imagery in the description of elements of nature and the landscape. In this way the transporting verse of the English Romantic poets is invoked, with their sublime fascination with sex, death and the mystery and beauty of the natural world, as well as their obsession with classical mythology. The Romantics' work is often excerpted in the rituals, as well as later poets who wrote of nature, including Whitman, Lampman and Duncan, and earlier works, such as those by Andrew Marvell and translated portions of *The Bacchae*. The use of the verse of other authors within the ritual texts of neo-pagan ritual is a method which first gained prominence with Gerald Gardner.

In addition to being a ritual author and librarian, DesRosiers was an award-winning gardener and environmental activist, and his love of flora and passion for ecology is reflected in his selection of poetic passages (as well as the original poetry and prose he wrote) for the Provider Cycle texts. Line after line celebrates the beauty of nature in sensual, often anthropomorphic terms: *"She shall tread on frail arbutus in the moist and mossy nooks"*, *"a flower-encircled glow of fruitage and of wine"*, *"a throng of little virgin clouds stood waiting for the Sun"*, *"Oh, lavish, brown, parturient earth"*, *"the hot green spaces of midsummer darkness"*.[328] The Provider Cycle is not only a piece of ritual theatre meant to heal the planet, but in its unapologetic eroticism urges participants and observers to explore their sensual connections to the natural world and, by extension, to one another.

The eroticized context of the ritual cycle occurs most prominently in three aspects: its invocation of the Corn Maiden/Earth Goddess figure; its invocation of the Harvest Lord/God figure; and its description and performance of the fertility rites themselves. In Wicca, the act of simulated sexual union known as 'The Great Rite' is performed as a standard part of most rituals, often symbolized by the insertion of a dagger into a chalice. This is representative of the union of opposite forces in nature and the cosmos as well as the sexual act. But there are also occasions where 'The Great Rite' is performed in more elaborate form, with the participants using a form of etheric energy exchange. Sometimes, actual intercourse may take place as an adjunct working to the ritual – most often this is done in private while the other coveners temporarily leave the room, or in the circle while the other coveners have their backs turned.

This conceit is explicit in The Provider Cycle rites, and the declamatory *"Brothers and Sisters, turn away. The Mystery is at hand"* in the 'Rite of Sowing' is but one example of language which suggests several possibilities in performance, depending upon the

---

328 The Provider Cycle, written and revised between 1972 and 1978, has never been published in a conventional way. Members of the coven have handwritten or typewritten copies, and it is available to members or others with a password on the coven website. The page numbers given in this article are from the online version.

participants and any ritual purposes agreed upon in advance. It is more or less agreed that the physical sexual act greatly intensifies the magical working, even as covens are aware such activity must be approached in a discreet and serious manner. Nevertheless, in The Provider Cycle's thirty-year performance history, the etheric expression of the *'Great Rite'* has traditionally been seen as powerful enough for most purposes.

In some cases lengthy passages provided the main structural elements of a ritual, such as the lines from Longfellow's *The Song of Hiawatha* which provide the narration for the *'blessing of the cornfields'* pantomime in the *'The Rite of the Seasoning'*, which takes place three times for each full moon during the summer months:

> *You shall bless tonight the cornfields,*
> *Draw a magic circle 'round them*
> *To protect them from destruction,*
> *Blast of mildew, blight of insect,*
> *From the birds, the thieves of cornfields,*
> *From the beasts who steal the corn-ear!*
> *In the night, when all is silence,*
> *In the night when all is darkness,*
> *When the Spirit of Sleep and Silence*
> *Shuts the doors of all the dwellings,*
> *So that not an ear can hear you,*
> *So that not an eye can see you,*
> *Rise up from your bed in silence,*
> *Lay aside your garments wholly,*
> *Walk around the fields we planted,*
> *'Round the borders of the cornfields,*
> *Covered by your tresses only,*
> *Robed with darkness as a garment.*
> *Thus the fields shall be more fruitful;*
> *For the passing of your footsteps,*
> *Will draw a magic circle round them,*
> *So that neither blight nor mildew,*
> *Neither burrowing worm nor insect*
> *Shall pass o'er the magic circle.*

This passage occurs about two-thirds of the way into the ritual, after the participants have recited a number of invocations to the sun and the earth, calling for good weather, for rain, and for an abundant season of harvest. While this segment is being recited, the two players representing the Harvest Lord and Corn Maiden perform the action suggested: they walk three times in a circle as if walking around the cornfields. They remove their ritual robes, as instructed in the poem.

When they have walked three times around the circle, they then perform the *'Great Rite'*. While this action takes place, the following segment of the poem is chanted as accompaniment:

> *When the noiseless night descended*
> *Broad and dark o'er field and forest,*

When the mournful south wind
Sorrowing sang among the hemlocks,
And the Spirit of Sleep and Silence
Shut the doors of all the dwellings,
From their bed they rose together.
Laid aside their garments wholly,
And with darkness clothed and guarded,
Unashamed and unaffrighted,
Walked securely 'round the cornfields,
Drew the sacred, magic circle
Of their footprints 'round the cornfields.
No one but the Midnight only
Saw their beauty in the darkness,
No one but the west wind
Heard the pantings of their bosoms,
In reverence the darkness wrapped them
Closely in his sacred mantle,
So that none might see their beauty,
So that none might boast "I saw them."[329]

Here the language of the poetry takes on an additional layer of erotically-charged meaning, since the participants are enacting a symbolic (or, in some cases perhaps, actual) act of sexual intercourse. The poem not only instructs the participants to disrobe, but also normalizes the experience of ritual nudity with language suggesting they should be *'unashamed'* and that they are *'clothed and guarded'* with darkness (in fact the interior of magical temple rooms are usually very dim, lit only with candles). The last line *'So that none might boast 'I saw them"* also reiterates the usual practice of having the coveners turn their heads away while the *'Great Rite'* takes place. It is a stroke of luck and ingenuity for DesRosiers to have hit upon a passage which more or less requires ritual nudity. This oft maligned aspect of pagan witchcraft practice is described by Hutton as being a desirable and perhaps necessary component of ritual performance:

"... in combination with other components normally present, such as candlelight, incense and music, it conveys a very powerful sense that something abnormal is going on; that the participants in the circle have cast off their everyday selves and limitations and entered into a space in which the extraordinary can be achieved. If the experience generates a degree of nervousness – which is initially the case for most people – then this can have the effect of increasing their sensitivity and receptivity and so call forth more powerful ritual performances from them."[330]

---

329 The Song of Hiawatha, XIII, ll. 36-59 and 76-95, in The Poetic Works of Henry Wadsworth Longfellow, New York, 1891, 170-71.

330 "A Modest Look at Ritual Nudity", in Ronald Hutton, Witches, Druids and King Arthur, London, 2003, 194.

It is worth noting that the novel (and television mini-series) *Harvest Home*, from which a significant amount of text is borrowed for the provider Cycle, as well as the titles of each ritual, also has as its dramatic climax an act of ritualized intercourse between the Harvest Lord and the Corn Maiden. The women of the village of Cornwall Combe form a circle in a cornfield and surround the Lord and Maiden. After their act of consummation, the Harvest Lord is sacrificed by having his throat slit with a sickle, and then torn apart by the women wielding old-fashioned garden tools; in effect, he is hoed and harrowed into the ground, so that his body may nourish the crops and propitiate *'the Mother'*: the goddess mentioned throughout the novel. In the Provider Cycle, the final ritual, entitled *'Harvest Home'*, has as part of its stage directions that a sickle is laid upon the altar, to be used at the appropriate time. Usually a small hand held sickle is used, and the act of violence is carefully (and harmlessly) pantomimed.

Another poet (and an avowed naturist, incidentally) whose work is frequently used in the cycle is Walt Whitman, whose Leaves of Grass is surely one of the most eloquent and sensual paeans to nature ever written. Its use in The Provider Cycle allows Whitman's invocation of nature's beauty and valour to double as an invocation of the deities or god-forms associated with the dramatis personae, including Persephone, Demeter, Apollo, Hecate, etc. Here, in the *'Rite of the Seasoning'* (which takes place three times, for each of the full moons of the summer months), with slightly revised words from Whitman's *'Return of the Heroes'* (also known as *'A Carol of Harvest'*) participants celebrate the beauty and fertility of the earth as seeds are ritually planted and blessed:

> *For the lands, and for these passionate days, and for*
> *ourselves,*
> *Now we awhile retire to Thee, O soil of summer's fields,*
> *Reclining on Thy breast, giving ourselves to Thee,*
> *Answering the pulses of Thy sane and equable heart,*
> *Tuning a verse for Thee.*
> *O Earth that hast no voice, confide in us a voice,*
> *O bounty of our lands – O boundless summer growths,*
> *O lavish brown parturient earth – O infinite teeming womb,*
> *A song to narrate Thee.*[331]

The changes from Whitman's original are minor: *'I'* is changed to *'we'*, and *'autumn's fields'* become *'summer's fields'*. DesRosiers changes *'harvest of our lands'* to *'bounty of our lands'* to reflect the earlier seasonal timing of this ritual. But since the terms *'bounty'* and *'harvest'* also correspond to specific ritual actions, namely the vaunting of the Earth Goddess' fertility and the sacrifice of the Harvest Lord, the intentional editing and recontextualization takes

---

331 Walt Whitman, "The Return of the Heroes", ll. 1-9, in Leaves of Grass and Other Writings, ed. Michael Moon, New York, 1965, pp. 301-302.

on an additional layer of meaning. The word *'harvest'* may mean gathering of crops, and also functions as a synonym for *'slay'*.

Since the ritual cycle unfolds over several months, such terms may be altered to reflect seasonally appropriate timing. The sickle displayed upon the altar, and which is later used in the pantomimed slaughter of the Harvest Lord during the *'Harvest Home'* rite, may be used equally effectively for cutting sheaves of wheat, or slitting the throat of the young lord. The descriptions of the flora and fauna of the first half (the first three rituals) of the cycle are full of vigour, colour and juicy vibrancy; the second half portends decay, dormancy and death. In the first half of the year, the Harvest Lord and the Sun are glorified, and the Goddess in her Virgin/Maiden aspect. In the second half of the cycle, the Earth is emphasized in her guise as Mother/Crone/Deathbringer, whereas the Harvest Lord has become a vehicle for propitiation of the fields. Within this thematic context we may again observe double meaning in words like *'seed'*. This image occurs again and again in The Provider Cycle: *"Seeds Elemental in the Womb-Matrix"*, *"O seed we planted in the dark furrow!"*, *"Blessed be this seedtime and our new-sown seed, blessed be the seed implanted in a fertile field"*, *"the image of our longing is the full head of seed"*, *"for the seed of today is the flower and fruit of the morrow"*, etc. The planting of seeds bears grain and fruit for sustenance; symbolically, modern pagans view the planting of *'seeds'* in a ritual framework as representative of goals and aspirations.

But *'seed'* is also used in its arcane sexual sense, referring to semen. Ritualized copulation in the fields is one of the oldest forms of sympathetic magic known to humanity – this act is still performed in some parts of the world to encourage crop growth. In the climactic scene of Thomas Tryon's horror novel *Harvest Home*, which lends so much of its structure and language to The Provider Cycle (three of the ritual titles and a great deal of prose text are drawn from it), the ritualized sexual union (called *'the making of the corn'*) of the Harvest Lord and Corn Maiden is immediately followed by an orgiastic frenzy, as the women caress the Harvest Lord's naked body, and then by a gruesome act of human sacrifice, in which the women gathered to perform the rite attack the Harvest Lord with garden hoes and hack him apart, scattering his flesh throughout the soil. In this way, the Lord's *'seed'* is spilt upon the earth, providing a powerful, symbolic, sympathetic component to the women's rite, and his decaying flesh quite literally nourishes the soil, ensuring future growth. The following summer, a child is born to the Corn Maiden. The circle is complete.

Mircea Eliade discusses modern fertility rites as re-enactments of rites of creation myths of Terra Mater, and as having *"religious significance. Sexual union and the orgy are rites celebrated in order to re-actualize primordial events."*[332] In a passage which may well have

---

332 Mircea Eliade, Myths, Dreams and Mysteries, New York, 1975:186.

inspired Tryon, Eliade elaborates upon the purpose of the ritual dismemberment of the sacrificial victim:

"This bloody rite evidently corresponds to the myth of the dismemberment of a primordial divinity. The orgy which accompanies it enables us to glimpse another meaning as well: the fragments of the victim's body were assimilated to the seed that fecundates the Earth-Mother."[333]

The next lines continue with more excerpts from *Leaves of Grass*, whose form DesRosiers truncates considerably, although leaving individual lines intact:

> *And Thou orb aloft full-dazzling! O sun of noon rufulgent!*
> *Our special word to thee. Hear us, O illustrious!*
> *Thy lovers we, for always we have loved Thee.*
> *Thou that with fructifying heat and light;*
> *Thou that to fields and weeds and little wild flowers givest so liberally;*
> *Shed, shed Thyself on us and ours.*
> *Nor only launch Thy subtle dazzle and Thy strength for these;*
> *But prepare the later afternoon of our Day – prepare our lengthening shadows,*
> *Prepare our starry nights.*[334]

DesRosiers decided to capitalize 'Thee' in keeping with the tendency of neo-pagan writers to refer to Earth as a proper name, or deity. He also changed the spelling of 'rufulgent' to 'refulgent' but this may have been an error in transcription. He replaces 'grapes' with 'fields' – another deferral to seasonal accuracy – and replaces 'mine and me' with the converse 'us and ours'. DesRosiers also felt the need to change "Prepare the later afternoon of me myself" to "But prepare the latter afternoon of our Day".

DesRosiers then leaves Whitman behind for the moment and continues with excerpts from two poets within this same invocation (spoken by all present): three lines from Friedrich Hölderlin's *To the Fates*, written in 1799, followed by four lines from a more contemporary poem *On Growing Old*, by John Masefield. Although from very different sources, these excerpts sustain the same powerful, sensual language of Whitman's poetry:

> *Only one summer, grant us, Powerful Spirits!*
> *One autumn, one, to ripen all our songs,*
> *So that our hearts, sated with sweet delight, may more willingly die.*
> *Let us have joy and beauty, wisdom and passion,*
> *Bread to the soul, rain where the summers parch,*
> *Give us but these, and though the darkness close*
> *Even the night will blossom as the rose.*

---

333 Ibid., 1975:1988.

334 Walt Whitman, "Thou Orb Aloft Full-Dazzling", ll. 1, 5-7, 15, 23-25 (*Leaves of Grass*, 388).

The first three lines are adapted from these four of Hölderlin's:

> *Grant me just one summer, powerful ones,*
> *And just one autumn for ripe songs,*
> *That my heart, filled with that sweet*
> *Music, may more willingly die within me.*

Or in another translation:

> *A single summer grant me, great powers, and*
> *A single autumn for fully ripened song*
> *That, sated with the sweetness of my*
> *Playing, my heart may more willingly die.*[335]

In Masefield's case, the transcription is faithful but for one important change. In his poem, he addresses *'Beauty'* as a proper name or concept. Masefield's original line is *"Let us have joy and wisdom, Beauty, wisdom and passion"*. DesRosiers changes this to *"Let us have joy and beauty, wisdom and passion"* and beauty is here merely one of several qualities wished for.[336] The larger context here is the idea of a selfless and humanistic view of one's individual existence. The Harvest Lord may remain innocent of the knowledge of his fate, but at the moment of his sacrifice he is given the ability to understand the value and importance of his death. His role as a martyr allows him a Christlike compassion, and ability to rise above the fear of death or the narcissistic view of the unique quality of one's existence. The Provider Cycle's creation during the era of one of the world's worst wars in terms of the sacrifice of young lives lends an additional layer of pathos and cultural relevance.

"Never forget: we are alive within mysteries"

In *'The Rite of Good Gathering'* (a rite which serves as a harvest festival that usually takes place in late August or early September), DesRosiers takes a passage from Whitman's poem *A Carol of Harvest for 1867*. The changes are somewhat more involved, and the recontextualization is profound. Whitman refers to America's riches in terms of both her natural resources and her human ones, specifically soldiers during the Civil War. DesRosiers changes *'America'* to *'Earth'* but the image of sacrifice in exchange for abundance works powerfully here:

> *Fecund America! To-day,*
> *Thou art all over set in births and joys!*
> *Thou groan'st with riches! thy wealth clothes thee as with a*
> *swathing garment!*
> *Thou laughest loud with ache of great possessions!*

---

335 The first of these two translations is by James Mitchell in The Fire of the Gods Drives Us to Set Forth by Day and by Night, San Francisco, 1978, and the second is by Walter Kaufmann in Twenty German Poets: A Bilingual Collection, New York, 1963:59. Hölderlin's original lines ("An die Parzen") are: "Nur einen Sommer gönnt, ihr Gewaltigen! / Und einen Herbst zu reifen Gesange mir, / Daß williger mein Herz, von süßen / Spiele gesättiget, dann mir sterbe."

336 John Masefield, Poems, New York, 1967:166.

> *A myriad-twining life, like interlacing vines, binds all thy vast*
> *demesne!*
> *As some huge ship, freighted to water's edge, thou ridest into*
> *port!*
> *As rain falls from the heaven, and vapours rise from earth, so*
> *have the precious values fallen upon thee, and risen out of*
> *thee!*
> *Thou envy of the globe! thou miracle!*
> *Thou, bathed, choked, swimming in plenty!*
> *Thou lucky Mistress of the tranquil barns!*
> *Thou Prairie Dame that sittest in the middle, and lookest out*
> *upon thy world, and lookest East, and lookest West!*
> *Dispensatress, that by a word givest a thousand miles – that*
> *giv'st a million farms, and missest nothing!*
> *Thou All-Acceptress – thou Hospitable – (thou only art*
> *hospitable, as*
> *God is hospitable.)*[337]

DesRosiers makes the following changes:

> *Fertile Earth! Today Thou art all over set in births and joys!*
> *Thou groanest with riches, Thy wealth clothes Thee as a royal*
> *garment,*
> *Thou laughest aloud with ache of great possessions.*
> *Thou envy of the world! Thou miracle!*
> *Thou bathed, immersed, swimming in plenty!*
> *Thou bounteous Mistress of the tranquil barns!*
> *Dispensatress, that by a word givest a thousand miles, a*
> *million farms,*
> *and misses nothing.*
> *Thou ll-acceptress! Thou Hospitable!*
> *Thou only art hospitable as God is hospitable.*

Whitman bemoans the loss of human life amidst natural beauty and fecundity; DesRosiers' purpose is to reawaken this same sentiment in ritual fashion, not only with regard to a neo-pagan view of the world, but an anti-war one. At the same time, it is an invocation of the Earth Goddess as personified by the Corn Maiden, and therefore the words of praise and wonderment for America/Earth is also contextualized as a language of seduction. Here we have again the threefold thematic elements: the Eternal Return, the sacrifice of the young man, and the romantic tragedy. The chosen one, whether the soldier or the sacrificial king, gives his life for others.

Christianity's appropriation of the sacrificed king trope is easily traced to pre-Christian myths of dying vegetation gods, whose lives are forfeit to fertilize the fields. The image of dead soldiers, the killing fields of war, offers a powerful symbolic parallel to this idea of youthful vigour offered up to provide an assurance of life, abundance

---

337 Walt Whitman, "The Return of the Heroes", ll. 23-26, 30-35 (Leaves of Grass, 302).

and protection of a community. The fear of starvation is not so very different from the fear of invasion, perhaps; Hutton compares the fear of starvation of ancient peoples to the very modern sentiment of fear of a dying planet, devoid of vegetation.[338]   Just as ancient peoples strove to protect their crops with magic, many modern pagans use magic and ritual as expressions of environmental awareness and stewardship, to protect the topsoil and groundwater, without which our potential for food growth would be seriously depleted.

Occult scholar Colin Wilson referred to the nineteenth-century pagan revival as *"fundamentally a revolt against coarse-grained reality"*.[339] Regarding the Romantics, he says:

"Their chief weakness was that they did not think. But their strength was an ability to be carried along on a flood of emotion that took them a long way towards mystical insight. The Romantics used the imagination to release pent-up frustrations and to conjure up the kind of world they would like to live in."[340]

If the Romantics and occultists were rebelling against the coarse-grained realism of the increasing industrialization of England, those drawn to paganism and magic in the United States during the occult revival of the late 1960s-early 1970s were responding to more than the myriad distractions of the counter-culture.

Wilson's description of a childlike, emotionally-driven approach to social change is appropriate for the neo-pagan hippies, as well. The Vietnam War prompted many young people to examine the most basic elements of human nature, contemplating not only danger and death but the true meaning of freedom and personal integrity. Consciousness-raising aimed at shared understanding of diverse social groups necessitated examining what stood in the way of human co-operation. The poisoning of the planet (perpetrated by a growing corporate based agricultural industry, and writ large in the chemical wasting of Southeast Asia by defoliants like Agent Orange) prompted not only the back-to-the-earth movement with its attendant organic gardening and vegetarianism, but a culture of environmental activism that spawned an interest in earth-based spirituality.

Just as the language and gestures of anti-war protests were augmented with the teachings of Gandhi and the Reverend Martin Luther King, the fight to save the earth was enhanced by the words of poets and naturalists like Walt Whitman, Wendell Berry and Rachel Carson. The earlier revival of paganism engendered some of the best loved and most artful poetry in the English language; it is little wonder that these words are used over a century later to revive the same imagery, ideals and ideology that inspired their creators, in

---

338 Hutton, The Pagan Religions of the Ancient British Isles, 1993:325.
339 Colin Wilson, The Occult: A History, New York, 1971:325.
340 Ibid., 1971:323.

rites designed to heal the planet and its people and to awaken a personal connection to the living Earth.

Bibliography

Blain, Jenny, Ezzy, Douglas and Harvey, Graham (eds.) (2004) *Researching Paganisms*. AltaMira Press.

Brown, Allan (2000) *Inside The Wicker Man*. Sidgwick and Jackson.

Eliade, Mircea (1975) *Myths, Dreams and Mysteries*. New York: Harper & Row.

Frazer, Sir James George (2009) *The Golden Bough: A Study in Magic and Religion*. Oxford World Classics.

Hölderlin, Friedrich (ed. John Mitchell) (1978) *The Fire of the Gods Drives Us to Set Forth by Day and by Night*. San Francisco.

Hutton, Ronald (1993) *The Pagan Religions of the Ancient British Isles: Their Nature and Legacy*. Riley-Blackwell.

Hutton, Ronald (2003) *Witches, Druids and King Arthur*. Hambelton Continuum.

Kauffman, Walter (1963) *Twenty German Poets: A Bilingual Collection*. Random House.

Krzyswinska, Tanya (2002) *A Skin for Dancing In: Possession, Witchcraft and Voodoo in Film*. Greenwood Press.

Longfellow, Wadsworth (1891) *The Poetic Works of Henry Wadsworth Longfellow*. New York.

Luhrmann, T.M. (1991) *Persuasions of the Witch's Craft: Ritual Magic in Contemporary England*. Harvard University Press.

Masefield, John (1967) *Poems*, New York.

Norton, Rictor. *The Homosexual Pastoral Tradition: An Era of Idylls* http://www.infopt.demon.co.uk/pastor01.htm (1974, 1997)

Whitman, Walt (eds. Michael Moon) (1965) *Leaves of Grass and Other Writings*. New York.

Wilson, Colin (1971) *The Occult: A History*. New York.

Ascending To The Imperishable: Star Lore And Death In Ancient Egypt

By Dave Moore

Dominating the skyline of present-day Cairo, the Great Pyramid at Giza, undoubtedly the most famous relic of Ancient Egypt, has for millennia been a source of inspiration, mystery and intrigue. Hidden deep within its confines are a number of strange and unexpected architectural features which may provide a fascinating glimpse into the way the Ancient Egyptians viewed the afterlife and the fate of those souls who travelled there.

1. Shafts and Pyramids

The Great Pyramid of Giza is the oldest and largest of the three pyramids of the Giza Necropolis on the outskirts of Cairo, Egypt. One of the original Seven Wonders of the World and the only one still physically extant, the Pyramids (and the Great Pyramid in particular) are the quintessential symbol of Ancient Egypt.

Built for funerary purposes by the fourth-dynasty pharaoh Khufu (who reigned from 2589 to 2566 BCE), the Great Pyramid, with an original height of 146.5 m, the Great Pyramid contains a number of internal chambers and passageways (Figure 1).

Some of these chambers and passageways are part of the initial construction whereas others were added later, mainly by treasure-seekers and robbers digging their way in to search for rumoured treasure (the most extensive *'explorations'* of this type were carried out in 832 CE by workers under the direction of the Abbasid caliph Al-Ma'mum; they forcibly broke into the pyramid and created what is now the main tourist entrance).

The largest chamber inside the Great Pyramid is known as the King's Chamber, and consists of a primary chamber (with dimensions of 11.48 × 5.24 × 5.33 m) topped by a number of shallow load-bearing *'relieving'* chambers situated immediately above (Figure 2). The King's Chamber is lined with pink granite, and the only known furniture or decoration is a roughly-finished coverless red granite sarcophagus. It is not known if this was actually used – no remains or grave goods have ever been found in the sarcophagus.

Set into the northern and southern walls are two small openings. In the early sixteenth century the English traveller and poet George Sandys observed of these openings that:

"...in the walls, on each side of the upper room, there are two holes, one opposite to another, their ends not discernable, nor big enough to be crept into - sooty within, and made, as they say, by a flame of fire which darted through it."[341]

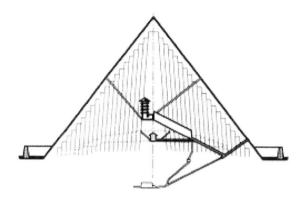

Figure 1: North-South Cross-Section of the Great Pyramid of Giza showing internal structure including the 'ventilation' shafts from the King's Chamber (adapted from Trimble 1992.)

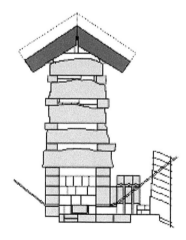

Figure 2. North-South cross-section of the King's Chamber, showing the "relieving" chambers and the shafts (adapted from Lohner 2006)

---

341 Sandys, 1621.

Their true nature was not determined until the infamous explorations of the Great Pyramid by the British Egyptologist Howard Vyse in 1837. Vyse, who was fond of using dynamite as an archaeological tool, ascertained that both openings were actually entrances to two small shafts that travelled upwards and outwards at an angle to eventually reach the middle of both the northern and southern sides of the Pyramid.

Following the publication of Vyse's findings,[342] attention was drawn to the Queen's Chamber,[343] another prominent internal feature of the Great Pyramid. Situated almost directly beneath the King's Chamber, the Queen's Chamber is a small chamber that sits exactly at the centre of the pyramid. Like the King's Chamber, no traces of remains have ever been discovered in this chamber. One side of the chamber contains a niche, and traces of a stairway and an offering table have been detected. No openings similar to those in the King's Chamber were detected until in 1872 a British engineer, Waynman Dixon, found a crack in the southern wall masonry, and subsequently discovered sealed-over entrances to two shafts similar to those already known in the King's Chamber.

Unlike the shafts explored by Vyse in the King's Chamber above, both the Queen's Chamber shafts do not travel all the way to the outside of the Pyramid. Both shafts (which measure 0.2 × 0.2 m square) extend from the northern and southern walls at an angle before ending in mysterious stone doors still some distance from the surface. Currently the subject of active research, in 1993, 2002 and more recently in early 2011,[344] robots have crawled up the southern shaft and drilled their way through the stone door, only to reveal a further door. What is beyond this second door in the southern shaft is currently unknown.

---

342 Vyse, 1840.

343 The Queen's Chamber is named as such due to early Arab explorers mistakenly equating the geometry of the room with the then-extant Arab burial tradition of buying males in tombs with flat roofs and females in tombs with gabled roofs.

344 Hooper, 2011.

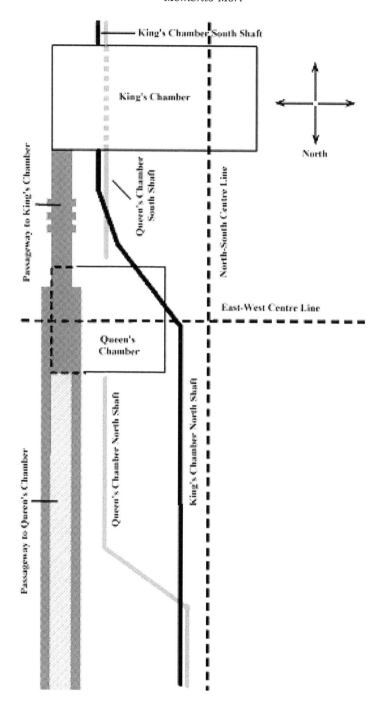

Figure 3. Plan View of the King's and Queen's Chambers along with their associated shafts (adapted from Lawton & Ogilvie-Herald 1999)

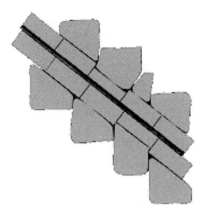

Figure 4. Shaft Cross-Section
(adapted from Gantenbrink 1999.)

The geometry of the shafts, and the spatial relationship of the King's and Queen's Chamber, is complex and is shown in Figure 3. It is important to note that the shafts do not run straight to the outside of the Great Pyramid, they twist and turn to an extent, and hence not even the King's Chamber shafts can be used for any visual purposes, although they each have an overall inclination, which are as follows:[345]

Shaft	Inclination
King's Chamber North	32° 28'
King's Chamber South	45° 14'
Queen's Chamber North	41° 28'
Queen's Chamber South	39° 30'

The four shafts were constructed in identical fashion, by cutting the roof and walls from one limestone block and using a second block to seal and form the floor. These sets of stones were then laid at an angle to the normal horizontal construction of the rest of the pyramid using wedge-shaped blocks (Figure 4).

2. Just Ventilation Shafts or Something Else?

After the publication of Vyse's findings, the consensus amongst Egyptologists developed that these shafts were built for 'merely' ventilation purposes. That when Vyse and his men had finally cleared the shafts in the King's Chamber an immediate rush of cooler air entered the King's interior of the pyramid from outside contributed heavily to this consensus. However, by the middle of the

---

345 Data from Belmonte, 2001.

20th century, some Egyptologists openly began to postulate that the shafts also may have had other purposes. This was driven largely by their uniqueness – no other pyramid featured these shafts. For example, in 1961, the respected authority I.E.S. Edwards stated that:

"The object of these shafts is not known with certainty; they may have been designed for the ventilation of the chamber or for some religious purpose which is still open to conjecture"[346]

But by 1969 Ahmed Fakhry had written:

"They are usually referred to as 'air channels,' but most Egyptologists believe that they had a religious significance related to the soul of the king."[347]

What transformed the views amongst academia of the nature of the shafts? The answer was the publication of a seminal paper in 1964 jointly authored by the astronomer Virginia Trimble and the Egyptologist Alexander Badawy,[348] in which they discovered that the alignments of the various shafts in the Great Pyramid coincided with the position in the sky of spiritually-important (to the ancient Egyptians) groups of stars at the time of the pyramid's construction.

As a result, the standard view of the purpose of the shafts changed entirely to one where the shafts appeared to have a specific ritual purpose, and more recent work on the possible archaeo-astronomical significance of the Giza Complex as a whole, along with reinterpretation of textual references in ancient Egyptian texts, have reinforced this hypothesis to the point where it is now the accepted explanation for the shafts.

Hence by 1997, Mark Lehner, perhaps the foremost expert on the Great Pyramid in Egyptology in the modern age, stated in his influential text *The Great Pyramids*:

"A symbolic function should also be attributed to the so-called "air-shafts," which had nothing to do with conducting air. No other pyramid contains chambers and passages so high in the body of masonry as Khufu's and so the builders provided the King's Chamber with small model passages to allow the king's spirit to ascend to the stars."[349]

But what is the evidence to suggest that these shafts are not simply for ventilation? And what are their connections to ancient Egyptian belief systems? Why did Lehner state that the purpose of the shafts was to allow the king's spirit to *"ascend to the stars"*? And which stars did he mean? And what Ancient Egyptian funerary practises and beliefs were involved? To answer all these questions, we must first look at the writings of the ancient Egyptians themselves.

---

346 Edwards, 1961:126.

347 Fakhry, 1969:118.

348 Trimble and Badawy, 1964, republished in Trimble, 1992.

349 Lehner, 1997:114.

3. The Imperishable Ones

The oldest set of religious texts in existence is the *Pyramid Texts,* which date back at least to the reign of the fifth dynasty pharaoh Unas, approximately 200 years after Khufu.[350] Probably pre-dynastic in origin,[351] and found exclusively carved on the walls and sarcophagi of the tombs of a number of pharaohs and their queens, they take the form of a series of magical spells and rituals written for the purpose of protecting the remains of the royal personage in question, reanimating his or her body after death, and then guiding them to the heavens (Figure 5).

Figure 5. Pyramid Texts carved on the walls of the Pyramid of Teti I (2323-2291 BCE).

However, their destination in the afterlife was not symbolic or metaphorical, but rather *an actual place* – a specific cosmological location within the dome of the night sky as viewed by ancient Egyptian sky watchers.

According to the *Pyramid Texts*, the fate of the soul of a pharaoh was to become a star that travelled in the sky with the other stars, and the *Pyramid Texts* were the means to allow the soul to reach its predestined fate. The spells contained within list all the ways the pharaoh could travel to the afterlife, including the use of ramps, stairs, ladders, and most importantly, flying. The spells could also be used to call upon the gods for help, and even threatening them if they didn't comply with the demands for help.

---

350 2353 to 2323 BCE.

351 Lurker, 1980:99.

One particular verse[352] is important when analysing the eventual fate of the pharaoh:

> *"Sah is encircled by the Duat.*
> *Pure and living in the horizon*
> *Sepedet is encircled by the Duat*
> *Pure and living in the horizon*
> *I (the king) am encircled by the Duat*
> *Pure and living in the horizon.*"[353]

The *Duat* was the ancient Egyptian underworld, and one of the three realms of existence, the other two being the Earth and the Sky. It was most notable as the temporary home of the sun god Ra each night as he travelled from west to east before rising again in the morning. Ra's nightly journey was perilous as he had to combat the countless forces of chaos led by Apophis, which did everything they could to prevent him from rising again.

Aiding Ra in this battle were the forces of light and order, represented by the great deities of the Egyptian pantheon, and a host of other beings, including *Hu* (Authority), *Sia* (Intellect) and *Heka* (Magic). They all sailed with the sun in his night barque on the waters of the Duat, accompanied with the deceased pharaoh, and eventually, from the time of the Middle Kingdom,[354] the souls of all the blessed dead.[355]

The Duat was also the realm of Osiris, the god of the underworld, the afterlife and the dead, and the oldest son of Geb, the Earth god, and Nuit, the sky goddess. Burial chambers formed gates between the mundane world and the Duat, and spirits could use tombs to travel back and forth from the Duat. It was viewed as a dark reflection of the mundane world, with realistic features such as rivers, isles, lakes, mounds and caverns, as well as more fantastic geography like lakes of fire, walls of iron and trees made of turquoise.

It was into this eternal battle that the soul of the deceased pharaoh was thrust. Two other references in the same verse give further clues to his fate.

Both *Sah* and *Sepedet* are stellar asterisms[356] that have been identified as parts of two modern-day constellations: Orion and Canis Major. At the time of the *Pyramid Texts*, Sah was associated with the three belt stars of Orion[357] (Figure 6) and Sepedet with the

---

352 All translations from the Pyramid Texts are, unless indicated, from Belmonte, 2001.

353 PT 216, 151.

354 The Middle Kingdom period lasted from 2055 to 1650 BCE and included the Eleventh to Fourteenth Dynasties.

355 Full details of the travails that Ra faced in his nightly journey can be found in the funerary texts The Book Of Amduat, The Book of Caverns and The Book of Gates.

356 In astronomy, an asterism is a recognized pattern of stars in the night sky. It may form part of an official constellation, or be composed of stars from more than one.

northern stars of Canis Major (Figure 7), which includes Sirius, the brightest star in the sky.[358]

According to the *Pyramid Texts*, the fate of the pharaoh's soul was to travel in the sky with *Sah*:

"O King, you are this great star, the companion of Sah, who traverses the sky with Sah, who navigates the Duat with Osiris; you ascend from the east of the sky, being renewed at your due season and rejuvenated at your due time."[359]

And with *Sepedet*:

"Your sister is Sepedet, your offspring is the Morning Star, and you shall sit between them on the great throne which is in the presence of the Two Enneads."[360]

However, this eternal companionship with *Sah* and *Sepedet* was not the only fate for his soul; ancient Egyptian mysticism is remarkably multi-faceted in this regard. Both *Sah* and *Sepedet* appear in the southern sky as viewed from the Earth's surface at Giza. However, there is also an important reference in the *Pyramid Texts* which refers to the *northern* sky:

"The sky is clear, Sepedet lives, because I am a living one, the son of Sepedet and the Two Enneads have cleansed themselves for me in Meskhetiu, the imperishable"[361]

Meskhetiu has been identified as part of a group of stars that were called The Imperishable Ones - stars that never rise, never set and were always visible all year round. We now call such stars circumpolar – stars that are located sufficiently close to the Celestial Poles that their entire sidereal cycle is visible (sunlight not withstanding of course). They were particularly significant to the Ancient Egyptians because as they were always visible, it appeared as if they never died, and therefore, in perhaps the supreme act of sympathetic symbolism, by joining these eternal stars the soul of the pharaoh also became eternal:

---

357 Almost a thousand years later than Khufu, the ceiling of the tomb of the Eighteenth-Dynasty vizier Senenmut contained a detailed astronomical map on which the column associated with Sah featured three large stars arranged vertically and bearing a striking resemblance to the Belt of Orion (Novakovic, 2008).

358 At the time of the Old Kingdom, the Egyptians didn't recognise constellations as we would now know them (the oldest of our present-day constellations are of Babylonian origin). Individual stars and asterisms were much more important, especially when it came to funerary practises, as individual stars were equated with individual souls (Legon, 1995). It was not until considerably later that the concept of constellations was introduced into Egyptian astronomy, around the time of the Nineteenth Dynasty, at which point the Sah became associated with the constellation of Orion as a whole. Most recent translations of the funerary texts (for example Faulkner et al., 2008), use this convention and translate Sah literally as Orion.

359 PT 446, 882.

360 PT 609, 1707.

361 PT 302, 458.

"You shall set me to be a magistrate amongst the spirits, the Imperishable stars in the north of the sky..."[362]

"I have gone to the great island in the midst of the Field of Offerings on which the swallow-gods alight; the swallows are the Imperishable Stars."[363]

"I will cross to that side on which are the Imperishable Stars, that I may be among them."[364]

Can we identify these particular stars? As it happens, yes we can, but there is a difficulty. Due to the effects of the wobble in the Earth's axial tilt over long periods of time, the whole sky appears to shift in a great circle over a period of approximately 26,000 years. This is known as the *Precession of the Equinoxes* and was discovered by the Greek astronomer Hipparchus of Nicea *c.* 130 BCE.

What this means is that stars that are now circumpolar as viewed from Egypt (Figure 8) may not have been around the time of the construction of the Great Pyramid. Fortunately, with the advent of modern astronomical software[365] it is easy to calculate how the northern sky would have appeared to the Ancient Egyptians (Figure 9).

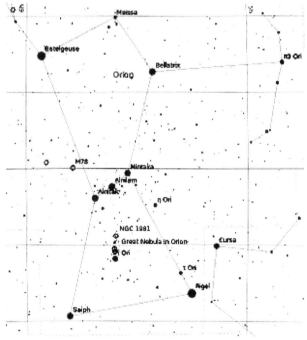

Figure 6. The constellation of Orion. The "Belt" is the line of three stars in the middle of the constellation.

---

362 PT 519, 1220.

363 PT 519, 1216.

364 PT 520, 1222

365 All astronomical maps in this text were generated by the author using the open-source Planetarium software Stellarium, available free at http://www.stellarium.org.

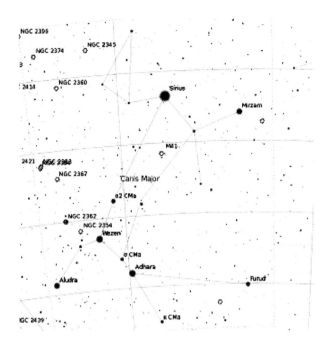

Figure 7 The constellation of Canis Major.

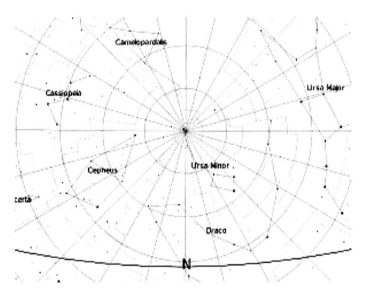

Figure 8. Circumpolar Stars of the Present Era (as viewed from Giza looking north). The thick line is the horizon, and the grid lines converge upon the North Celestial Pole (NCP). The star currently located at the NCP is Polaris, the Pole Star.

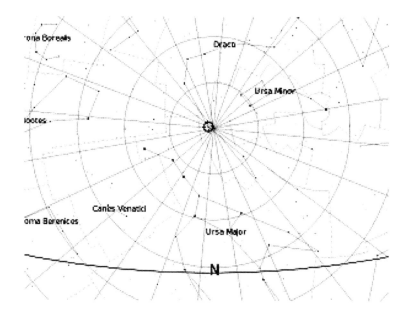

Figure 9. Looking North from the Location of Giza as it appeared in 2600 BCE, showing the effects of Precession. The circled star is the equivalent Pole Star for that epoch, now known as Thuban or Alpha Draconis.

The effects of precession in the millennia since the construction of the Great Pyramid have shifted the North Celestial Pole away from the then pole star, Thuban, towards the current pole star, Polaris. In the future, Polaris will also gradually shift away and other bright stars such as Vega and Alpha Cephei will approach the location of the Pole in the intervening millennia, however, only Polaris and Thuban accurately mark the location of the NCP over an entire processional cycle. In 26,000 years time, Polaris will again be the Pole Star.

This means that we must study the sky as it appeared to the Ancient Egyptians, not how it appears now, as there are easily visible differences between the two.[366]

Returning to the question of the specific identity of the imperishable stars, *Meskhetiu* has been identified as a group of stars that we now recognise as the Plough or Big Dipper - the brightest asterism of the constellation of Ursa Major, the Greater Bear (as is prominently shown in (Figure 9). The Ancient Egyptians did not view these stars as a bear, but rather as a bull's leg.

As well as *Meskhetiu,* other possible stellar asterisms are also mentioned amongst the *Pyramid Texts*. One such is the Mooring

---

366 The effects of precession are such that at the time of the building of the Pyramids, the Southern Cross, Crux, which is now in the deep southern sky and only comfortably visible from the Southern He\misphere, was visible in Southern England at the latitude of Stonehenge.

Post, which some archaeo-astronomers such as Dr E.C. Krupp[367] have associated with the area of the sky around the Northern Celestial Pole and some of the stars of what is now the constellation of Draco:

"The doors of the sky are opened for you, the doors of the firmament are thrown open for you, even those which keep out the plebs. The Mooring Post cries to you, the sun-folk call to you, the Imperishable Stars wait on you."[368]

Although there is no firm evidence that the Ancient Egyptians recognised a Pole Star as we now recognise Polaris, some archaeo-astronomers[369] have speculated they recognised the concept of the Celestial Pole, and the former argues that the *Pyramid Texts* directly refers to the Celestial Pole and the area of the sky specifically surrounding it as a goal of the pharaoh in the afterlife, citing further references in the *Pyramid Texts*:

"...and you will give satiety to me at the Pole, at that which is the foremost of its flagstaffs."[370]

This view is gaining currency amongst Egyptologists; Jane Sellers in her magisterial *The Death of Gods in Ancient Egypt* states that, in relation to the Northern Celestial Pole:

"this region was seen as 'foremost of the flagstaffs' and was a hoped for final destination for the spirit of the deceased."[371]

Another specific reference in the *Pyramid Texts* to an asterism in the night sky is that of the *Two Adzes*:

"May you stand at the head of the Imperishable Stars, may you sit on your iron throne from which the dead are far removed, your adzes having hacked up the mansion of your sky of water."[372]

"...and the king spends day and night propitiating the Two Adzes in Unu."[373]

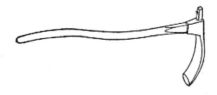

Figure 10. A modern adze (from Hodgson 1909).

There is specific funerary significance of the usage of the term *adze* here. An adze is a tool used for smoothing or carving rough-cut

367 Krupp, 2003:105.

368 PT 463, 876.

369 Belmonte, 2001, and Krupp, 2003, both argue convincingly for this hypothesis.

370 PT 519, 1218.

371 Sellers, 2003:176.

372 PT 666, 1926.

373 PT 259, 312.

wood in hand woodworking, but a variant of this, the *ahnetjer*, was used in the *Opening of the Mouth* ceremony, a specific funerary rite that involved the symbolic animation of a mummy by magically opening its mouth so it could breathe and speak. Detailed in many Ancient Egyptian texts, including the *Pyramid Texts* and the *Book of the Dead* (a later collection of funerary rites used for people other than just the Pharaohs and their spouses), this rite consisted of numerous parts, including a spell designed to be used by the dead themselves as part of the process of their own ascension into the heavens and which refers to the asterism Sah by name:

"May Ptah open my mouth, and may the god of my town loose the swathings, even the swathings which are over my mouth.

Moreover, may Thoth, being filled and furnished with charms, come and loose the bandages, the bandages of Set which fetter my mouth; and may the god Tmu hurl them' at those who would fetter [me] with them, and drive them back.

May my mouth be opened, may my mouth be unclosed by Shu with his iron knife, wherewith he opened the mouth of the gods.

I am Sekhet, and I sit upon the great western side of heaven.

1 am the great goddess Sah among the souls of Annu.

Now as concerning every charm and all the words which may be spoken against me, may the gods resist them, and may each and every one of the company of the gods withstand it them."[374]

From these texts we can conclude that celestial objects in both the northern and southern skies played an important role in the pharaoh's plans in the afterlife. It is with this fate of the pharaoh's soul in mind that we can begin to answer questions about the purpose of the shafts emanating from the King's and Queen's Chamber.

4. Stellar Alignments

The chief effect of precession upon a particular star or asterism is that the altitude of culmination[375] changes slowly over time, and therefore, given a particular altitude it is possible to backwards-calculate a corresponding date upon which the star culminated at that exact altitude. Therefore it should be feasible to ascertain if in the past the shafts ever pointed to any significant groups of stars, such as Sah and Sepedet or the Imperishable Ones. And it was these calculations that Trimble and Badawy were the first to carry out in 1964. Examining the case of the King's Chamber shafts first, the northern shaft has an overall inclination of 32° 28' from the

---

374 Translation from Budge, 1895.

375 The highest point a star reaches in the sky over the course of each sidereal day; this always occur at the meridian, a line running from due South to due North through the zenith, nadir and the two Celestial Poles. The Sun of course always culminates at local solar noon.

horizontal. As the latitude of the Giza Necropolis is approximately 30□ North (29° 8' 51" to be exact), this means that, circumstantially at least, the shaft almost points directly to the Northern Celestial Pole, around which the circumpolar stars revolve (Figure 11).

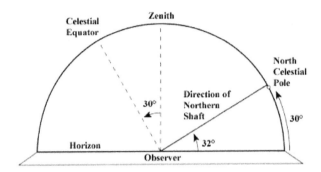

Figure 11. Celestial Geometry of the Northern King's Chamber Shaft (adapted from Trimble, 1992).

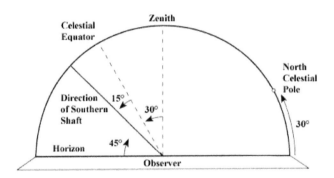

Figure 12. Geometry of the Southern King's Chamber Shaft (adapted from Trimble, 1992).

The southern shaft, which has an inclination of 45° 14' to the horizontal, has a slightly different geometry (Figure 12). Both of these shafts appear to have significant alignments. Around the time of the construction of the Pyramid,[376] the Northern Celestial Pole was almost exactly marked by the star (Figure 9) Thuban (Alpha Draconis) that appeared not to move at all over the course of 24 hours and the year. At this, Thuban culminated at almost the exact altitude pointed to by the shaft. Although not as bright as the current pole star, under a clear dark sky it is fairly prominent.

The southern shaft, on the other hand, also seems to have a significant correlation. Around the time of the construction of the

---

376 And also a few hundred years on either side, from approximately 3000 to 2500 BCE.

pyramids, the shaft was aligned such that for a star to culminate exactly at that point in the sky, the star would have to have a declination[377] of almost 15° South (15 degrees below the Celestial Equator) and Trimble and Badawy calculated that one prominent group of stars would have this almost exact declination during the reign of Khufu: the three stars that make up Orion's Belt, or Sah.[378] What's more, further calculations have revealed that no other bright stars would pass within a degree and a half[379] of the shaft angle during that period.[380]

So it would appear that the King's Chamber shafts align to religiously significant parts of the Sky. What about the Queen's Chamber shafts? As these are uncompleted, and show signs of historic settlement,[381] it is harder to establish this, but the angles of the shafts can still be examined.

The southern shaft has an overall alignment of 39° 30', and whenever the effects of precession are taken into account this points almost directly at the culmination point of *Sepedet*, or Sirius.[382] On the other hand, the northern shaft (with an overall alignment of 41° 28') does not appear to be aligned with any significant star. Some authors in the *'Alternative Archaeology'* field such as Robert Bauval or Graham Hancock have suggested that the shaft is aligned to the star Kocab in Ursa Major, but there are several problems with this idea. Firstly, unlike Sirius, there is no evidence of this star having any religious significance to the Ancient Egyptians, and it is not mentioned in any primary texts dating from the era of the construction of the Great Pyramid. Secondly, the data for the alignment of the Queen's Chamber southern shaft that both authors used to support their idea was subsequently shown to be erroneous,[383] and with the confirmed alignment data, the northern shaft does not appear to point to any particularly significant star.[384]

5. Souls, Stars and Passages

That we can only find confirmed alignments for three of the four shafts suggests one of two conclusions. Firstly, that the alignments are nothing but chance; yet the textual references and the accuracy of the shafts that would suggest that this is not the case, at least for

---

377 Declination is the Celestial equivalent of latitude, and ranges from 90☐ N to 90☐ S.

378 Due to daylight (the proximity of the Sun in the sky), such culminations would of course not be visible for approximately half the year.

379 Trimble, 1992, pp. 8.

380 Although this does not sound like much, in the sky it is actually three times the diameter of the Full Moon.

381 According to Gantenbrink, 1999.

382 Belmonte, 2001.

383 Lawton & Ogilvie-Herald, 1999:354.

384 Belmonte, 2001, speculatively suggests Mizar, the second star in the handle of the Plough, but offers no evidence to back this up.

the shafts where we can find alignments. Secondly, that only the King's Chamber shafts are significant; this idea is supported by the fact that only the King's Chamber shafts actually reach the outside of the pyramid, or that there is something yet to be discovered about the southern shaft. Explorations of the Queen's Chamber shafts are ongoing, and plans are already being made for penetrating the mysterious doors at the end of each shaft to ascertain if they lead to anywhere else.[385]

That said, it is not enough to demonstrate *correlation*. *Causation* must also be demonstrated, and one does not imply the other.[386] It is not enough to show that the shafts align with religiously-significant groups of stars. This could be, as mentioned above, mere coincidence. The shafts could be merely decorative, or in the case of the King's Chamber, for ventilatory purposes. And additionally, how can we be sure that the purpose of the shafts was actually funerary, i.e. to allow the passageway of the soul of the Pharaoh to the Imperishable Ones?

As it turns out, such passageways are a common feature in Egyptian funerary monuments - the tomb of the Third-Dynasty ruler Djeser,[387] located within the famous Step Pyramid of Sakkara (which predates the Pyramids at Giza) contains a number of slots and apertures designed to allow the soul of the deceased to pass through various walls, a feature that also appears in the northern walls of the serdabs (enclosed tomb structures) of the mastaba tombs of the fifth dynasty. It is also worth nothing that as a rule the Ancient Egyptians didn't *'ventilate'* their tombs.[388]

With the establishment that religiously-motivated passageways were commonplace in ancient Egyptian funerary structures, and the particular alignments of the King's Chamber shafts at least, it is a reasonable conclusion that their purpose was to allow the soul of the deceased pharaoh (in the case of the Great Pyramid, Khufu) to travel to meet its destiny, as part of the Imperishable Ones that lived eternally in the sky, and part of the god-constellation of *Sah*; this idea is accepted by most current Egyptologists.[389] Unfortunately we cannot yet say the same for the Queen's Chamber shafts.

---

385 Hooper, 2011.

386 Famously summarised by the Astronomer Carl Sagan as "correlation does not imply causation".

387 Also known as Zoser.

388 Krupp, 2003:108.

389 Although some authors do offer a non-stellar/funerary explanation for the shafts, e.g. Sarovitch (2005) and Wall (2007).

Bibliography

Belmonte, J.A. (2001) *On the Orientation of Old Kingdom Egyptian Pyramids,* in *Journal for the History of Astronomy, Archaeoastronomy Supplement,* 32(26):S1-S20.

Budge, E.W. (1895) *The Book of the Dead.* London: British Museum.

Davis, V.L. (1985) *Identifying Ancient Egyptian Constellations,* in *Journal for the History of Astronomy, Archaeoastronomy Supplement,* 16(9):S102-S104.

Edwards, I.E.S. (1961) *The Pyramids of Egypt.* Baltimore: Penguin Books.

Fakhry, A. (1969) *The Pyramids.* Chicago: University of Chicago.

Faulkner, R.O., Andrews, C. & Wasserman, J. (2008) *The Egyptian Book of the Dead: The Book of Going Forth by Day.* San Francisco: Chronicle Books.

Gantenbrink, R. (1999) *The upuaut project.* [online] Available at <http://www.cheops.org> [Accessed 07 November 2011].

Haack, S.C. (1984) *The Astronomical Orientation of the Egyptian Pyramids,* in *Journal for the History of Astronomy, Archaeoastronomy Astronomy Supplement,* 15(7):S119-S125.

Hodgson, F.T. (1909) *Light and heavy timber framing made easy.* Chicago: Drake & Co.

Hooper, R. (2011) *First images from Great Pyramid's chamber of secrets,* in *New Scientist,* 2814 [online] Available at <http://www.newscientist.com/article/mg21028144.500-first-images-from-great-pyramids-chamber-of-secrets.html> [Accessed 08 November 2011].

Lawton, C. and Ogilvie-Herald, I. (1999) *Giza the Truth.* London: Virgin Publishing Ltd.

Legon, J.A.R. (1995). *Osiris and Orion.* [online] Available at < http://www.legon.demon.co.uk/osirion.htm> [Accessed 06 November 2011].

Lehner , M. (1997) *The Complete Pyramids.* London: Thames & Hudson.

Lohner, F. (2006) *Building the great pyramid.* [online] Available at: <http://www.cheops-pyramide.ch/khufu-pyramid/cheops-great-pyramid.html> [Accessed 06 November 2011].

Lurker, M. (1980) *The Gods and Symbols of Ancient Egypt.* London: Thames & Hudson.

Krupp, E.C. (2003) *Echoes of the Ancient Skies: The Astronomy of Lost Civilizations.* New York: Courier Dover Publications.

Novakovic, B. (2008) *Senenmut: An ancient Egyptian astronomer, Publications of the Astronomical Observatory of Belgrade,* 85:19-23.

Sarovitch, A.P. (2005) *Explaining the Shafts in Khufu's Pyramid at Giza,* in *Journal of the American Research Centre in Egypt,* 42:1-12.

Sandys, G. (1621) *The Relation of a Journey begun an. Dom. 1610, in four books.* London: W. Barrett.

Sellers, J. (2003) *The Death of Gods in Ancient Egypt.* Rev. Ed. London: Penguin Books.

Spence, K. (2000) *Ancient Egyptian chronology and the astronomical orientation of pyramids,* in *Nature,* 408:320-324.

Trimble, V. (1992) *Visit to a small universe.* New York: Springer.

Trimble, V. & Badawy. A. (1964) *Astronomical investigation concerning the so-called air-shafts of Cheops's pyramid,* in *Mitteilungen der Institut Fur Orientforschung,* 10:183-187.

Vyse, R.W.H. (1840) *Operations Carried on at the Pyramids of Gizeh in 1837.* London: J. Fraser.

Wall, J. (2007) *The star alignment hypothesis for the Great Pyramid shafts,* in *Journal for the History of Astronomy,* 38(131):199-206.

Image Sources

1. Adapted from original image in book. Original image @ http://www.amazon.com/Visit-Universe-Masters-Modern-Physics/dp/0883187922, P. 4.

2. Adapted from original image online. Original image @ http://www.cheops-pyramide.ch/khufu-pyramid/great-pyramid/kings-chamber-plan.gif

3. Adapted from original image in book and online. Original image @ http://www.ianlawton.com/ss2fig1.gif

4. Adapted from original image online. Original image @ http://cheops.org/startpage/thefindings/schacht2.JPG

5. Public Domain image. Original image @ http://en.wikipedia.org/wiki/File:Hieroglyph_Text_from_Teti_I_pyramid.jpg

6. Original Diagram by Me.

7. Original Diagram by Me.

8. Original Diagram by Me.

9. Original Diagram by Me.

10. Public Domain image. Original image: http://en.wikipedia.org/wiki/File:Timber_framing_adze.png

11. Adapted from original image in book. Original image @ http://www.amazon.com/Visit-Universe-Masters-Modern-Physics/dp/0883187922, P. 4.

12. Adapted from original image in book. Original image @ http://www.amazon.com/Visit-Universe-Masters-Modern-Physics/dp/0883187922, P. 6.

ARS MORIENDI

BY HUMBERTO MAGGI

> *"The issue of our death is never pressed far enough. Death is*
> *the only wise adviser that we have. Whenever you feel, as you*
> *always do, that everything is going wrong and you're about to*
> *be annihilated, turn to your death and ask if that is so. Your*
> *death will tell you that you're wrong; that nothing really*
> *matters outside its touch. Your death will tell you, 'I haven't*
> *touched you yet.'"*
> ~ Carlos Castaneda (Journey to Ixtlan)

When the 15th century began, the peoples of Europe were living in the Kingdom of Death. Atra mors, the Great Pestilence, drastically reduced the population, reaping with indifference the young and the old, saints and sinners, beggars and kings. The far reach and total disregard displayed by death in the choosing of its victims gave rise to an iconographic theme very peculiar to the Western art: the skeleton, on foot or mounted on a horse, walking in a field of exposed corpses, a gruesome image that ended up dramatically rendered in Arcana XIII of the Tarot. It is after the 15th century that the skeletal figure carrying a large scythe and clothed in a black cloak with a hood makes its appearance, replacing the by then almost forgotten classical themes of the just and gentle Thanatos - usually represented as a bearded man with wings or, sometimes, as a boy. The new image was in agreement with the experience of death in the 15th century, which was very often sudden, painful and brutal. This was the death sprouting out of the *Book of Revelations*, bringing with it an abysmal sense of doom which would give rise to a trembling culture deeply focused on the end of the world, the cataclysmic event to be awaited with terror and hope at the same time.

"When the Lamb opened the fourth seal, I heard the voice of the fourth living creature say, "Come and see!" I looked and there before me was a pale horse! Its rider was named Death, and Hades was following close behind him. They were given power over a fourth of the earth to kill by sword, famine and plague, and by the wild beasts of the earth."[390]

---

390 Revelations 6:7-8.

Nude woman holding a sundial, standing on a skull, Engraving
made by Master MZ, Germany, 1500-1503.

The two versions of the renewed death image made their way into
the Tarot. We can see Death standing on its feet in the Visconti
Sforza Tarots and riding over a pile of bodies in the Visconti Tarots of
Yale, both from the end of the 15th century. This double tradition is
today represented in the two most popular decks from the 20th
century: the Rider-Waite and the Thoth Tarot of Crowley, where
respectively we see Death riding and Death standing.

The version of the Death card we find in the Rider-Waite,
published in 1909, inherits and sum up very properly the entire

iconographic tradition of death consecrated in the 15th century. In the Rider-Waite Tarot card a skeleton mounted on a horse, wearing black armour, lifting a flag above a crowned body, moves toward a kneeling child, a maiden crowned with flowers and a bishop with his hands lifted in prayer. Although this image of Death riding has its origin in the aforementioned excerpt of the *Book of Revelations*, where we see the Lamb breaking the Fourth Seal to set free the last and most terrible of the four riders, and was already in use in the 4th century, the tragic combination of the Hundred Years War with the Great Plague was necessary to inspire the artists to adopt it as a zeitgeist theme. As Andrea Vitali wrote in his essay *Death*:

"Up until the XIII century, a tightly Christian figuration of death doesn't exist. From the middle of the XV century, with the advent of the great epidemics, the plague that reaped million of victims, the fear of the incumbent death had a certain effect even on the figurative art of profane kind. At that time The Legend of the Three Dead and the Three Living, in which three characters who in their lives had been rich and powerful talk about themselves and about vanitas (vanity) to similar persons of high rank, in the presence of death, was widely publicized."[391]

The new iconography of death, like the *Legend of Three Dead and the Three Living* (which was very popular and widespread in the 15th century), had a very specific cultural goal to serve as memento mori. The legend, also known as The Three Dead Kings, drew from necromantic ideas and from the redefinition of the cult of the ancestors under the development of Christianity. The tale runs that three kings go into a boar hunt and get lost in the midst of a strange fog, where they meet the walking corpses of the three kings who went before them.

> *"Then speaks the last king, he looks in the hills*
> *He looks under his hands and holds his head*
> *But a dreadful blow goes cold to his heart*
> *Like the knife or the key, that chills the knuckle*
> *These are three demons that walk on these hills*
> *May our Lord, who rules all the world, show us the quickest*
> *way out!*
> *My heart bends with fright like a reed*
> *Each finger of my hand grows weak with fear*
> *I'm forcefully afraid of our fate*
> *Let us quickly flee, therefore*
> *I can give no counsel but worry*
> *These devils will make us cower*
> *For dread lest they shut each escape."*[392]

---

391 Eletronically published by the Le Tarot Associazione Culturale at www.letarot.it

392 Text in Thorville-Petre, T. (ed.) *Alliterative Poetry of the Later Middle Ages: An Anthology*, London: Routledge, 1989:148–157.

The Three Living and the Three Dead Kings, by the Master of the
Hausbuch, circa 1485–1490.

The dead kings had first to reassure the living that they were not
demons – this is very significant in the context of the critique against
magic that was prevalent at the time. The assurance of their
identities as departed souls or revenants would be out of context in
classical times, when the use of ghosts in magical practices was that
the apparitions were devils in disguise. The identity of the dead kings
is further confirmed by the content of their messages, as they then
proceed to reproach their heirs for neglecting their memory and not
having masses said for their souls, but in Medieval Europe the first
assumption would be that the apparitions were devils in disguise.
From this we infer they were sentenced to Purgatory, the middle
realm of unredeemed souls created by the theologians of the 11th
century, for their confessed life of pleasure seeking.

This is at the centre of the Christian view of the memento mori.
Confronted with the harsh realities of the time and the futility of long
term aspirations, Europeans had to choose between mundane
hedonism and commitment to devotion. The *Decameron* from the
14th century, with its idylls of love and sex in the midst of the Black
Death epidemic, thus stands in sharp contrast with the *Ars Moriendi*
of the following century.

Ars Moriendi, or *The Art of Dying*, may be seen as the Christian
equivalent of the *Bardo Thodol* and the so called *Book of the Dead* of
the Egyptians. Differentiating it from these two, however, its focus is
not set upon the trials of the soul after the event of the death, but in
the proper preparations for the event. This critical difference is a
consequence of the eschatological change brought about by the rise
and development of Christianity: all the contradictory views of the
Christian afterlife (going to Heaven versus being resurrected, being
condemned to Hell but awaiting the Last Judgment, being sentenced

to Purgatory by a just God but having the penalties assuaged by the living) were nonetheless in agreement that the fate of the soul was sealed at the moment of the death. There was nothing that the departed soul could do to better his new conditions, if sentenced to Purgatory or condemned to Hell.

This new eschatological view had a strong impact on the magic of the West. In Classical times, ghosts were one of the main resources of magical practice, and the cult of the ancestors figured prominently in the practical aspect of religion. The axis of these dealings rested on the twofold principle that the dead need help and that the dead can provide help. Ancestors not forgotten remained protective of their families, and the restless dead could be employed to achieve magical results. Under Christian dogmatism, the dead remained at the mercy of the care of the living if they were in Purgatory: the living should not forget and must help them with masses, prayers and the acquisition of indulgences from the Church; but the souls in Purgatory could not be employed or forced to act for the living.

We see the seeds of this change already in the 2nd century, in the writings of Tertullian. This argument on behalf of the Christian faith was developed very soon and did not confine itself to a critique of magic, but could be used also to disparage every other religion, as we see in the use Tertullian made of the concept of idolatry:

"A famous text promises to evocate even souls that have been laid to rest at their proper age, even souls separated from their bodies by a just death, and even souls dispatched with prompt burial. What then shall we say of magic? The same almost everyone: that it is a deceit. But the nature of its deceit is apparent only to Christians, because we know the superhuman powers of evil, by virtue of an awareness developed through opposition to them, not, of course, through association with them. Our dealings with this multifarious pestilence of the human race, this deviser of all error, this destroyer of salvation and soul alike, are not to invite it but to overpower it and expel it. So too the nature of magic is apparent to us. It is of course a second idolatry, in which demons pretend that they are dead people, just as in the case of idolatry proper, demons pretend that they are gods. And why not? For the gods too are dead."[393]

There was a very important reason behind Tertullian's attack on the necromantic practices, as they were based in the ancient concepts of the afterlife as being a shadowy destiny of the souls of men, whilst the popularity of Christianity rested specifically in its better offer of an idyllic post mortem destination. A necromantic success would be seen as a proof that the Christian descriptions were wrong. When we look at the archetypical necromantic experience as described by Homer in the *Odyssey*, we are confronted with legions of souls who *'just flit about as shadows'* and are called *'the powerless folk of the dead'*.[394] Even Tiresias, favoured by

---

393 Tertullian, De Anima 57.
394 Homer, Odyssey 10.494-5.

Persephone as the only soul to retain its wits after death, seems to partake of the needy state of the dead as he had to ask Odysseus to be allowed to drink from the sacrifice first to be able to give the infallible information required. The Christian beliefs had to account for the ingrained old conceptions of both the Greek Hades and the Jewish Sheol, and managed to make the transition by elaborating upon the new idea of the *Harrowing of Hell:* no matter what the Homeric and Old Testament books said about the destiny and state of the dead, Jesus Christ's *descendit ad inferos* changed radically the previous situation by releasing the souls of the unbaptised just who died before his advent. The doctrine is explicitly declared in the Catechism of the Catholic Church:

"By the expression 'He descended into Hell', the Apostles' Creed confesses that Jesus did really die and through his death for us conquered death and the devil 'who has the power of death'. In his human soul united to his divine person, the dead Christ went down to the realm of the dead. He opened Heaven's gates for the just who had gone before him."[395]

The influence of the eschatological view of the Christian afterlife then removed in large part the use of the ghosts in magic, but they were replaced with demons. We saw this in the legend of the Three Dead Kings when the departed had to convince the living that they were not demons in disguise, because that was the prevalent view from the religious authorities of the age. Of course, being mainly an individual endeavour, magic was not in need of conforming wholeheartedly to the official canons, and also did not have to be free of every contradiction. In fact, when it came to spirit summoning and exorcism, the mind of the magician could store many different interpretations about what was going on.

In the Portuguese versions of the so-called *Book of Saint Cyprian* we can see clear examples of this. The book is a large compilation of exorcisms, prayers and magical secrets, but lacking the ceremonial preparations and practices to be found in the Spanish versions published around the same time. One of the oldest known editions of the complete Portuguese book can be seen in the Library of Lisbon, in an example that the Galician anthropologist Felix Castro Vicente believes to be prior to 1893. Some excerpts from it quoted below show varied examples of necromantic practices and unorthodox views about the souls in the Purgatory and their use in magic, but at the same time in the same book we can find a long explanation about the true nature of ghosts with an exhortation to pray for them. The Devil's role as prescribed by the Catechism of the Catholic Church, being the one *'who has the power of death'* is also acknowledged, as in his name of Lucifer he is invoked in the majority of the necromantic spells. In this way, the ancient appellations to the gods of the underworld are carried over to the world view of the Christian

---

395 The Catechism of the Catholic Church, Part 1, Section 2, I. The Creeds: Chapter 2, Article 5, 636-637.

conjurer, who has somehow to deal with all the inherent contradictions between the religion he professes and the practice of magic.

Three necromantic spells from the Portuguese *Book of Saint Cyprian:*

Sorcery which can be done with mallows plucked in a graveyard or from a churchyard

Pluck three mallow plants, take them to your house and put them under the mattress of your bed, saying every day when you go to bed:

So and so, as these mallows were plucked in the cemetery and under me are kept, so and so to me will be bound and tied by the power of Lucifer and the liberal magic, and only when the bodies from the cemetery or from the church from where these came talk, is when you will leave me

The words here mentioned must be repeated during the nine following days, to achieve a good effect.

Sorcery which is made with five nails taken from a dead man's coffin, that is, after it has already been taken from the grave

Enter a cemetery and take from there five nails from a deceased person's coffin, but always with the thought fixed on the sorcery you will do.

After that scratch on a wooden board a sign of Solomon where you must have a sign of the person you will bewitch; this sign must be nailed over the aforementioned sign of Solomon.

Manner in which the nails shall be nailed and the words that must be said while they are being nailed

1° nail (say the name of the person to be bewitched) – *So and so, I beg you, in the names of Satanaz, Barrabaz and Caifaz, that you be bound to me, as Lucifer is bound in the depths of hell.*

2° nail – *So and so, I seize and tie you inside the sign of Solomon; as the Cross of Jesus Christ in this sketch was buried and the blood of Jesus upon it was drawn, so I cite and notify so that you do not fail me in this, by the drawn blood of Jesus Christ.*

3° nail – *So and so, I bind you to me, for eternity, as Satanaz is bound to hell.*

4° nail – *So and so, I fasten and bind you inside this sign of Solomon, so you do not have repose or rest unless when in my company, this by the power of Satanaz and Maria Padilha and all her family.*

5° nail – *So and so, only when God stops being God and the dead person whom these nails served speaks, is when you shall leave me.*

We declare that when the last word is spoken a great blow must be done to the nail.

In the end of all that keep the wooden board and when you want to break the spell burn it.

The magic of the needle passed three times in a dead person

This magic is very simple and Saint Cyprian declares in chapter XXI of his work that it was discovered by a demon or a pythonic spirit from the XII century.

Thread a string of Galician linen in the eye of a needle, then pass the needle under the skin of the deceased three times, saying the following words:

So and so (say the deceased's name), this needle in your body I will pass, so it acquires the force to charm.

After the said operation is done keep the needle and you will work with it the following sorceries:

1° - When you pass by a girl and you wish her to follow you, it is enough to make a stitch in the dress or in any other part, and leave an edge of string; she will follow you to wherever you wish. When you no longer want the said girl to follow you, you must remove the loose thread of string attached to the dress. It is necessary to keep this as a great secret to avoid undergoing what happened to me: I suffered great harm for doing the said magic and declaring the manner and why I did it; because of this you must never reveal this secret to anyone.

2° - When you wish a girlfriend of yours to never stop loving you and to not love another, do the following: Take one object of the said girlfriend or boyfriend and give it three stitches in the form of a cross, saying the following words: (first call the name of the deceased in whom you passed the needle).

First stitch: *So and so, when you speak is when so and so will leave me.*

Second stitch: *So and so, when God stops being God is when so and so will leave me.*

Third stitch: *So and so, as long as these stitches remain put and your body stays in the grave, so and so will not have repose or rest whilst not in my company.*

In this way you can bewitch or charm all the people that please you.

We assert that this spell not only has the power to do good, but also has power to do evil. It all depends on the words used. For instance, instead of saying as above, say instead: '*When this deceased speaks is when you, so and so, will have health*', and all the rest like that.

The *Book of Saint Cyprian* is an important example of the survival of the ancient magical techniques centred on necromancy, as they prove to be mere variations of themes we find, for instance, in the *Greek Magical Papyri.* The erotic utilization of necromantic practices as seen above, for instance, helps to establish an important point of contact between these two sources. We also find in the *Book of Saint Cyprian* the use of dolls in erotic spells and spells for causing harm, a practice common in the Mediterranean cultures since the 4th century BCE.

The survival of these techniques seems to have occurred mainly due to popular traditions of folk magic, as the *Book of Saint Cyprian* emerges in the end of the 19th century as a large collection of spells and prayers that have as their main characteristics their brevity and practicality. Necromantic practices using a dead cat from the Book and the Papyri, for instance, can be instructively compared.

Great magic of the fava beans

Kill a black cat, bury it in your backyard, put one fava bean in each eye, another under the tail and another in each ear hole. After all this is done, cover it with soil, and go to water it every night, at midnight, with a little water until the fava beans sprout, being ripe; and when you see that they are then harvest them at the base.

After the harvest, take them to your house and put them one by one in your mouth. When, however, it looks to you that you are invisible, it is because that fava bean has the force of the magic needed, and so, if it please you to enter into any place without anyone seeing, first put the aforesaid fava bean in your mouth.

This works through one occult virtue, without it being necessary to make a pact with the devil, like the witches do....

Warning to whoever makes use of this magic

When you go to water the fava beans there will appear to you many ghosts, with the intent of scaring you, so you did not achieve your intent. The reason is simple. It is because the demon is envious of whosoever will use this magic, without delivering himself to him body and soul, as the witches do, the ones who are called women of virtue. However, do not get scared because they will not do you any harm, and to this you must first of all make the sign of the Cross, and at the same time say the Creed.

Cat ritual for many purposes

Take a cat, and make it into an Esies by submerging its body in water. While you are drowning it, speak the formula to its back. Take the cat and make three lamellae, one for its anus, one for [its ear holes], and one for its throat, and write the formula concerning the deed in a clean sheet of papyrus, and wind this around the body of the cat and bury it. Light seven lamps upon unbaked bricks, and make an offering. Take its body and preserve it by immuring it either in a tomb or in a burial place.

The Papyri spell on the right is abridged, and I inserted the word *'ear holes'* between brackets where the text is found to be corrupted, as it is clear from the sequence of the spell that the second lamellae is destined to it. The word *'Esies'* in the spell, according to the Hans Dieter Betz's edition, is an epithet applied to the sacred dead. A similar spell to the one from the *Book of Saint Cyprian* can be found in the French *Grimorium Verum*, replacing the dead cat with a human skull. It is interesting to compare the two, because the *Grimorium Verum* spell is clearly dependent on demonic assistance, while the *Book of Saint Cyprian* states emphatically that the power of the spell works through an occult virtue, and even against the interference of ghosts at the service of the Devil. Another point of interest is the use of beans, as beans are mentioned in connection with funeral rites, necromancy and the souls of the dead at least since the 6th century BCE - which once again points to a survival of very ancient necromantic secrets finally preserved in written form in the *Book of Saint Cyprian.*

In the next magical secret from the *Book of Saint Cyprian*, we can see the mingling of a concept derived from the cult of ancestors with the idea of necromantic pahedros so important to the *Magical Papyri.*

Recipe to be happy in the things that are undertaken

Take a living toad and cut off its head and its feet on a Friday, soon after the Full Moon of the September month. Put these pieces in oil of the elder tree for 21 days, retrieving them after this time at the first bell's tolls of midnight. Then, exposing them during three consecutive nights to the beams of the moon, calcinate them in a clay pot that has never been used before, mixing it later with the same amount of soil from a cemetery, but specifically from the place where there is buried someone related to the person for whom the recipe is made. The person that possesses this can be assured that the spirit of the deceased will watch over them and over all things they undertake, because the toad will not lose from sight the interests of the person.

This spell touches upon the subject of the spirit pots which the seminal work of Aaron Leitch, *Secrets of the Magickal Grimoires,* brought to attention, after he made comparisons between the Brass Vessel of Solomonic magic and legend with many similar shamanic techniques found throughout the world. The most advanced and complex spirit pot operation I know is the creation of the Prenda in Palo Mayombe. The best description and explanation of this we find in the very elegant work of Nicholaj Frisvold, *The Garden of Blood and Bones.*

Witch Feeding Demonic Imps, 16th century

The use of the toad in magic and Witchcraft is as ancient as typical, as we can see in the introduction to Andrew Chumbley's study on the amulet of the toad bone:

"The purpose of this essay is to examine the magical lore, beliefs, and practices involving the 'toad-bone' amulet, a magical object which is literally what its name suggests: the bone of a toad. Throughout Europe and further afield, occult praxes involving this amulet type have occurred in various forms over a remarkable period of some two thousand years. Its recorded uses begin with Pliny's 1st century recipes for various frog/toad charms for love, protection, and agrarian fertility. Later, during the medieval, renaissance, and early modern periods, forms of toad-derived amulet - a magical bone, stone, or powder - recur widely throughout the lore of magic, alchemy, and witchcraft."[396]

Toads were traditionally associated with familiars spirits in Europe, a fact that must have been inspired by the Book of Revelations, wherein are mentioned *'three unclean spirits like frogs'* who came out from the mouths of the dragon, the beast and the false prophet.[397] These unclean spirits are further identified as *'spirits of devils'*, which very possibly influenced the artistic representations of witches with their assistant spirits.

Following the deep influence of the Christian eschatology on the magic of the West, the *Book of Saint Cyprian* turns full circle and states a reason for the employment of the toad in which necromancy and demonism share equal parts:

"In the book about his life whilst he was a sorcerer, he says [Saint Cyprian] that the reason why the toad has great force in magic and

---

396 Chumbley, Andrew. The Leaper Between: An Historical Study of the Toad-bone Amulet; its forms, functions, and praxes in popular magic. 2001.

397 Revelations 16:13.

sorcery is because the demons share part of it, because it is the food Lucifer gives to the souls that are in hell."[398]

In the *Book of Saint Cyprian* we also find a short spell concerning the summoning and exploitation of the souls in the Purgatory. We are again treading familiar ground, as the souls in the Purgatory must be seen as the equivalent of the restless dead from Classical necromancy. As a tribute to contradiction, after this spell I quote from another chapter of the same book, an exhortation in favour of the sentenced souls which does not lack a practical side.

Way to demand the souls from purgatory to force them to do whatever you wish

On a Tuesday, at midnight sharp, you must go to the main door of a church, and when you are there knock three times at the door, saying in a loud voice these words:

Souls, souls, souls! I demand from you, from the part of God and the Holy Trinity, that you follow me.

These words being spoken, walk three times around the church, but do not look behind because it can result in a great fright and you can be impaired without voice forever.

About the ghosts who appear in the crossroads, or souls from the spiritual world who in a mission from God come to this corporeal world in search of prayers to be purified from the mistakes they made in this world against God Our Lord.

What are the ghosts?

"They are visions that appear to certain individuals of weak spirit, and to those who believe that the souls of those who have ceased existing visit this world. Because ghosts appear only to the believers in spiritual beings and not to the incredulous, because from this they take no profit, or worse, they receive curses.

Ah! What will happen to the one who acts like that! Unhappy in this world, who did not care for anything except deriding the servants of the Lord, who come to this world searching for relief and find punishment? Double are their torments!

Ah! What will happen to you on the day in which you will be sentenced? If you do not have good friends who had asked for you to the Supreme Judge? If you do not have protection you shall be punished with the rigor of justice!

So, cultivate good friends so in that tremendous day there will be good friends to beg the Creator for you; do as the husbandman that

---

398 O Grande Livro de S. Cypriano ou Thesouro do Feiticeiro. Published by the Livraria Econômica in Lisbon, probably before 1893.

harvests in the day of Saint Michael, lay in the ground good foundations.

Note it well, brothers, these words which are not simply the work of the point of the pen but are inspired from the bottom of the heart: When a vision appears to you, do not exorcise it because then it will curse you, it will prejudice all your affairs, and everything will go awry to you; but when you feel a vision resort to prayer, the one that in this book is mentioned with the title Prayer for the good spirits, because you soon will relieve that beggar who searches for alms from the charitable souls.

Look, brothers: the devil sometimes appears as a ghost, because the demons were angels and they do not have bodies to cover themselves; because of that I recommend that when you see a ghost with an animal figure, then it is certain to be a demon, and you must exorcize it and do a ✠ to it. But, if the ghost is in human shape, it is not a demon, but a soul who searches for relief of its punishments. You must do quickly the prayer from this book, because doing that you have nothing to lose, because the soul that you freed will be with you whenever you call it. If you do not believe in me, do the experiment and then you will see.

Pray, pray for those wretched spirits and call them in all your dealings and in everything that pleases you, then you will be successful; I swear.

Happy is the creature who is chased by the spirits, because it is certain that person is a good creature, whom the spirits chase so they may pray to the Lord for them, that they are worthy of being heard by the Creator. It is for that reason they are chased by the ghosts. Now, there are many spirits who do not adopt the system of appearing as ghosts, but appear in the houses of their relatives, making noise at night, dragging chairs, tables and everything in the house; one day they kill a pig, the other a cow, and so everything goes awry in that house for lack of intelligence of its inhabitants, because if they resorted soon to the prayers, they would be freed from the spirit and would make one work of charity, and in the last day of their lives the doors of heaven would be open for them. Note well, brothers, these words, and consecrate them in your heart, because I pretend that for sake of this work many souls will be saved; and not that absurdities be committed."

This excerpt agrees with the ancient necromantic view we mentioned before, that the dead at the same time need and can provide help, and is also of interest as it tries to differentiate between souls and demons. It accepts the manifestation of both kinds of spirits as possible and gives to the owner of the book a means to properly identify and deal with each of them. All this stays inside the Christian worldview, but goes against many fundamental doctrines of the traditional Catholic and Protestant churches.

This mix of demon summoning and necromancy became a constant in the grimoire genre. The *Pseudomonarchia Daemonum* compiled in the 16th century presents the demon Bune, who *'maketh the dead to change their place, and devils to assemble upon the sepulchres of the dead'*, together with Bifrons who *'changeth dead bodies from place to place'* and *'seemeth to light candles upon the sepulchres of the dead'*. [399] The *Grimorium Verum* lists the demon Frucissière as one who can resuscitate the dead and shares with the *Grand Grimoire* a complex magical secret (one could say magical quest) for speaking with the dead.[400] This spell includes attendance of a Mass of the Nativity at midnight, a walk to the cemetery, a call to the Infernal Powers, the throwing of human bones inside a church, walking five thousand and nine hundred steps to the West, and (finally!) laying stretched on the ground facing the Moon. A phantom should then appear to grant some kind of ecstatic experience mysteriously described as *'the sight of the object that was most beloved to you, and provides the greatest delight of all'*. This magical secret should not be underestimated: I know after my own experience the almost unbelievable power that some spirits have to grant unto you an ecstatic experience.

The initial call to the Infernal Powers in this magical secret is a perfect example of the mix we mentioned:

"Infernal Powers, you who scatter the turbid throughout the entire Universe, abandon your abode of darkness and leave your prison beyond the river Styx. If it is in your power to control the one who interests me, I conjure you in the name of the King of Kings to make him appear to me in the hour and moment that I will indicate to you."

The magician is then forced to bend or to simply ignore the basic tenets of any orthodox form of Christianity to work with the dead or with the damned. The simple spell from the *Book of Saint Cyprian* and the magical secret shared by the *Grimorium Verum* and the *Grand Grimoire* do exactly that, assuming that the Infernal Powers could release a condemned soul (i.e. a soul in Hell) and that the souls from Purgatory can be forced to act in the behalf of the practitioner.

Both categories of souls, those sentenced to Purgatory and those condemned to Hell, now correspond in function to the ancient category of the restless dead. The difference between the old and the new interpretation lies in the fact that the deceased could become a restless dead after the circumstances of his death and burial, but to the Christians a soul would be condemned or sentenced depending on the circumstances of the life it lead. Restless ghosts were the ones

---

399 The Pseudomonarchia Daemonum, or The False Monarchy of Demons, was first published as an Appendix to De praestigiis daemonum by Johann Weyer, published in Basel in 1563. Recently republished as an Appendix to Joseph H. Peterson's The Lesser Key of Solomon.

400 Grimorium Verum, or The True Grimoire, is a late work published in the 18th century. The best available editions are Joseph H. Peterson's and Jake Stratton-Kent's.

who died before their time, before marriage and the ones deprived of prompt and proper burial. Souls in Hell or Purgatory belonged to the unbaptised, the sinners and the ones who died without repenting and confessing their sins – circumstances of death and burial were not considered relevant anymore. In fact, the restless category named biothanatoi, *'those dead by violence'*, which included the fallen in battle and the executed, depending on the circumstances of the life lived could become then the Christian equivalent of the heroes worshiped throughout the Greek-Roman world. The faithful who suffered, fought or were executed (usually keeping their virginity or chastity) for their beliefs were now adored as a new category of the dead: the saints of the new religion.

The Magical Eschatology

When we look at the two main pillars of Western culture, Greece and Israel, we see that they shared a very ancient eschatological view of the afterlife as a gloomy destination for most of the departed. The Greek Hades was not an encouraging prospect for the dying. There the damned souls would be condemned to the great pit of Tartarus, whilst the vast majority of mankind was destined to an emotionless semi-life in the Asphodel Meadows. The Sheol of the Jews looked even worse: a place of darkness away from the light of God was the final destination for all and every soul.

For the Greeks, however, things could become even more terrible if the dead became restless. The restless ghosts could not achieve by themselves the plain where the asphodel flowers could be eaten, and had to await indefinitely on the borders of Hades. Those were the multitude of the dead that Odysseus had to keep at bay after crossing the river Oceanus to summon the ghost of the prophet Tiresias, a menacing and pitiful crowd of brides, bachelors, old men who had suffered much, tender maidens with their fresh grief, warriors wounded by spears, and men killed in battle:

"From all sides they crowded en masse round the pit with a terrible cry. Fear gripped me and turned me pale. Then I roused my men and gave them order to flay and burn the sheep that lay there jugulated by the pitiless bronze, and to pray to the gods, to strong Hades and dread Persephone. I myself drew my sharp sword from thigh and sat there, and I did not allow the powerless folk of the dead to approach the blood before I made inquiry of Tiresias."[401]

The singular fact about these descriptions is that, in the end, it seems that the restless dead were the kind of dead who through suffering managed to keep their consciousness, whereas the others seem to sleepwalk among the flowers and vanish as time goes by. These restless dead, however, were a *'powerless folk'*, who could only be rescued by the living. The rescue could happen in three ways: (1) the ghost could be laid and finally pass to the realm of forgetfulness;

---

401 Homer, Odyssey, 11.13.

(2) the ghost could become a magical assistant, a parhedros; (3) the ghost could be worshipped as an ancestor or a hero.

If we choose to ignore the dogmatic differences in the many religious and magical systems where there is an active exchange between the living and the dead, what remains is the universal fact that the state and capacity of the dead seems to be improved after some kind of offering is made by the living. The main idea behind the necromantic practices in every culture and every age, its fundamental concept, is the offer of energy. Be it under the guise of a fire, smoke, blood, food or prayer, it is always energy which is being promised to the spirits of the dead.

The cult of the ancestors would strengthen the ghosts of the family who would be able to look after the interests of the living, the necromantic sacrifices would empower the restless for a time, and the experience of martyrdom followed by cultic adoration could create a very powerful new kind of dead – the saints.

The category of saints came to substitute for the classical hero cults. If I am allowed to quote from the Wikipedia:

"By the historical period the word 'hero' came to mean specifically a dead man, venerated and propitiated at his tomb or at a designated shrine, because his fame during life or unusual manner of death gave him power to support and protect the living. A hero was more than human but less than a god, and various kinds of supernatural figures came to be assimilated to the class of heroes; the distinction between a hero and a god was less than certain, especially in the case of Heracles, the most prominent, but a typical hero."[402]

The heroes were not the only type of blessed dead, but together with the ancestors, they were the only ones who could intervene on the behalf of the living. The other blessed souls, a joyful minority of mortals chosen by the gods to live in the Fortunate Isles ruled by Cronos, and the initiated in the Mysteries accepted in the Elysian Fields ruled by Rhadamanthus, were useless for the living.

Orphism seemed to acknowledge the fact that there is a possibility of eluding the losses of conscience, memory and mobility and, in the end, achieve a better existence after death, through initiation and an ascetic life. The ars moriendi of the Orphic adept would start with the first initiation and was followed beyond the grave, to where he carried the instructions engraved in the golden leaves that were buried with him.

I am inclined to think that the great advantage Christianity had over the other religions two thousand years ago was the fact that it offered a very cheap and easy way of achieving a happy afterlife, with many options of payment available. All that was necessary was a formal acceptance of the new faith, a weekly ritual participation and the manifestation of regret at the time of death for the sins committed. The Christian adept would be exempt from Hades and

---

402 http://en.wikipedia.org/wiki/Hero_cult

Sheol without having to realize great deeds or follow some initiatory path like Orphism – a privilege not open anyway to the great mass of the poor and the enslaved that supported the splendour that was Rome.

Ars moriendi magicæ

To interpret the ancient initiatory ideas in modern terms, we could postulate that certain practices and experiences can allow us to effectively transfer our consciousness to an energetic matrix which could successfully survive the death of the body. These energetic matrices could be helped by other inorganic entities and by offerings made by the living.

The entirety of the written work of Carlos Castaneda, for instance, had a magical eschatology as its aim. The development of awareness, the recapitulation, the lucid dreaming, the alteration of the perception and of the consciousness and the loss of the human form all had the objective of eluding another dreadful description of the afterlife he called the Eagle:

"The power that governs the destiny of all living beings is called the Eagle or the Indescribable Force. Providing the luminous shell that comprises one's humanness has been broken, it is possible to find in the Indescribable Force the faint reflection of man. The Indescribable Force's irrevocable dictums can then be apprehended by seers, properly interpreted by them, and accumulated in the form of a governing body. Thus the rule was formed. The rule is not a tale. The rule states that every living thing has been granted the power, if it so desires, to seek an opening to freedom and to go through it."[403]

The destiny of the souls in Castaneda's account is to float up to the Eagle's beak to be devoured as awareness, as the power symbolized by the Eagle is the origin and the end and the great manipulator of the energetic *'fibres which exude awareness and make consciousness possible'*. To avoid the final dissolution, we should become a man or woman of knowledge, an intrepid sorcerer who refuses to be consumed and dedicates his or her life to preventing it. The magical way to do it is to use the best of our ability and training to profit from the almost impossible chance the Eagle grants to the ones who really desire it – at the moment of death.

We are here not far from the post mortem teachings of the *Bardo Thodol* and the Orphic *Golden Leaves*. The *Bardo Thodol* repeatedly states that the departed must concentrate to identify the manifestations of the Clear Light, which dawn upon him at certain intervals after the last expiration. The loss of consciousness must be avoided, not allowing sleep to come before the final breath, and the living have the task of reading the book to help the soul to concentrate and remain focused. The Orphic initiate should also strive to avoid the loss of memory as he departs, as we can see in the

---

403 Castaneda, Carlos. The Eagle's Gift, 1982.

beautiful reconstruction the philologist Richard Janko made of the hypothetical source text of the Orphic golden tablets:

"You will find on the right in Hades' halls a spring, and by it stands a ghostly cypress-tree, where the dead souls descending wash away their lives. Do not even draw nigh this spring. Further on you will find chill water flowing from the pool of Memory: over this stand guardians. They will ask you with keen mind what is your quest in the gloom of deadly Hades. They will ask you for what reason you have come. Tell them the whole truth straight out. Say: 'I am the child of Earth and starry Heaven, but of Heaven is my birth: this you know yourselves. I am parched with thirst and perishing: give me quickly chill water flowing from the pool of Memory.' Assuredly the kings of the underworld take pity on you, and will themselves give you water from the spring divine; then you, when you have drunk, traverse the holy path which other initiates and bacchants tread in glory. After that you will rule amongst the other heroes."[404]

In Castaneda's elaborated tale, we also find a mention of the help which the dead can give us. The lineage of sorcerers spread across time and the many visible and invisible worlds left not just the oral knowledge to be passed from master to pupil, their efforts also created projections which guide the beginner:

"The old sorcerers deliberately placed different facets of their attention on material objects. By unravelling another facet of our attention we might become receptors for the projections of ancient sorcerers' second attention. Those sorcerers were impeccable practitioners with no limit to what they could accomplish with the fixation of their second attention."[405]

There seems to be an agreement between many ancient or ancient inspired systems that the survival of the soul is a difficult task. The fear of death of course helps us to ignore and deny that there is any reason why the transition to the afterlife should not be as unjust as anything else in the universe we live in, and that only a few are born with the necessary awareness and will to find the elusive path. But there was never, in truth, one single religion that preached an equality for every human in the afterlife so, in the end, the difference between eschatologies becomes just a matter of statistics...

Ars moriendi thelemica

The word *'death'* appears seventeen times in the *Book of the Law*: Aiwass reciting for Nuit says it twice; in Hadit's chapter fourteen; and Crowley included an invocation from the Stele of Revealing on in the final chapter where the word appears once.

---

404 Richard Janko, "Forgetfulness in the Golden Tablets of Memory," Classical Quarterly 34 (1984) pp.89–100, especially pp. 99.

405 Castaneda, Carlos. The Eagle's Gift, 1982.

As it proposes itself to be a complete guide for mankind in the so called *'New Aeon'*, the *Book of the Law* presents precepts and instructions both to life as to death; but it follows the same path dictated by the books of Orpheus, and being an initiatory work it necessarily ends up being elitist in its teachings.

The palace of initiation described in Nuit's chapter seems to be a place of beauty, luxury and love, but is not complete without a memento mori, *'the emblems of death'*. In the palace of Nuit, the adept is invited to enjoy all the good things of life, rich foods, sweet wines and love, but he is advised to keep concentrated and focused on his true and sole aim. Here carpe diem meets memento mori as the two faces of the same coin, the coin that sooner or later we have to offer to the ferryman.

"There are four gates to one palace; the floor of that palace is of silver and gold; lapis lazuli & jasper are there; and all rare scents; jasmine & rose, and the emblems of death. Let him enter in turn or at once the four gates; let him stand on the floor of the palace. Will he not sink? Amn. Ho! warrior, if thy servant sink? But there are means and means. Be goodly therefore: dress ye all in fine apparel; eat rich foods and drink sweet wines and wines that foam! Also, take your fill and will of love as ye will, when, where and with whom ye will! But always unto me."[406]

Nuit's promises include not just the best things of life, joy, peace, rest and ecstasy, but something that for me has the ultimate value, the thing I have been searching for since the dawn of my consciousness, the difficult certainty about the true nature of death:

"I give unimaginable joys on earth: certainty, not faith, while in life, upon death; peace unutterable, rest, ecstasy; nor do I demand aught in sacrifice."[407]

The god of the third chapter does not say the word even once, as he appears to be solely focused on the task at hand and urges us to do the same. But we have the teachings of the second chapter, where Hadit tries to enlighten us about the knowledge of death, which we should know well before confronting the wisdom of the Lord of the Aeon. Death is not to be feared, and neither the hereafter. Death should be commemorated with a feast greater than the feasts prepared for the fire, for the water and for life itself. There *is* death, but it is *'for the dogs'*, and here maybe we are talking again that death is a gateway for freedom just for a few, just for the kings to whom there is dissolution and the eternal kisses of Nu...

The art is long and life is short, the opportunity is told by many traditions to be fleeting, the experiment *is* very dangerous... and we know very well how difficult the judgment can be. But we also know that he that lives long and desires death much, is ever the King among the Kings.

---

406 Liber al vel Legis. 1.51.
407 Liber al vel Legis. 1.58.

Bibliography

Betz, Hans Dieter (1997) *The Greek Magical Papyri in Translation, Including the Demotic Spells: Texts v. 1*. University of Chicago Press.

Castaneda, Carlos (1975) *Journey to Ixtlan: Lessons of Don Juan*. Penguin Books.

Castaneda, Carlos (1982) *The Eagle's Gift*. Penguin Books.

Chumbley, Andrew (2001) *The Leaper Between: An Historical Study of the Toad-bone Amulet; its forms, functions, and praxes in popular magic*.

Crowley, Aleister (1977) *The Book of the Law*. Red Wheel/Weiser.

Dalai Lama (trans.) (2006) *The Tibetan Book of the Dead*. Penguin Classics.

Frisvold, Nicholaj de Mattos (2011) *Palo Mayombe: The Garden of Blood and Bones*. Scarlet Imprint.

Homer, & Rieu, E.V. (trans) (2003) *Odyssey*. Penguin Classics.

Janko, Richard (1984) *Forgetfulness in the Golden Tablets of Memory*, in *Classical Quarterly* 34:89–100.

Leitch, Aaron (2005) *Secrets of the Magickal Grimoires: The Classical Texts of Magick Deciphered*. Llewellyn Publications.

Ogden, Daniel (2002) *Magic, Witchcraft and Ghosts in the Greek and Roman World: A Sourcebook*. Oxford University Press.

Peterson, Joseph H. (2007) *Grimorium Verum*. Createspace.

Peterson, Joseph H. (2001) *The Lesser Key of Solomon: Lemegeton Clavicula Salomonis*. Red Wheel/Weiser.

Stratton-Kent, Jake (2010) *The True Grimoire*. Scarlet Imprint.

The Bible: Authorized King James Version. (2008) Oxford World Classics.

The Catechism of the Catholic Chuch, online at Libreria Editrice Vaticana, Citta del Vaticano, 1993, http://www.vatican.va/archive/ENG0015/_INDEX.HTM

Thorville-Petre, T. (ed.) (1989) *Alliterative Poetry of the Later Middle Ages: An Anthology*, London: Routledge.

PRAYER FOR THE GOOD SPIRITS

FROM THE BOOK OF SAINT CYPRIAN

TRANSLATION FROM THE ORIGINAL PORTUGUESE, AND INTRODUCTION BY HUMBERTO MAGGI

All the magical-religious traditions associated with the name of Saint Cyprian of Antioch have their common roots in a text first known in the 4rd century BCE, named *Confessio*. The *Confessio* is a Christian *tour de force* against paganism and magic, where we see described in detail the long training and studies of Cyprian, a rich and gifted youth dedicated by his parents to Apollo. Through his many travels in search of knowledge, Cyprian became the paragon of magicians, with the story putting him on the same level as other legendary figures like Solomon and Simon Magus. But the aim of the writer of this strange tale is to equate all Cyprian's achievements to demonolatry, as in the end all pagan wisdom and magical knowledge are identified as snares of the Devil. And the *coup de grace* is given when all the power Cyprian received from his arts is defeated by a young Christian virgin, armed only with her faith and the Sign of the Cross. The defeated magus then acknowledges God as more powerful than the Devil and renounces his old master. He then raises himself in the faith becoming a bishop and dying a martyr.

"Although there remains a possibility that there were three eastern martyrs named Cyprian, Justina, and Theoctistus whose relics were translated from Nicomedia to Caelian Hill in Rome during the fourth century, the entire hagiographical romance of Cyprian of Antioch, the pagan magician turned Christian bishop and martyr, has been widely regarded as pure fiction. In addition to the fact that no bishop named Cyprian appears in the well-known lists of bishops of Antioch, source-criticism of the legend has shown conclusively that neither the plot nor even the majority of the names of the characters in the legend are original, but were borrowed from other literary works."[408]

From this piece of Christian propaganda two currents arose. The first, identifying the saint as being especially apt to intervene against magic due to his dark past, attributed to him prayers and exorcisms of great efficiency and virtue. The second, taking liberties with the

---

[408] Bailey , Ryan: The Confession of Cyprian of Antioch: Introduction, Text, and Translation

original legend, speaks of forbidden books and spells from his devilish days which would had survived the burning made by the converted Cyprian. Both currents soon got mixed and are to be found in the late Iberian grimoires carrying the name of the saint.

The following prayer comes from the *O Grande Livro de S. Cypriano ou Thesouro do Feiticeiro,* published in Lisbon at the end of the 19th century. It is a kind of benign exorcism which aims at helping the souls which come back to this world in search of religious help, souls who appear to the living as ghosts and apparitions. These souls can become the source of many problems when their needy state is not acknowledged and the ignorant living curse them in their fear. However, if properly addressed with the prayer, these souls become helpful after the prayer alleviates their torments.

PRAYER TO ASK GOD FOR THE GOOD SPIRITS who come to this world seeking prayers so they may be purified from the evil they made in this world, and to restitute some debt or theft

This prayer must be said in any place where it is needed, or in which a spirit or ghost wanders. At the end of this prayer the Creed and the Act of Constriction are said.

Leave, Christian soul, this world in the name of God the All-Powerful Father who created you; in the name of Jesus Christ, Son of the living God, who suffered for you; in the name of the Holy Spirit, who abundantly communicated to you. Leave this body or place where you are, because the Lord receives you in his kingdom; Jesus, listen to my prayer and be my shelter as you are the shelter to the Holy Angels and Archangels; to the Thrones and Dominations, to the Cherubims and Seraphims; to the Prophets, to the Holy Apostles and to the Evangelists; to the Holy Martyrs, Confessors, Monks, Religious and

Hermits; to the Holy Virgins and wives of Jesus Christ, and to all the Saints of God, who concedes to give you a place of rest, and the enjoyment of the eternal peace in the holy city of Sion, where you will praise him through all the centuries. Amén.

LET US PRAY

Merciful God, clement God, God who after the greatness of your infinite mercy forgives the sins of this spirit who is in pain for having committed them, and who gives him the liberal absolution from the past faults and offenses; put the eyes of your compassion on this your servant who wanders in this world in penance; open to him, Lord, the doors of heaven, be propitious when you listen to him and grant him the absolution of all his sins; because with all his heart he asks this from you through his humble confession. Renew and repair, oh most merciful father, the shards and ruins of this soul, and the sins he made and acquired, or by weakness, or by cunning and deception of the devil. Accept him to become part of the body of your Triumphant Church. As a living member of your Church, freed by the precious blood of your Son, have compassion, Lord, to his moans, let his tears and sobs move you, let his and our entreaties touch you. Shelter and help him who had put his hope only in your mercy, and instate him in your friendship and grace, by the Love you have for Jesus Christ your beloved Son, he who with you lives and reigns through all the centuries of the centuries. Amén.

Ò soul who wanders atoning for your faults, I entrust you to God Almighty. Brother of mine most dear, for whom I ask God to give shelter and favour as a creature of his, so that paying with death the punishment of this life you come to see the Lord as the sovereign artificer, he who formed you from the dust of earth; when your soul leaves your body the shining army of the Holy Angels will come to escort you, defend you and celebrate you; let the glorious college of the Holy Apostles favour you, being advocates of your cause; let the triumphant legions of the invincible martyrs shelter you; let the most noble company of the illustrious confessors receive you in their midst, and with the gentle perfume of the lilies and of the white lilies they bring in their hands, symbol of the perfumed smoothness of their virtues, let them comfort you; let the choirs of the happy and content Holy Virgins receive you; let all that blissful company of celestials and courtiers with tight embraces of true friendship give you entrance into the glorious bosom of the Patriarchs; let the face of your Redeemer Jesus Christ present itself to you pitiful and pleasant, and let him give you a place between the ones that forever serve in his presence. Never let you experience the horror of the eternal darkness, or the noises of its flames, nor the penances that torment the condemned. Le the damned Satanaz surrender with all his allies, and when you pass by him, in the company of the Angels, let the miserable tremble and fearfully retreat to the dense blackness of his dark abode.

Go, soul; let your martyrdom be finished, because you no longer belong to this corporeal world, but to the celestial one. Let God who favours you free you, and disband all enemies who abhor you, let them flee from your presence; dispel like the smoke in the air and like the wax in the fire the rebellious and damned demons; and let the just and content sit in safety with you at the table of your God. Let the infernal armies confuse themselves and in affront retreat, and the ministers of Satanaz will not dare to hinder your way to heaven. Let Christ free you from hell, he that for you was crucified; free yourself from these agonies in which you walk in this world, tormenting and being tormented.

Christ, who gave his life for you, let Christ, Son of the living God, place you in the fields and forests of Paradise, which never dry or whither, and as the true shepherd he will recognize you as a lamb of his flock. Let him absolve you from all your sins, and seat you at his right hand between the chosen and the predestined; let God make you so joyous that forever assisting in his presence you shall know with blissful eyes the manifest truth of his divinity, and in the company of the courtiers of heaven you will enjoy the sweetness of his eternal contemplation through all the centuries. Amén.

DEATH AND THE LADY

19TH CENTURY ENGLISH BROADSIDE BALLAD

Dating from the 19th century (the date of publication is usually placed between 1880-1890), this broadside ballad is firstly a moral instruction, secondly an anti-capitalist agenda, and finally a reminder of the inevitable. It is set as a dialogue between Death and a rich, relatively young, lady of society, to whom Death comes as quite a shock. What follows is the lady's bargaining for a longer life, her entreaties to medical science, to Death's sense of fairness (!), her *'compassion'* towards those whose suffering is not relieved by Death, and her plea for a pardon not only from Death but from God for her sins. The essential message of the ballad seems to be not only that all shall die, regardless of the wealth they obtain in life, and also that if one lives a good, honest and virtuous life one should not be afraid to die. The piece ends with a vivid and evocative description of death as a marketplace where all shall eventually meet, irrespective of their rank in society or their wealth: it paints death as the great equalizer, and reminds us of the old saying in reference to material goods, *'You can't take it with you.'*

> DEATH: *Fair lady, lay your costly robes aside.*
> *No longer may you glory in your pride;*
> *Take leave of all your carnal vain delight,*
> *I'm come to summon you away to-night.*
>
> LADY: *What bold attempt is this? Pray let me know*
> *From whence you come, and whither I must go:*
> *Shall I, who am a lady, stoop or bow*
> *To such a pale-faced visage? Who art thou?*
>
> DEATH: *Do you not know me? I will tell thee then:*
> *Tis I that conquer all the sobs of men;*
> *No pitch of honour from my dart is free:*
> *My name is Death. Have you not heard of me?*
>
> LADY: *Yes, I have heard of thee time after time;*
> *But, being in the glory of my prime,*
> *I did not think you would have come so soon:*
> *Why must my morning sun go down at noon?*
>
> DEATH: *Talk not of noon - you may as well be mute*
> *This is no time at all for vain dispute;*
> *Your riches, garments, gold and jewels bright.*

Your houses and lands must on new owners light.

LADY: My heart is cold! It trembles at the news!
There's bags of gold, if you will me excuse;
And seize on those (so finish thou the strife)
Who wretched are and weary of their life.
Are there not many bound in prison strong.
In bitter grief of some who've languish'd long.
Who could but find the grave a place of rest
From all the grief with which they are oppres'd.
Besides, there's many with a hoary head,
And palsied joints, from whom all joys are fled;
Release thou them whose sorrows are so great.
But spare my life to have a longer date.

DEATH: Though thy vain heart to riches is inclined,
Yet thou must die end leave them all behind;
I come to none before their warrant's seal'd,
And when it is they must submit and yield.
Though some by age be full of grief and pain,
Till their appointed hour they must remain:
I take no bribe - believe me, this is true -
Prepare yourself to go; I'm come for you.

LADY: But if, O if, you could for me obtain
My freedom, and a longer life to reign,
Fain would I stay. If thou my life would spare.
I have a daughter, beautiful and fair,
I wish to see her wed, whom I adore.
Grant me but this - I'll ask no more.

DEATH: This is a slender, frivolous excuse;
I have you fast, and will not let you loose.
Leave her to Providence, for you must go
Along with me, whether you will or no:
Death commands the king to leave his crown.
He at my feet must lay his sceptre down.
Then if to kings I don't this favour give,
But cut them off can you expect to live
Beyond the limit of your time and space?
No - I must send you to another place.

LADY: You learned doctors, now exert your skill.
And let not Death obtain of me his will;
Prepare your cordials, let me comfort find.
My gold shall fly like chaff before the wind.

DEATH: Forbear to call; their skill will never do,
They are but mortals here as well us you:

I give the fatal wound- my dart is sure -
'Tis far beyond the doctors' skill to cure.
How freely can you let your riches fly,
To purchase life, rather than yield to die;
But while you flourish here, with all your store,
You would not give one penny to the poor.
Though in God's name their suit to you they make.
Yon would not spare one penny for his sake;
My Lord beheld wherein you did amiss,
And calls you hence to give account of this.

LADY: O heavy news! Must I no longer stay?
How shall I stand at the great judgment day!

Down from her eyes the crystal tears did flow,
She said, None knows what I do undergo.
Upon my bed of sorrow here I lie.
My selfish life makes me afraid to die;
My sins are great, manifold, and foul.
Lord Jesus Christ, have mercy on my soul!
And though I do deserve thy righteous frown,
Yet pardon, Lord, and send a blessing down:

Then, with a dying sigh, her heart did break,
And did the pleasures of this world forsake.
Thus may we see the mighty rise and fall
For surely Death shews no respect at all,
To those of either high or low degree:
The great submit to Death as well as we.
Though they are gay, their life is but a span.
A lump of clay, so vile a creature's man;
Then happy they whom Christ has made his care,
Who die in the Lord, and ever happy are.
The grave's the market-place where all must meet,
Both rich and poor, both small and great:
If life were merchandize that gold could buy
The rich would live, the poor alone would die.

DEATH, BE NOT PROUD

FROM HOLY SONNETS (SONNET 10)

BY JOHN DONNE

This classic poem, believed to have been written around 1610 but not published until after the author's death in 1633, is often read in the modern world at funerals. It is a sonnet addressed to Death, and is essentially both triumphant and rebellious in tone. It discusses the fear that death has over people, suggesting that Death himself swells with pride for the fear he brings in his wake, but reminds us – and Death – that the process of dying is just like falling asleep. Sleep brings peace and ease, so more so must Death! When we finally come to die, the author says, we will fall asleep and then *'wake eternally'*, referring to an afterlife, and it is this life after death that destroys death. The poem ends not with a traditional *'memento mori'* addressed to the reader, but instead to Death: *"Death, thou shalt die."*

> *Death, be not proud, though some have callèd thee*
> *Mighty and dreadful, for thou art not so;*
> *For those whom thou think'st thou dost overthrow*
> *Die not, poor Death, nor yet canst thou kill me.*
> *From rest and sleep, which but thy pictures be,*
> *Much pleasure—then, from thee much more must flow;*
> *And soonest our best men with thee do go,*
> *Rest of their bones and soul's delivery.*
> *Thou'rt slave to fate, chance, kings and desperate men,*
> *And dost with poison, war, and sickness dwell ;*
> *And poppy or charms can make us sleep as well,*
> *And better than thy stroke. Why swell'st thou then?*
> *One short sleep past, we wake eternally,*
> *And death shall be no more. Death, thou shalt die.*

I Am Stretched On Your Grave

Anonymous Irish poem, 17th century

This poem, written in the 17th century in Irish Gaelic, and titled *"Táim sínte ar do thuama"* (*"From the cold sod that's o'er you"*) was translated from the Irish by Frank O'Connor, into the version reproduced in the left column below, which in turn was first put to music in 1979 by the band Scullion on their album of the same name.[409] An original translation from the Irish can be found from 1847, where it appears in *Irish Popular Songs* by Edward Walsh (reproduced in right column below.)[410] It is a poem that expresses a raw and powerful grief of love unfulfilled, as a young man mourns the loss of his betrothed. He describes his wish to share her *'chaste pillow'* – to die with her so they might *'now sleep together'*. Despite his sadness at their unfulfilled love, he praises her virginity and thanks Jesus that they did not give into passion – presumably because she died pure and therefore went to Heaven. The openness of the grief is highlighted in the poem by the fact that the lover sits watch over (or lies upon) the grave of the deceased young woman, and cries aloud to the air and earth. He smells like the grave in which his love is interred, and his heart is a black hole of pain. He longs and yearns for death to come in his infinite mercy, that he might be reunited with his betrothed. It is a poignant and honest rendition of the grief felt when those we love so much are taken away from us too early.

Modern version (one of many)

I am stretched on your grave,
And will lie there forever.
If your hands were in mine,
I'd be sure we'd not sever.
My apple tree, my brightness,
It's time we were together,
For I smell of the earth
And am worn by the weather.

Original published version, 1847

From the cold sod that's o'er you,
I never shall sever –
Were my hands twin'd in yours, love,
I'd hold them forever.
My fondest, my fairest,
We may now sleep together,
I've the cold earth's damp odour,
And I'm worn for the weather!

This heart filled with fondness,

---

409 Modern renditions of the poem as a song are sung by Sinead O'Connor, Kate Rusby, Dead Can Dance, and even the steampunk band Abney Park.

410 Walsh, Edward. Irish Popular Songs, pp. 149-153. W.H.Smith, 1847.

Memento Mori

Is wounded sad and weary;
A dark gulf beneath it,
Yawns jet-black and dreary;
When death comes, a victor,
In mercy to greet me,
On the wings of the whirlwind,
In the wild wastes you'll meet me!

When my family thinks
That I'm safe in my bed,
From night until morning,
I am stretched at your head,
Calling out to the air
With tears hot and wild,
My grief for the girl
That I loved as a child.

When the folk of my household
Suppose I am sleeping,
On your cold grave, til morning,
The lone watch I'm keeping;
My grief to the night wind,
For the mild maid to render,
Who was my betrothed,
Since infancy tender!

Do you remember
The night we were lost,
In the shade of the blackthorn
And the chill of the frost?
Thanks be to Jesus
We did what was right,
And your maidenhead still
Is your pillar of light.

Remember the lone night
I last spent with you, love,
Beneath the dark sloe-tree,
When the icy wind blew, love –
High praise to the Saviour,
No sin-stain had found you,
That your virginal glory,
Shines brightly around you!

The priests and the friars
Approach me in dread
Because I still love you,
My love, and you're dead.
I still would be your shelter
Through rain and through storm.
And with you in your cold grave,
I cannot sleep warm.

The priests and the friars,
Are ceaselessly chiding,
That I love a young maiden,
In life not abiding –
O! I'd shelter and shield you,
If wild storms were swelling,
And O! My wreck'd hope,
That the cold earth's you dwelling!

So I'm stretched on your grave,
And will lie there forever.
If your hands were in mine,
I'd be sure we'd not sever.
My apple tree, my brightness,
It's time we were together,
For I smell of the earth
And am worn by the weather.

Alas for your father,
And also your mother,
And all your relations,
Your sister and brother,
Who gave you to sorrow,
And the grave 'neath the willow,
While I craved as your portion,
But to share your chaste pillow!

O, DEATH

AMERICAN FOLK SONG, DATE UNKNOWN

This song is obscure in its origins, though it is currently believed to have originated with the Appalachian region of the USA, which stretches from the southern state of New York to northern Alabama, Mississippi and Georgia. It is sung as a repetitive, melancholy, morose dirge, and has seen many versions over the years. Whilst it is certain to have dated further back, it was originally popularized in the 1920s by the country and blues musician Moran Lee *'Dock'* Boggs. It was later brought back by folk artists such as Mike Seeger and Bob Dylan. More recently, Ralph Stanley performed the song for the film *"Oh Brother, Where Art Thou?"*, and Jen Titus did the same for the TV series *"Supernatural."*

The song is reminiscent of *"Death and the Lady"*, the English broadside ballad dating to the 19th century, in which a young, rich young woman pleads with death not to take her so early. She offers death wealth in exchange for her life, but death does not accept. He is very firm on the matter: no wealth, no land, no silver or gold will satisfy him. Nothing will satisfy him but her soul. When death comes for you, these songs say, he cannot be bargained with nor reasoned with.

"O, Death" is also interesting because it describes vividly the physical process of death, a feature not often found in poetry or songs around the world. It places the human being very much at the mercy of death, bound by his laws, and in this particular song not even religion or religious intervention can help.

> *O, Death. O, Death.*
> *Won't you spare me over 'til another year?*
> *Well, what is this that I can't see*
> *With ice cold hands takin' hold of me.*
> *"Well I am death, none can excel*
> *I'll open the door to heaven or hell."*
> *'O, death' someone would pray*
> *'Could you wait to call me another day?'*
> *The children prayed, the preacher preached*
> *Time and mercy is out of your reach.*
> *"I'll fix your feet 'til you can't walk*
> *I'll lock your jaw 'til you can't talk*
> *I'll close your eyes so you can't see*
> *This very hour, come and go with me*
> *I'm death I come to take the soul*
> *Leave the body and leave it cold*
> *To draw the flesh off of the frame*
> *Dirt and worm both have a claim."*

O, Death. O, Death.
Won't you spare me over til another year?
My mother came to my bed
Placed a cold towel upon my head
My head is warm my feet are cold
Death is a-movin upon my soul
Oh, death how you're treatin' me
You've close my eyes so I can't see
Well you're hurtin' my body
You make me cold
You run my life right outta my soul
Oh death please consider my age
Please don't take me at this stage
My wealth is all at your command
If you will move your icy hand.
"The old, the young, the rich or poor
All alike to me, you know
No wealth, no land, no silver no gold
Nothing satisfies me but your soul."
O, Death. O, Death.
Won't you spare me over til another year?

TO HIS COY MISTRESS

BY ANDREW MARVELL

This 17ᵗʰ century piece is one of the editor's favourite pieces of poetry. Written as a young man attempting to woo his lady love, it is clear what this particular gentleman has in mind! The piece begins by praising the lady's features, her kindness, and stating that if the gentleman had all the time in the world he would be happy to take all of it to appreciate her in a chaste fashion, woo her in a courtly way, before eventually considering moving onto something more passionate. It continues by stating very clearly, however, that the young lovers do not have all the time in the world, but are very much in a race against time. The lady's good looks will one day fall into ruin, and her body will become food for worms. Why, then, does she hold her chastity so dearly? What good is it in death?

*Death is the ultimate goad to action. We have so little time on
this planet, such a limited number of breaths and heartbeats...
we must make every single one of them count. This poem
reminds the reader to seize the day, because nobody is
promised tomorrow.*
Had we but world enough, and time,
This coyness, lady, were no crime.
We would sit down and think which way
To walk, and pass our long love's day;
Thou by the Indian Ganges' side
Shouldst rubies find; I by the tide
Of Humber would complain. I would
Love you ten years before the Flood;
And you should, if you please, refuse
Till the conversion of the Jews.
My vegetable love should grow
Vaster than empires, and more slow.
An hundred years should go to praise
Thine eyes, and on thy forehead gaze;
Two hundred to adore each breast,
But thirty thousand to the rest;
An age at least to every part,
And the last age should show your heart.
For, lady, you deserve this state,
Nor would I love at lower rate.

But at my back I always hear

Time's winged chariot hurrying near;
And yonder all before us lie
Deserts of vast eternity.
Thy beauty shall no more be found,
Nor, in thy marble vault, shall sound
My echoing song; then worms shall try
That long preserv'd virginity,
And your quaint honour turn to dust,
And into ashes all my lust.
The grave's a fine and private place,
But none I think do there embrace.

Now therefore, while the youthful hue
Sits on thy skin like morning dew,
And while thy willing soul transpires
At every pore with instant fires,
Now let us sport us while we may;
And now, like am'rous birds of prey,
Rather at once our time devour,
Than languish in his slow-chapp'd power.
Let us roll all our strength, and all
Our sweetness, up into one ball;
And tear our pleasures with rough strife
Thorough the iron gates of life.
Thus, though we cannot make our sun
Stand still, yet we will make him run.

DÈY

TRADITIONAL HAITIAN SONG OF MOURNING

TRANSLATED BY KIM HUGGENS

This traditional Haitian mourning song has been performed by many artists over the years, as well as sung by countless Haitians. It is a mournful yet powerful song that starts low and sad, rises in strength and power in the middle and ends on a crescendo not only of expressed anger and loss but also of determination to rise up out of oppression and darkness. Whilst it is used sometimes to mourn the loss of an individual, more specifically Dey mourns the death of Haiti, *'Ayiti cheri'*, as its people suffer under the weight of poverty, political oppression, social unrest and economic uncertainty. It is a collective song, stating that *'We are singing/calling "Dey-o,'* and expressing grief (*'Woy'* is a Haitian sound of surprise, an exclamation, akin to *'alas!'*,[411] and to sing *'Dey'* is specifically to sing in mourning, from the French *deuil*) Most of the song is simple in its form and expression of sadness and frustration, yet certain terms are explicitly Haitian in nature, such as *'desounen'* (literally, *'going down'*), which refers to part of the funerary rites for a dead person in which the spirit of the deceased is separated from the lwa so each may go to their proper places, but in this case is applied to the entire country. It should also be noted that Haitians give their country a family name, *'Toma'*, which appears in the second verse of the song. The *konbit*, or gathering place, at the end of the song refers specifically to a community area in towns and villages of Haiti in which people would gather for community events or work. It therefore signifies both shared trials and challenges, and shared triumphs.

Haitian Kreyòl	English Translation
Dèy o m'rele dèy o,	*Dèy, oh, I'm calling out dèy, oh!*
Ayiti woy.	*Woy, Haiti!*
Dèy o mwen chante dèy o,	*Dèy, oh, I'm singing out dèy, oh!*
Ayiti woy.	*Woy, Haiti!*
Ayiti cheri, men pitit ou mouri,	*My dear Haiti, your children are dying,*

---

411 With thanks to Kath Glover for this particular translation of the term.

Men lòt yo toutouni	They are going naked
Sa ka pote dèy la pou ou woy.	Bringing the song of mourning for you.
Dèy o m'rele dèy o,	Dèy, oh, I'm calling out dèy, oh,
Ayiti woy.	Woy, Haiti!
Dèy o n'ap rele dey o,	Dèy, oh, we're calling out dèy, oh,
Ayiti woy.	Woy, Haiti!
Ayiti Toma, men san ou nan Djaspora,	Haiti Toma, without you in the diaspora,
Men peyi a ap kaba	The country will end
Sa ka pote dèy la pou ou woy.	So we are bringing the song of mourning for you.
Dèy o n'ap rele dey o	Dèy, oh, we are calling out dèy oh,
Ayiti woy.	Woy, Haiti!
Dèy o mwen chante dey o,	Dèy , oh, I am singing dèy oh,
Ayiti woy.	Woy, Haiti!
Ayiti desounen,	Haiti is 'going down'
Ayiti je fèmen,	Haiti's eyes are closed
Ayiti detounen,	Haiti is being hijacked
Sa ka pote dèy la pou ou woy.	So we are bringing the song of mourning for you.
	Haiti I am calling you
Ayiti m'rele ou,	I am calling for you, I'm calling for you,
M'rele ou pou ou rele m,	You must send for your blood,
Fòk ou rele tout san ou,	You must bring the land (people) together,
Fòk peyi a sanble assemble,	Woy, woy, for the gathering
	Haiti, rise, Haiti, stand,
Woy, Woy pou konbit la	People are dancing in the gathering place
Ayiti a leve, Ayiti a kanpe	to bring the song of mourning for you, woy.
Ayiti a danse nan konbit la	
dèy la pou ou woy.	

In Memoriam

Peg Aloi

Peg holds dear many departed ancestors and loved ones, most recently her friend Derek Miller, as well as her beloved father Daniel Anthony Aloi, and her friends Adam Schleimer and J.P. Slota, who died too young.

Emily Carding

Remembering with great love the indomitable Jane Dagger, who was Nanny Ogg and Granny Weatherwax rolled into one. She feasts now with the ancestors, on whose shoulders we all stand, (which must make for quite a party). I also send love to my mother's mother and remember childhood canal walks fondly and the gifts she passed down from all her grandmothers before her.

Sophia Fisher

To Rudolph, Juil, Jesse, Brinley and John; and to Carol, Louis and Mimi, who would all have loved to meet the boys. With love, honour and respect.

Kyle Fite

"Behind The Glasses Of Ghuedhe" is dedicated to the memory of my Father, my Friend and Spiritual Brother Dennis O'Brien, my Grandfather Walter and all those whose lovely lives have deeply touched mine ere departing into the Great Mystery. Honour and Respect to the Baron Samedhi, Mamman Brigitte, Papa Ghuedhe and the Ghuedhe Spirits who remind us from Death of the Life which dances through All. *"Absent Friends Shall Live By Love"* - Killing Joke

Kim Huggens

In fond and loving memory of my Aunty Mary, a woman with infinite patience for the whimsies of a precocious child, who let her win a little too often at draughts. In honour also of my father's mother, Nell Huggens, and his father whom I never really knew. With gratitude to Charles Beecham and Bill Padgham who were dedicated guides in my years with St. John Ambulance. Finally, with the greatest respect I remember Granny Hannam, my great-grandmother, whose influence and guidance is felt so strongly in my mother's line still.

Ivy Kerrigan

I would like to dedicate my article to my little brother Daniel who died more than 14 years ago though it still seems like yesterday, my Grandmother Annie Kerrigan who is an endless source of inspiration, my Grandfather Harold John William Cook who I wish I'd known better, and to all my other ancestors both known and unknown who have had a hand in who I am today. You reside forever in my heart and will not be forgotten.

Humberto Maggi

I consider myself blessed for reaching my 44 years with very few close deaths. I remember my grandma, who was innocent, and Rose, a very dear friend of mine, whose spirit reached the shores of Amenti.

Dave Moore

In memory of Elizabeth Moore (1912-1996), who taught me to dream.

Mogg Morgan

Every month over three days of the new moon I light candles on an ancestral shrine in remembrance of departed friends and other immortals. Amongst them I number several household pets that have shared my life over the years, as well as my mother who died a few years back and a dear friend who died of a broken heart at the height of the AIDS epidemic.

Here's a prayer, adapted from the Ancient Egyptian *Pyramids Texts* that I find evocative and comforting

> *"Oh my mother Nuit,*
> *spread your wings over me,*
> *so I am wound,*
> *as mummies in a cloth are bound,*
> *and become one with the imperishable stars*
> *that are in you,*
> *and shall not die."*

Tylluan Penry

Tylluan and Mr Penry remember their beloved ancestors, known and unknown. It is their untold struggles for survival that have made us who we are today.

Karen F. Pierce

In memory of my beloved grandparents, Mary, May (Lally) and Gordon; and of Darkle, a treasured friend who is waiting across the Rainbow Bridge.

Caroline Tully

Caroline honours the memory of her own beloved dead; thanking her paternal line through which she became a witch and her maternal line by which she became an artist.

Julian Vayne

I wish to remember all those brave souls who have transgressed the limits of culture to discover pleasure, freedom and power. Those witches, those natural philosophers, those psychonauts who, down the centuries, have had their lives cut short by execution. May we honour their work, their sacrifice. May we be inspired by their bravery and, with dignity and strength, seek to oppose the murderous culture of fear wherever it exists.

INDEX

If you enjoyed this book, you may also enjoy some of the other titles published by Avalonia.

A Collection of Magical Secrets by David Rankine (editor)

Artemis: Virgin Goddess of the Sun & Moon by Sorita d'Este

Defences Against the Witches' Craft by John Canard

From a Drop of Water (anthology, various contributors) edited by Kim Huggens

Heka: Egyptian Magic by David Rankine

Hekate Her Sacred Fires (anthology) edited by Sorita d'Este

Hekate Liminal Rites (history) by Sorita d'Este & David Rankine

Odin's Gateways by Katie Gerrard

The Priory of Sion by Jean-luc Chaumeil

Seidr: The Gate is Open by Katie Gerrard

Stellar Magic by Payam Nabarz

The Book of Gold by David Rankine (editor) & Paul Harry Barron (translator)

The Cosmic Shekinah by Sorita d'Este & David Rankine

The Gods of the Vikings by Marion Pearce

The Grimoire of Arthur Gauntlet by David Rankine (editor)

The Guises of the Morrigan by David Rankine & Sorita d'Este

The Isles of the Many Gods by David Rankine & Sorita d'Este

The Temple of Hekate by Tara Sanchez

Thracian Magic by Georgi Mishev

Thoth: The Ancient Egyptian God of Wisdom by Lesley Jackson

Visions of the Cailleach by Sorita d'Este & David Rankine

Vs. (anthology, various contributors) edited by Kim Huggens

Wicca Magickal Beginnings by Sorita d'Este & David Rankine

These and many other titles are available from our website, **www.avaloniabooks.co.uk** and all good metaphysical bookshops.

Lightning Source UK Ltd.
Milton Keynes UK
UKHW030632100321
380099UK00009B/921